William Wordsworth
and the Hermeneutics of Incarnation

Literature & Philosophy

A. J. Cascardi, General Editor

This series publishes books in a wide range of subjects in philosophy and literature, including studies of the social and historical issues that relate these two fields. Drawing on the resources of the Anglo-American and Continental traditions, the series is open to philosophically informed scholarship covering the entire range of contemporary critical thought.

Already published:

J. M. Bernstein, *The Fate of Art: Aesthetic Alienation from Kant to Derrida and Adorno*
Peter Bürger, *The Decline of Modernism*
Mary E. Finn, *Writing the Incommensurable: Kierkegaard, Rossetti, and Hopkins*
Reed Way Dasenbrock, ed., *Literary Theory After Davidson*
David Jacobson, *Emerson's Pragmatic Vision: The Dance of the Eye*
Gray Kochhar-Lindgren, *Narcissus Transformed: The Textual Subject in Psychoanalysis and Literature*
Robert Steiner, *Toward a Grammar of Abstraction: Modernity, Wittgenstein, and the Paintings of Jackson Pollock*

William Wordsworth *and the* Hermeneutics *of* Incarnation

David P. Haney

The Pennsylvania State University Press
University Park, Pennsylvania

Library of Congress Cataloging-in-Publication Data

Haney, David P., 1952–
    William Wordsworth and the hermeneutics of incarnation / David P. Haney.
        p.   cm.
    Includes bibliographical references and index.
    ISBN 0-271-00911-X (alk. paper)
    1. Wordsworth, William, 1770–1850—Philosophy. 2. Incarnation in literature. 3. Hermeneutics. I. Title.
PR5892.P5H36   1993
821'.7—dc20   92-29464
                                                                                                      CIP

Copyright © 1993 The Pennsylvania State University
All rights reserved
Printed in the United States of America

Published by The Pennsylvania State University Press,
Barbara Building, Suite C, University Park, PA 16802-1003

It is the policy of The Pennsylvania State University Press to use acid-free paper for the first printing of all clothbound books. Publications on uncoated stock satisfy the minimum requirements of American National Standard for Information Sciences—Permanence of Paper for Printed Library Materials, ANSI Z39.48–1984.

*For my parents, Joe and Jean Haney,
who taught me to read*

"There must be a way I have missed," he says, and looks mournfully back on his story. "There must be a way whereby the word becomes flesh. There must be a way whereby the flesh becomes word. Whereby loneliness becomes communion without contamination. Whereby contamination becomes purity without exile. There must be a way, but I may not have it now. All I can have now is knowledge."
—Robert Penn Warren,
World Enough and Time: A Romantic Novel, 460

Or to put it another way, the best thing about philosophy is that it fails. It is better that philosophy fail to totalize meaning—even though, as ontology, it has attempted just this—for it thereby remains open to the irreducible otherness of transcendence.
—Emmanuel Levinas,
an interview with Richard Kearney,
in *Face to Face With Levinas,* 22

Our destiny, our being's heart and home,
Is with infinitude—and only there;
With hope it is, hope that can never die,
Effort, and expectation, and desire,
And something evermore about to be.
—William Wordsworth,
The Prelude (1805), 6.538–42

Contents

Preface and Acknowledgments — xi

Abbreviations — xv

Introduction: Incarnation and the Generation of Meaning — 1

1 Hegel and the Problem of Jesus — 47

2 Words, Things, and Death — 69

3 Ending *The Prelude:* Incarnation and the Autobiographical Exit — 103

4 *The Excursion:* Incarnation and Philosophical Poetry — 141

Notes — 235

Works Cited — 253

Index — 261

Preface and Acknowledgments

According to Emmanuel Levinas,

> A book is interrupted discourse catching up with its own breaks. But books have their fate; they belong to a world they do not include, but recognize by being written and printed, and by being prefaced and getting themselves prefaced with forewords. They are interrupted, and call for other books and in the end are interpreted in a saying distinct from the said. (*OTB* 171)

Given the hermeneutic premises of this book, it is more than a little presumptuous to reduce Wordsworth's incarnational thought to a few hundred pages of analysis, particularly in the wake of readers from Coleridge to Geoffrey Hartman who have devoted some of the best critical thought of their eras to Wordsworth. My only solace is that my interrupted discourse, whether or not it actually does catch up with its own breaks, will in turn be interrupted in the kind of critical conversation of which Hans-Georg Gadamer says "the more genuine a conversation is, the less its conduct lies within the will of either partner" (*TM* 383).

Whatever is worthwhile in this book is the result of conversations that extend back twenty years, to my first experience of Wordsworth's depth in Bob Ward's undergraduate course on the Romantics. My current view of Wordsworth has its dim origins in an ungainly Ph.D. dissertation on *The Prelude,* written in the heady critical atmosphere of the State University of New York at Buffalo in the late seventies, and patiently read by

Homer Brown, Irving Massey, and Bill Warner. I owe Irving Massey an incalculable debt; without his fortuitously timed encouragement I would never have returned to the academic world I had almost forgotten after a decade's absence.

Tony Cascardi gave me excellent critical advice, and his interest in the book's early stages helped to effect both the manuscript's completion and my association with Penn State's Literature and Philosophy series. Thanks also to Philip Winsor and Cherene Holland of Penn State Press for orchestrating the manuscript's acceptance and guiding it through the editorial process, and to Andrew Lewis for his thorough and sympathetic copyediting. I am happy that Donald G. Marshall lifted the veil of the manuscript reviewer's anonymity so that I can thank him for his careful and extremely helpful reading. Kenneth Johnston was kind enough to include what became part of Chapter 2 in the English Romanticism panel at the 1990 MLA convention; there I received invaluable critiques from two leaders of contemporary Romantic criticism: Thomas McFarland and Geoffrey Hartman.

Three supportive department heads deserve thanks: Harry Pagliaro at Swarthmore College and Bert Hitchcock and Dennis Rygiel at Auburn University. I would like to thank my colleagues in the English department at Auburn for providing a rare atmosphere of collegiality and mutual respect. Those colleagues deserving more specific thanks, for having read this manuscript in whole or in part, include Miller Solomon, who keeps me from taking myself or Wordsworth too seriously; Don Wehrs, whose historical and philosophical breadth keeps sending me back to the library; and Dan Latimer, a careful reader and a quietly original, good-humored critic. David Hiley helped me in two major ways: as a dean in the College of Liberal Arts he helped unlock the mysteries of the grant proposal and gave me a good deal of practical encouragement; as a philosopher he helped me see, in both his writing and his conversation, how literature and philosophy can interact productively. Many of the ideas in this book were formulated and tested in an informal reading group at Auburn that he organized in 1989; I also thank the other members of that group for a year of intense, intelligent, generous, and for me very productive conversation.

I have benefited greatly from Raimonda Modiano's careful reading of my discussions of sacrifice and gift exchange. Sheila Kearns helped me understand, among other things, the importance of death in Wordsworth's autobiographical rhetoric. Richard Sha's comments helped give coherence to an early version of Chapter 4, and he suggested several essential secondary resources. Conversations about Romanticism with

Bill Kumbier have sharpened my thinking at several crucial points over the past fifteen years.

I am grateful to the National Endowment for the Humanities for a summer stipend in 1990 that enabled me to write much of Chapter 4 and to Auburn University's College of Liberal Arts for a summer research grant in 1991 that allowed me to complete the introductory chapter.

An earlier version of part of Chapter 1 appears in *Bodies: Image, Writing, Technology*, ed. Juliet Flower MacCannell and Laura Zakarin (State University of New York Press, 1993), as "The Romantic Incarnation of Thought." An earlier version of Chapter 3 appeared in the Winter 1990 issue of *Studies in Romanticism* as "Incarnation and the Autobiographical Exit: Wordsworth's *The Prelude*, Books IX–XIII (1805)."

Finally I want to thank Lisa and Jim for giving me the kind of happy, loving life that makes thinking and writing possible.

Abbreviations

OTB   *Otherwise Than Being or Beyond Essence* by Emmanuel Levinas
PrW   *The Prose Works of William Wordsworth*
TI   *Totality and Infinity: An Essay on Exteriority* by Emmanuel Levinas
TM   *Truth and Method* by Hans-Georg Gadamer

Complete publication data pertaining to these sources can be found in Works Cited.

Introduction: Incarnation and the Generation of Meaning

In this book I explore the implications of Wordsworth's statement in his third "Essay Upon Epitaphs," that language should be an "incarnation" of thought:

> If words be not (recurring to a metaphor before used) an incarnation of the thought but only a clothing for it, then surely will they prove an ill gift; such a one as those poisoned vestments, read of in the stories of superstitious times, which had power to consume and to alienate from his right mind the victim who put them on. Language, if it do not uphold, and feed, and leave in quiet, like the power of gravitation or the air we breathe, is a counter-spirit, unremittingly and noiselessly at work to derange, to subvert, to lay waste, to vitiate, and to dissolve. (*PrW* 2:84–85)

This passage has received a great deal of attention in the last two decades, particularly after Paul de Man's "Autobiography as De-facement," which claims that this distinction between incarnation and counter-spirit does not hold, and after Frances Ferguson's *Wordsworth: Language as Counter-Spirit*, which explores the conflict between the desire for an incarnational language and the tendency of language to become, as Wordsworth put it, "counter-spirit." I justify a book-length treatment of this familiar topic with the assertion that the notion of language as incarnation has ramifications that go far beyond the questions of linguistic representation to which discussions of it are usually restricted. I argue that Wordsworth's incarnational poetics does not simply secularize a Christian concept in the service of a theory of representation, but rather pursues a critical, nonrepresentational, historically engaged, concrete hermeneutic of both thought and language.

In his 1963 essay "English Romanticism: The Spirit of the Age," M. H. Abrams located the source of Wordsworth's mixed style in the paradox of the Incarnation:

> The ultimate source of Wordsworth's discovery [of the interaction of high and low themes]... was the Bible, and especially the New Testament, which is grounded on the radical paradox that "the last shall be first," and dramatizes that fact in the central mystery of Christ incarnate as a lowly carpenter's son who takes fishermen for his disciples, consorts with beggars, publicans, and fallen women, and dies ignominiously, crucified with thieves. This interfusion of highest and lowest, the divine and the base, as Erich Auerbach has shown, had from the beginning been a stumbling-block to readers habituated to the classical separation of levels of subject matter and style. (115)

The next quarter-century of Romantic criticism shifted away from Abrams's vision, expressed most completely in *Natural Supernaturalism*, of Romanticism as a Hegelian secularization of Protestantism, toward an emphasis on the complex blindness of Romantic language, and returned to history only via a "new" historicism antithetical to Abrams's Hegelianism and faith in a traditional history of ideas. Recent criticism has usefully enlarged our stock of analytical tools and has enabled a healthy self-consciousness about historical generalization, but we have lost the force of this insight into the paradox of Wordsworth's incarnational thought. Despite vociferous protests to the contrary, neither deconstruction nor the many varieties of ideological criticism are very good at discussing paradoxical combinations such as those presented by the Incarnation, except as distortions or repressions of some impossibly pure dream of representational presence (for the deconstructionists) or ideological power (for the ideological critics).

If we see Christianity, based on the paradox of high and low described by Abrams, as "mixed" from the start, in the radical sense of a "mixture" that is prior to either of the mixed terms, then Wordsworth's use of incarnation to link thought and language cannot be contained within the familiar binary oppositions, such as presence and absence, blindness and insight, or ideology and history, that are usually employed to understand Wordsworth. I argue, against Abrams, that the Hegelian secularization of the Protestant tradition is an inadequate explanation of Romantic thought because it ignores the theology that remains and because it falls prey to an insufficiently self-conscious history of ideas and theory of language. However, though I will borrow from their methodologies, I also argue against critics such as Paul de Man, the early Frances Ferguson, and Andrzej Warminski, whose brilliant analyses of Romanticism's self-consuming rhetoric have tended to oversimplify or simply dismiss the theological, historical, and ethical side of Wordsworth's thought.[1]

I hope a close study of Wordsworth's use of the concept of incarnation will bring to light a kind of interdisciplinary cross-section of Romantic thought and practice: strands of the history of ontology, epistemology, linguistics, ethics, aesthetics, and theology (not necessarily in that order) all pass through the core of Wordsworth's incarnational thought and can be seen in a new perspective if we slice into that concept with the tools provided by recent philosophy and literary theory. My metaphor suggests that I am going to "murder to dissect," in explicit opposition to Wordsworth's sentiments in "The Tables Turned" (28), by adopting a pseudo-objective stance and applying certain theoretical tools to the "object" constituted by Wordsworth's poetry. Although some of that may be inevitable, another topic of this book (implicit when it is not explicit) is precisely the problem of how to study a body of thought that has been so influential in our own way of thinking. I do not agree with Jerome McGann's restrictively historical solution to this problem, but I do believe he is right to question the "uncritical absorption in Romanticism's own self-representations" (*The Romantic Ideology* 1) evident in various schools of Romantic criticism. Rather than attempt to escape Romanticism, however, I am attempting to embrace it—now, at a late point in its history—with as clear as possible a sense of how I am doing that.

A guiding principle here, to which I will return at several points, is Hans-Georg Gadamer's concept of *wirkungsgeschichtliches Bewußtsein*,[2] or (in the most recent attempt to translate this difficult phrase) "historically effected consciousness"—the idea that we operate within a horizon of real experience that is both other to and a product of the historical moment we are interpreting, that we find "ourselves" only by relating to an otherness with which we can share a conversational language: "The life of the mind consists precisely in recognizing oneself in other being" (*TM* 346). Gadamer is pointing to the fact that our own interpretive horizon is conditioned by the history of which it is a part. This is not reducible to the claim made by many recent critics, influenced by thinkers from Nietzsche to Marx to Foucault, that claims to philosophical objectivity are masked expressions of ideology; such a simple contrast between objectivity and ideology, and such a reduction of meaning to the expression of power, are inadequate. Nor is Gadamer's concept reducible, as some of his critics have maintained, to a Hegelian myth of history that simply reinstates the German intellectual tradition.[3] The point is rather that our dialogue with our own past is a conversation in which the very past we are analyzing helps to determine what we will say, and that this necessary prejudgment is not something to be removed but rather something to be worked with as the necessary foundation of any historical interpretation (and for Gadamer there is no nonhistorical interpretation).

One methodological implication of this concept for my work is that I attend equally to, while recognizing the differences among, at least three different kinds of writers: (1) Wordsworth and his contemporaries (such as Coleridge and Hegel) who are struggling with related problems, (2) our own contemporaries who are struggling with the same problems, often using the Romantics for support (such as Stanley Cavell and Gadamer), and (3) our own contemporaries who treat the Romantics as objects of historical and critical interest (most literary critics). Needless to say, many current thinkers (Geoffrey Hartman, for instance) are in both categories 2 and 3. The very concept of *wirkungsgeschichtliches Bewußtsein* prevents a firm distinction between those last two categories and enables us to see our task as dialectically related to the efforts of those in the first category. My use of the concept of "incarnation" also spans these categories: I see it as a concept, shared by Wordsworth and some of his contemporaries, implications of which are expressed, tested, and counteracted in his poetry; a philosophically and theologically important concept embedded in Wordsworth's and our own cultural and poetic heritage; and a theoretical concept by means of which we can interpret Wordsworth.

If I can escape the accusation of murdering to dissect, can I escape the accusation of imputing such an intention to Wordsworth? Or am I treating this nontheoretical poet as having created a "theory"" of incarnation? These are particularly hard questions because many aspects of incarnational thought mitigate against the very idea of a "theory"; the notion of a theory that can be applied to a variety of concrete situations is close to the idea of an objective, representational code or grammar, the very idea against which incarnational thought makes its claim. I argue in Chapter 4 that this problem is minor in *The Prelude,* because the autobiographical mode allows the enactment (we might even say the "incarnation") of incarnational principles, but it is at the core of *The Excursion*'s interest and failure, because that "philosophical" poem contains figures (particularly the Wanderer) charged with the impossible task of theorizing about antitheoretical incarnational principles.

INCARNATION AND ANIMISM

As a way of placing the story of Wordsworth's incarnational poetics into a broader Romantic context, I would like to begin with a relatively uncontroversial argument: Wordsworth's insistence that words should be "an incarnation of the thought" is part of the Romantic project of animating the world, attributing a force of life to a broadly defined concept of "nature." As he points out in the above passage from the third "Essay Upon Epitaphs," for language to incarnate thought is for it to take on power analogous to that of natural forces such as "gravitation" or "the air we breathe." The difference between thought's incarnation in language, which is analogous to the Christian story of the son of God becoming a mortal, and animism, which attributes life to the inanimate, is important and will be treated below. For now, I want to contextualize my specific argument about Wordsworth's incarnational language by treating it as a special case of a general desire to bring to life a world perceived as having died at the hands of Enlightenment thought.

This animation of the world occurred in the wake of the crisis of knowledge, articulated by Kant, to which both British empiricism and Continental rationalism had led. The tantalizing no-win situation presented by Kant—that in order to posit the existence of a ground for appearances we must deny ourselves access to that ground—led Coleridge to say in chapter 9 of the *Biographia Literaria,* "In spite therefore of his own declarations, I could never believe, it was possible for him to have meant no more by his *Noumenon,* or THING IN ITSELF, than his mere words express" (*Collected Works* 7.1.155). In order to prove that the world "in itself" could indeed be more to us than Kant's shadowy "beings of the understanding" (*Prolegomena* 126), most of the Romantics animated the world, turning it into a living being that could somehow make its own case by speaking for itself, whether by an expression of the "eternal language, which thy God / utters" in Coleridge's "Frost at Midnight," by Nature's manifestation in *The Prelude* of "that mutual domination which she loves / To exert upon the face of outward things" ([1850] 14.81–82),[4] or by means of the "Power in likeness of the Arve" that emanates from the inaccessible reaches of Mont Blanc in Shelley's poem.[5]

This Romantic animation of the world is of course historically self-conscious. Stephen Prickett argues, following Owen Barfield, that in ancient Hebrew "wind" and "breath" were parts of the same concept, before what Coleridge calls "desynonymy" separated the names for inner and outer forces. For Wordsworth to reanimate the world, particularly after its objectification by seventeenth- and eighteenth-century science (for example by granting consciousness to the wind at the beginning of *The Prelude*), is to construct a metaphor that acknowledges the history by which the ancient nondifferentiation of inner and outer had been lost.[6] Particularly after Kant, such an act raises many questions: what exactly *is* this world that is being animated? If we are animating it because we cannot know it, how can we intelligibly posit an antecedent for "it" in this sentence? If the world is to be treated as a being to be looked at or talked to, instead of as a dead object of knowledge, what is our ethical relationship to that world? What kind of ethical relationship can operate in the epistemological vacuum left by Kant's restriction? Is it a world outside or a world inside or both? What does it mean to "animate" something—must the granting of life be framed by death, as in Victor Frankenstein's project? How do we negotiate the conflict between bringing something to life in a poem (for example, speculating on the sources and ends of the procession on Keats's urn) and the apparently unavoidable act of fixing it as a frozen sign or "cold Pastoral"? To what extent does the animated world express its own life and to what extent does it function as a sign of something else, such as a "Power"?

A close look at Wordsworth's language of incarnation will, I hope, trace a somewhat new path through what must seem rather well-traveled territory. To demonstrate the range of this concept of animism, I use two recent works of North American philosophy, Charles Taylor's *Sources of the Self* and Stanley Cavell's *In Quest of the Ordinary*, that provide opposing perspectives on the Romantic desire to bring the world to life. These particular thinkers introduce arguments to which I will return later and suggest connections between these Romantic concerns and some broader philosophical issues, particularly the ethical nature of the modern self and the question of how to live in a skeptical universe, that are still very much with us.

Charles Taylor and Stanley Cavell have very different goals: Taylor narrates the history of the modern self in terms of how we build ontologies and epistemologies within inescapable moral frameworks. Cavell negotiates a position that takes into account the necessity of both the drive for skepticism and the drive toward the resolution of skeptical doubt. However, both accept the Kantian challenge to knowledge as more than merely an epistemological dilemma, Taylor because for him all epistemological stances are rooted in moral concerns,[7] and Cavell because for him our only meaningful response to Kant's epistemological problem is to move outside of epistemology in order to articulate a relationship with that which we cannot know.

Both are very interested in the phenomenon of Romanticism, and both base their interpretations of the period on the idea—more explicit in Cavell than in Taylor—of a world brought to life. Taylor's view of Romanticism is extremely traditional; he borrows heavily from M. H. Abrams's 1953 study, *The Mirror and the Lamp*. Still, the philosophical context in which he places this interpretation will help establish one border of the territory I want to explore. He claims "that the picture of nature as a source was a crucial part of the conceptual armoury in which Romanticism arose and conquered European culture and sensibility" (*Sources of the Self* 368). "Nature," he defines, after Herder, as a version of "the larger order in which we are set," specified by Herder in very animistic terms as "a great current of sympathy, running through all things" (369). Though it is a context within which we are set, this nature is an "inner" source, accessible only in and through individual acts of expression in which nature is both manifested and created:

> My claim is that the idea of nature as an intrinsic source goes along with an expressive view of human life. Fulfilling my nature means espousing the inner élan, the voice or impulse. And this makes what was hidden manifest for both myself and others. But this manifestation also helps to define what is to be realized.... A human life is seen as manifesting a potential which is also being shaped by this manifestation; it is not just a matter of copying an external model or carrying out an already determinate formulation. (375)

On this view, the bringing of the world to life allows for a close alliance of ontology, epistemology, and ethics. In the language of Wordsworth's "Tintern Abbey," our recognition of and participation in an ontology of "something far more deeply interfused" allows us to bypass the unintelligibility of the world and achieve a new kind of epistemology as

> with an eye made quiet by the power
> Of harmony, and the deep power of joy,
> We see into the life of things.
>
> (47–49)

The "soul / Of all my moral being" (110–11) can thus be "recognize[d] / In nature and the language of the sense" (108); expressive participation in an animated nature makes moral life (ethics), the positing of essential being (ontology), and knowledge of that being (epistemology) all parts of the same gesture. This way of bringing the world to life makes the Kantian difference between what really exists and what we can know, and the related problem of how we should act, largely irrelevant. If this expressive view of nature as source carries the day, then for language to be an incarnation of thought is merely one more effort to bring what used to be, from Locke onward, a manipulation of inanimate conventional signs into the realm of this all-encompassing life-force. Inner and outer are united and animated, not in the ancient Hebrew sense discussed above, but by the inner route of creative expressive force. Taylor is not uncritical toward this expressivism, but he does grant this Romantic fusion of expression and nature-as-source a major role in the construction of the modern self.

For Stanley Cavell, "Romanticism's bargain with the Kantian (buying back the thing in itself by taking on animism)" (*In Quest of the Ordinary* 65) is not as clearly advantageous a transaction. He uses the Romantics as a way of explaining how animism is not so much a solution to Kant's enforcement of skepticism regarding knowledge of things in themselves as it is a reformulation of the problem of skepticism. Cavell sees skepticism not as an expression of knowledge's impossibility but rather as an act of creating a metaphysical lack, of drawing a line around the boundaries of knowledge:

> What there is to be known philosophically remains unknown not through ignorance (for we cannot just not know what there is to be known philosophically, for example that there is a world and I and others in it) but through a refusal of knowledge, a denial, or a repression of knowledge, say even a killing of it. The beginning of skepticism is the insinuation of absence, of a line, or limitation, hence the creation of want, or desire; the creation, as I have put it, of the interpretation of metaphysical finitude as intellectual lack. (51)

This translation of skepticism into desire is already close to animism; the world about which we are skeptical is a possible murder victim and object of desire. When Cavell adds to this the notion of a reciprocal relation between material-object skepticism and other-minds skepticism, he begins to suspect "that skeptical doubt is to be interpreted as jealousy and that our relation to the world that remains is as to something that has died at our hands" (55). This transformation of skepticism into animism may be of intellectual profit, he says,

> if we come to see the idea of the jealousy of the world as bringing out an animism already implicit in the idea of doubting its existence—to the extent that the uncertainty created by this doubt is pictured less in terms of whether one's knowledge is well grounded (whether, for example, we can achieve assured knowledge of the world on the basis of the senses alone) than in terms of whether one's trust is well placed (whether we are well assured, for example, that we are not now dreaming that we are awake). (55–56)

This is related to Geoffrey Hartman's distinction between linguistic "truth" and "troth," the difference between words as marks of a representational truth and words as "signs of obeisance or identity or mutual recognition" (*Saving the Text* 135). It is also a broadening of the concept of skepticism from a purely epistemological exercise to a way of living in the world; in this sense Cavell's effort parallels that of David Hiley, who reminds us in *Philosophy in Question* that the epistemological skepticism developed in the seventeenth century and after is actually a narrowing of earlier Pyrrhonian skepticism, whose challenge we still need to meet; Pyrrhonism saw epistemological doubt not as an end in itself, but as a way to "sever the Socratic connection between knowledge and the virtuous or happy life" (10) and thereby enable an ethically more satisfying life.[8]

Cavell's skeptical animism is a very different notion of bringing the world to life from that which Taylor takes over from Abrams, though Cavell shares with Taylor the idea that the most useful response to Kant's epistemological problem is to be sought in a moral stance within our lived existence rather than in purely epistemological speculations. For Cavell, the world we see has life, not so that we may share a fundamental life-force, but so that it can adopt the role of an other of whom we can be jealous, and whom we are tempted to kill in an effort to get beyond the very human resistance it offers. In shifting from the problem of knowledge not only to ethics but also to a violent relation with the world, Cavell approaches Piotr Hoffman's extreme position that causality itself is a result of the violent relation with an other: "In his having an impact on me—in his emergence as the original causal power—the other injects causal *necessity* into the world" (Hoffman, *Violence in Modern Philosophy*, 11).

The Ancient Mariner's killing of the albatross is Cavell's paradigmatic example of Romanticism's struggle with an animated world. Playing on the Mariner's crossing of the geographical and metaphysical line that separates the everyday world of the Wedding Guest from the supernatural world in which the albatross is killed, Cavell notes that "the Mariner's seascape is an image of the skeptic's temptation and progress past (what presents itself to him as) the merely conventional limits of knowledge" (*In Quest of the Ordinary* 57). The killing of the bird—a part of that living world that confronts the skeptic—is part of this act of transgression: the Mariner

> may just have wanted at once to silence the bird's claim upon him and to establish a connection with it closer, as it were, than his caring for it: a connection beyond the force of his human responsibilities, whether conventional or personal, either of which can seem arbitrary. In dreaming his solution, to pierce it with his arrow, he split off the knowledge that the consequences of his act would be the death of nature, this piece of nature. (60)

In this conception, the animation of the world is a threat, not a promise; rather than offer us a way out of Kant's challenge, it presents the life of the world in frightening forms like Wordsworth's "huge peak, black and huge" that "as if with voluntary power instinct, / Upreared its head" and

> For so it seemed, with purpose of its own
> And measured motion like a living thing,
> Strode after [him].
> (*The Prelude* [1850] 1.378–85)

If to treat language as the incarnation of thought is to participate in this process of animating the world, then both Taylor's and Cavell's interpretations need to be taken into account. On the one hand, Wordsworth's incarnational poetics, like the Coleridgean symbol with which it shares a great deal of its theological basis, provides a link to moral sources that offer the possibility of a way of living that can see into the life of things. On the other hand, the translation of epistemological skepticism into this relation to a living world—Cavell's translation of the Kantian problem into a problem of animism—has a dark underside that is reflected in the deep link between the incarnational analogy and human mortality. As we shall see, for Wordsworth to draw on the Christian idea of incarnation for his theory of language is for him to acknowledge that this paradigmatic translation of spirit into event entailed the violent death of the God become man.

To view Wordsworth's poetry as split between engagement and fear is of course nothing new; from his own sense that he was "fostered alike by beauty and by fear" (*The Prelude* 1.302), to Geoffrey Hartman's analysis, in *Wordsworth's Poetry 1787–1814*, of the combination of fear of the autonomous imagination and engagement with the binding force of humanized nature,[9] to the ease with which his own poetics can be turned against him by deconstructionist or historicist readings, interpretations of Wordsworth have pointed to his doubleness. Recently, Gerald Bruns, in phenomenological terms that intersect my own, discussed the tension in Wordsworth between the "romantic hermeneutics" of *Einfühlung*, or complete identification with the consciousness of an other, and the fear that what one thus discovers might be the monstrousness of the other consciousness: "*Einfühlung* as 'the romantic way of knowing,' becoming what you know, sounds like a good idea until you run up against a monster. . . . Knowing as becoming what you know has its mortal risks" ("Wordsworth at the Limits of Romantic Hermeneutics" 404–5). For Bruns the phenomenologists Wilhelm Dilthey and Georges Poulet represent this Romantic hermeneutics, and Cavell represents the skeptical threat to this treatment of understanding as *Einfühlung*. The consequences for Wordsworth, according to Bruns, are as follows:

> Let's say that understanding another means re-experiencing the other's lived experience, call it (romantically) the other's "life of feeling." What we find in Wordsworth is something like a realism concerning the limits of such understanding, but perhaps it is more like what Cavell has in mind when he speaks of encountering the limits of the human, where the idea is that only by encountering these limits, where the human is caught in the moment of slipping into something else, something more-or-less or frightfully other-than-human, we are able to determine, with something like philosophical self-certainty, the existence of the human. (409)

I support everything in this quotation except the first sentence. For example, in Chapter 2 I develop the idea that understanding occurs en route toward death. That corresponds to what Bruns sees here as understanding occurring as it confronts its mortal limits. This idea goes back to Kant, for whom understanding occurs on the boundary of the phenomenal: "The setting of a boundary to the field of understanding by something, which is otherwise unknown to it, is still a cognition which belongs to reason" (*Prolegomena* 133).

Where I differ from Bruns, in emphasis at least, is in the notion that the other pole from this is a private version of understanding that desires to "re-experience the other's lived experience." I contend that the historicity of understanding in Wordsworth's incarnational thought preempts that kind of phenomenological subjectivity from the start. This is why I am opposing Cavell's skepticism, not to a concept of phenomenological intentionality, but to Taylor's expressivism. Inwardness does not entail becoming the other, but rather engaging "nature" through an inner route. For Wordsworth epitaphs do not so much engage what Bruns claims is an ultimately private "descent into the unconscious" ("Wordsworth at the Limits of Romantic Hermeneutics" 492), as they do an ultimately public, historical, dialogical "truth" defined interactively by Wordsworth in the first "Essay Upon Epitaphs" as "truth hallowed by love—the joint offspring of the worth of the dead and the affections of the living" (*PrW* 2:58). It is not identification with the deceased so much as it is a combination of his "worth" (objective in one sense, but also determined only through a process of valuing) with the living historical temporality of the reader. In this sense I see Wordsworth as already providing a corrective to what Gadamer sees as the error of Romanticism's "pantheistic metaphysics of individuality" (*TM* 198), exemplified by Schleiermacher's ultimately ahistorical interpretive principle, to be given support by later developments in the psychology of the unconscious, that the goal of interpretation is to recover the author's intention, "*to understand a writer better than he understood himself*" (*TM* 192). Bruns also sees Wordsworth's "Cavellian" skeptical side as performing a critique of successors to these Romantic theories of reading, such as Poulet's, but I think a close reading of Wordsworth's incarnational thought will show that this skeptical historicality is not just a corrective to a Romantic hermeneutics of subjective identification, what in the reading process is a "Husserlian idea of interpretation as the reproduction of an author's intentional experience" ("Wordsworth at the Limits of Romantic Hermeneutics" 414), but is a fundamental part of Wordsworth's whole experience of language.

THE METAPHOR OF INCARNATION

The Christian incarnation, whether seen as event, concept, or mystery, has been consciously employed as an example or a foundation (the difference often being obscure) for systems of meaning at least since commentators began struggling with the concept of the Son of God as the "Word" of God in the opening verses of John's gospel.[10] The notion of a human incarnation of the divine can be accepted as the primary given, which any system of meaning must take into account, or it can be employed as an illustrative example of or solution to problems of meaning that already exist in human communication. Though this difference may separate the theologians (who do the first) from the philosophers (who do the second), it is a difference that is hard to maintain, because the theological status of the Incarnation as the solution to the problem of human salvation in Judeo-Christian history is often indistinguishable from its philosophical status as a solution to problems such as the relationship between the finite and the infinite. Coleridge, of course, sought to efface such differences in a system that would unite theology, philosophy, and poetics. Without such a synthesis (but with the urging of Coleridge to unite philosophy and poetry), Wordsworth has a complex relationship to this difference. For him, incarnation is a naturally inherited metaphorical matrix, entering his language from the tradition of English religious poetry in which he, as a poetic descendent of George Herbert as well as Milton, was deeply steeped,[11] and from the interdependence of self, God, and land that he saw represented in the physical as well as spiritual presence of an English church, important both as a national institution and as a community center of worship that joined the living and the dead.[12] From another angle, the complexities of incarnation as a philosophical problem and solution would have entered Wordsworth's thought from German Idealism by way of Coleridge. Most important, the incarnational theory of language arises from Wordsworth's own experiments in search of poetry that remained rooted in experience yet refused to accept the compromise of a system of meaning to be paid for by renunciation of access to anything beyond the limits of our categories of understanding.

Though incarnation is used by Wordsworth to create what from our perspective may seem an artificial distinction between Romantic and Enlightenment systems of thought, the incarnational metaphor cannot be reduced to one side of an oppositional pair, as when we oppose Romantic "organicism" to Enlightenment "mechanism," or Romantic "symbol" to Enlightenment "allegory." The foundational role of the Incarnation and its Christian context in the culture that produced both Enlightenment and Romantic epistemology can provide a critical perspective that is not tied essentially to the binary oppositions within which Romanticism explicitly thought, even though it is a term that has been polarized by recent criticism in the service of that binary opposition. Its usefulness and flexibility as a critical concept thus resides in the fact that it provides a metaphorical structure that operates both "inside" and "outside" of Romanticism. From the inside, it can be studied as a metaphor that Wordsworth used to define his project, limiting it and setting it up in opposition to what he saw as the arbitrarily representational project of his predecessors. He saw himself as trapped between an abhorrent but inescapable system of representation for which language was no more than a series of arbitrary signs and an intuition of the possibility of harnessing the power of words as incarnations of thought, of making self-consciousness turn into language.

From the "outside," however, from a perspective that acknowledges the influence of incarnational thought on both the Enlightenment and Romanticism, the situation is problematic, because the Incarnation can be and has been used to legitimize both what Wordsworth promotes and what he contests. For example, Taylor points out that the groundwork for the so-called secularization of Enlightenment culture was laid within the Christian culture itself:

> In each case, the stimulus existed within Christian culture itself to generate these views which stand on the threshold. Augustinian inwardness stands behind the Cartesian turn, and the mechanistic universe was originally a demand of theology. The disengaged subject stands in a place already hollowed out for God; he takes a stance to the world which befits an image of the Deity. The belief in interlocking nature follows the affirmation of ordinary life, a central Judeo-Christian idea, and extends the centrally Christian notion that God's goodness consists in his stooping to seek the benefit of humans.
>   What arises in each case is a conception which stands ready for a mutation, which will carry it outside Christian faith altogether. (*Sources of the Self* 315)

Louis Marin argues that the memorialization of the Incarnation in the Eucharist helps construct precisely the Enlightenment relationship of arbitrary binary representation against which Wordsworth invokes his incarnational poetics. In his *Food for Thought*, the text Marin uses to support that argument is the influential treatise on reason written by Antoine Arnauld and others, published in 1662 as *La logique, ou L'art de Penser* and translated into English as *The Art of Thinking: Port-Royal Logic*. According to Marin, the system of representation offered in the *Port-Royal Logic* is founded on the Eucharist's memorialization of the incarnational connection between spirit and body. The Eucharistic utterance, "This is my body," which the authors of the *Port-Royal Logic* present as a mere example of how the relationship between signs and things is established, and as a demonstration of the compatibility of faith and reason, is, according to Marin, how the relationship between signs and things is legislated: "The complex and unitary space of the eucharistic model is organized in such a way that the binary oppositions pertaining to the classificatory criteria are dissolved into a mysterious unity that provides the theological and theoretical origin of their diversification" (*Food for Thought* 9).

The dual role of the incarnational analogy highlights the obvious fact that Wordsworth, like everyone in his situation, must object to his predecessors in the very language he inherited from them, and that a concept such as incarnation can have a variety of philosophical and political uses. As we shall see, to use the concept of the Incarnation (as memorialized in the Eucharist) as an instrument in the service of a subjective fiat is very different from Wordsworth's very anti-instrumental use of the concept. Nevertheless, from the "outside" incarnation can be seen as a metaphor that reaches back beyond Romanticism to the beginning of the history of meaning in the Christian West, and thus can be invoked in contextualizing and critiquing Wordsworth's "inside" perspective.

It is now a critical commonplace that the contrast between "mirror" and "lamp," as well as the equation of Romanticism and secularized Protestantism, fails to account for Wordsworth's linguistic relationship to the world. Still, in the preceding discussion I hope I have clarified my contention that it is also insufficient simply to reverse the terms of Romantic self-evaluation, and to argue reductively that the search for self always throws the Romantic poet back into a semiological[13] web from which he is trying to escape, that because of the pervasive workings of *écriture* symbol is always (already) allegory. As Hans-Georg Gadamer points out, Romantic hermeneutics itself made the mistake of simply inverting oppositions such as reason versus feeling and art versus nature, without escaping that structure of oppositions: "Precisely because romanticism has a negative attitude to this development [the Enlightenment 'conquest of mythos by logos'], it takes over the schema itself as an obvious truth. It shares the presupposition of the enlightenment and only reverses the evaluation of it" (*TM* 242).

Critics of Romanticism often repeat this mistake, either accepting or inverting Romantic pronouncements (often on the basis of absolutist positions on how language does or does not work) and failing to recognize the implications of images and thoughts that, while operating in complex ways within the binary oppositions that polarized both the Romantics' own writing and that of their critics, also point in directions that cannot be accommodated within such oppositions.[14] Paul de Man, whose reversal of Romantic self-evaluation set the tone for so much criticism of the 1970s and 1980s, argues in "Autobiography as Defacement" that "the language so violently denounced" in the passage from the third "Essay Upon Epitaphs" quoted above "is in fact the language of metaphor," the very language Wordsworth seems both to promote and to denounce, but within which he must write, suffering the consequences of a language of representation and death, which, in autobiography, "deprives and disfigures to the precise extent that it restores" (*The Rhetoric of Romanticism* 80–81). (De Man rather arbitrarily reads the *Essays Upon Epitaphs* as autobiography, and it goes without saying that problems will arise if memorials for the dead are used as models for self-representation.) Frances Ferguson, in *Wordsworth: Language as Counter-Spirit*, develops a related insight in tracing how "both language and consciousness may be simultaneously spirit and counter-spirit" (vii).

These readings of the incarnational relationship between thought and language fall into these binary oppositions (as, at times, does Wordsworth's own analysis) because they are limited by a perceived obligation to argue for or against the idealizing Coleridgean symbol, particularly after the tradition, extending from Coleridge to de Man, which pits symbolic unity against allegorical difference. As a result, modern readers who, whether or not they are explicitly deconstructive, devote their energies to the many fissures in Wordsworth's theory of language, assume too readily that for him and other post-Enlightenment writers the idea of incarnation represents a desired ahistorical transparency between thought and language that is undercut by the actuality of language as death-ridden counter-spirit. In J. Hillis Miller's *Disappearance of God*, for example, the Incarnation and its repetition in the Eucharist are seen as a "guarantee of communion" among God, man, nature, and language resulting from the event that "brought God back to earth, so that once more he walked among us as he had before the fall, when history had not yet begun" (3). In thus collapsing Christian history into a single relationship, Miller somewhat typically fails to distinguish between God's prelapsarian presence on earth and his very different entrance into postlapsarian history in the Incarnation. Similarly, David Ferry's discussion of *The Prelude*'s final books associates the "sacramental" in Wordsworth simply with harmonious nature (*The Limits of Mortality* 160, 169–70). The latest example of this trend is Karen Mills-Courts's *Poetry as Epitaph*, worth special notice because of the potentially misleading similarity between her terminology and mine. Though she very usefully contrasts "incarnational" and "representational" thought in Romanticism, her equation of incarnation with the kind of nostalgia for "presence" that Derrida attacks forces both the incarnational and the representational sides of her argument to remain within binary representational bounds, which I see incarnational thought as transgressing.[15]

Without denying the importance of such readings, I would like to argue for a more detailed and less polarized consideration of the "incarnation" side of the conflict between language as incarnation and language as counter-spirit. Missing from the analyses mentioned above is a recognition that incarnation is not simply a deeper connection between thought and language, a connection that pretends to deny history, but is rather a very historical relationship entirely different from that which sees language as a more or less adequate representation of thought. De Man, commenting on the *Essays Upon Epitaphs*, says that Wordsworth's contrast between the relationship of body to soul and clothing to body is "in fact a perfectly consistent metaphorical chain: garment is the visible outside of the body as the body is the visible outside of the soul" (*The Rhetoric of Romanticism* 80). To be fair to de Man, Wordsworth's own consistent pairing of these oppositions supports such a dualistic reading, and de Man gives at least some credence to the claim that these "two notions ... seem indeed to 'have another and a finer connection than that of contrast' " (79). On very different grounds, Stephen K. Land claims that despite his apparent intentions, "Wordsworth has emphasized rather than denied semantic dualism in his theory of language" because the body-soul comparison involves a greater difference than that between thought and language: "The ontological distinction between body and soul is incomparably greater than the relatively trivial distinction between thought and its verbal embodiment" ("Silent Poet" 160).

The distinction between thought and language is not at all trivial for Wordsworth, as the incarnational analogy attests. More important, his incarnational language needs to be addressed, not just in dualistic structural terms (whether the terms used by de Man or the very different ones used by Land) of relative distance between figural poles, but also in terms of what is entailed by the precisely nondualistic process of incarnational generation of meaning. A closer examination of the complex notion of incarnation will reveal the limitations of the dualistic views that simply oppose incarnation to clothing as comparable analogies for poetic language, limitations that Wordsworth's incarnational language struggles to overcome.

Hans-Georg Gadamer provides a way to release the concept of incarnation from the dualistic trap while illuminating its role in the production of meaning. Whereas de Man argues, by way of a contrast between visible exterior and inaccessible interior, that the relationship of difference obtaining between clothing and body is repeated in the relationship between body and soul, Gadamer insists on a clear distinction between incarnation and embodiment:

> Incarnation is obviously not embodiment. Neither the idea of the soul nor of God that is connected with embodiment corresponds to the Christian idea of incarnation. . . . The relation between soul and body as conceived in these theories [of embodiment rather than incarnation] . . . assumes that soul and body are completely different. (*TM* 418)

Similarly, Thomas De Quincey noted in a much more contemporaneous context that the point of the Romantic objection to the Enlightenment view of language as thought's dress is that poetic thought posits, not just a closer relationship between language and thought, but a different kind of relationship:

> If language were merely a dress, then you could separate the two; you could lay the thoughts on the left hand, the language on the right. But, generally speaking, you can no more deal thus with poetic thought than you can with soul and body. The union is too subtle, the intertexture too ineffable—each coexisting not merely with the other, but each in and through the other. An image, for instance, a single word, often enters into a thought as a constituent part. In short, the two elements are not united as a body with a separable dress, but as a *mysterious incarnation*. (*Collected Writings* 10:229–30, quoted in *PrW* 2:115n; emphasis added)

One of the premises for Wordsworth's distinction between incarnation and counter-spirit is that "words are too awful an instrument for good and evil to be trifled with: they hold above all other external powers a dominion over thoughts" (*PrW* 2:84). Thus we are faced not only with the danger that words will, like clothing, separate from their referents and enter the realm of what he calls "counter-spirit," but also with a different kind of problem in the notion of incarnation itself. This is the recognition that incarnation is not an ideal effacement of the difference between word and referent, but rather a process of spirit becoming event, a process by which (by analogy with Jesus entering the world) words move from the ideality of thought to become—for better *and* for worse—things and events in the world which are not simply separable from thought, but which must enter the realm of mortality.

The threat and the modernity of the incarnational link between word and thing lie in the recognition that this link is not an ahistorical idealization of language, but rather a concretization of thought, as thought is incarnated into the events of language. According to Gadamer, the Incarnation was not the denial of history, but rather its founding. The Augustinian and Thomist idea of meaning as incarnation presents words as events in the world, rather than signs of ideality:

> The uniqueness of the redemptive event introduces the essence of history into Western thought, brings the phenomenon of language out of its immersion in the ideality of meaning, and offers it to philosophical reflection. For in contrast to the Greek logos, the word is pure event. (*TM* 419)

Thus the significance of the incarnational metaphor for our understanding of Romantic poetics lies not in its intimation of a representational access to a kind of presence, but rather in both the problems and solutions of the transition from thought to the historical event of language in the world.[16] In the terms of J. L. Austin (whom Gadamer cites with approval), words such as those of the marriage ceremony can be thought of as "performatives," which effect action, rather than as "statements," which describe or represent something (*How to Do Things with Words* 4–6, 12–13). Like Austin, Wordsworth often uses marriage as a paradigmatic example of how language achieves its effects. As we shall see, Wordsworth's sense of the "performative" side of language is more radical than Austin's in the sense that words are not only events, but "things." In the incarnational transition from "spirit" to "event" the interesting problems occur on the human, "event" side of the relationship, the side of language and world rather than spirit and thought.[17]

A brief excursus into the history of the relationship between the theology of the Incarnation and the role of language in thought may help to clarify what, from the point of much current theory, might appear as incompatible goals of this study: to preserve the theological bases of Wordsworth's thought *and* to rescue this side of his thought from charges of a naive logocentrism. Those goals are incompatible only if we confuse incarnational thought with the thought of representational adequacy, which, I argue, post-Saussurean critiques of Wordsworth have done.

Saint Paul contrasted the Greek, Jewish, and Christian modes of apprehending the guiding principles of human existence in the following ways: "For Jews demand signs and Greeks seek wisdom, but we preach Christ crucified" (1 Cor. 1:22–23). This declaration establishes the fundamental difference that Christianity bases its thought not on the apprehension of abstract truth (Greek "wisdom") or representational structure (Jewish "signs"), but on the *event* of the Incarnate God's transition into a very mortal life. This distinction holds from Paul to Wordsworth, despite the many permutations undergone by thought about meaning between early Christianity and Romanticism. Still, early arguments in favor of incarnation and against representation had purposes very different from the arguments of the Romantics. Patristic and medieval thought about incarnation and language argued against representation as a way of arguing against the heresy of subordinationism that could result from a misreading of the opening of John's gospel:

> In the Beginning was the Word, and the Word was with God, and the Word was God. He was in the beginning with God; all things were made through him, and without him was not anything made that was made. In him was life, and the life was the light of men. The light shines in the darkness, and the darkness has not overcome it. (1:1–5)

Here we must back up from the Incarnation itself (God's becoming human) to its enabling source: the pre-incarnational relationship between the Father and the Son. Because John used human language to talk about the Son of God as the "Word" of God, an analogy between divine and human expression was inescapable: we have to depend on the human meaning of "word" if we are to understand, even through a glass darkly, what John is talking about. This puts the exegete in a double bind: there has to be a connection between God and his Word on one hand and human thought and language on the other, but to put that analogy in terms of actual spoken language, whose contingency and inadequacy to thought is all too evident, would be to commit the heresy of subordinating the Word to his source in the Father.

Augustine's solution, in *On the Holy Trinity*, was to see the comparison to the Word not in terms of actual spoken language, but in terms of an "inner word" produced by but consubstantial with thought, just as the Son was begotten by but consubstantial with the Father:

> That word of man ... which is neither utterable in sound nor capable of being thought under the likeness of sound, such as must needs be with the word of any tongue; but which precedes all the signs by which it is signified, and is begotten from the knowledge that continues in the mind, when that same knowledge is spoken inwardly as it really is. (210)

The analogy between divine and human language is mediated by this concept of an inner word that can be linked both to audible human language, which Augustine calls "the articulate sound of a word," so called "on account of that to make which outwardly apparent it is itself assumed" (209), and to the Word of God. Before we accuse Augustine of solving the problem by sneaking in a piece of representational trickery, however (such as, for example, creating a proto-Saussurean category of "signified" to mediate between material signifiers and elusive referents), we need to do justice to this concept of the inner word, which is not just a simple image of representational presence. This word precedes a specific language, but is actively produced in a process of begetting, continuing, and even speaking. This "true word concerning a true thing" is not a subordinate representation of the thing, but neither is it an idealization; it actively expresses knowledge gained from contingent human sources:

> All those things, then, both those which the human mind knows by itself, and those which it knows by the bodily senses, and those which it has received and knows by the testimony of others, are laid up and retained in the storehouse of the memory; and from these is begotten a word that is true. (212)

The point I want to emphasize here is that this combination of production and consubstantiality cannot be covered by the concept of representation, which, in classical, Enlightenment and post-Saussurean variations, insists on a separation between the word and what it represents. If we insist on drawing a sharp distinction between a pre-temporal "presence" and its contingent representation, we will not be able to understand

Augustine's concept. The inner word is ontologically prior to its contingent expression in any particular language, but it is still a process, not a simple presence, and is characterized by its potential for achieving historical utterance, just as John's description of the Son as the Word leads to the possibility of the Son as becoming human.

The processual character of the inner word is both a difference from and a similarity to the divine Word. As Gadamer notes, following Thomas Aquinas, the finitude of our thought requires a process of inner dialogue: "Because our understanding does not comprehend what it knows in one single inclusive glance, it must always draw what it thinks out of itself, and present it to itself as if in inner dialogue with itself" (*TM* 422). But this is not to say that human thought is temporal and divine thought is not; human thought is not tied to the temporality of linear narrative succession, because if it were, it would simply change with each successive thought and would have no means of connecting those thoughts (*TM* 423). Nor is the divine Word simply unitary and the human word multiple; there is a real multiplicity in the Word's appearance as event in the church: "It is one word that is proclaimed ever anew in preaching. Its character as gospel, then, already points to the multiplicity of its proclamation" (*TM* 427).

The inner word must be put into the context of events rather than representational structures in two other ways. First, as Augustine's biblical language of "begetting" implies, and as Gadamer emphasizes from his reading of Augustine and Aquinas, the articulation of the inner word is not the result of a reflective process by which we decide to link a word and a concept. On the contrary,

> in thinking, a person does not move from the one thing to the other, from thinking to speaking to himself. The word does not emerge in a sphere of mind that is still free of thought.... In fact there is no reflection when the word is formed, for the word is not expressing the mind but the thing intended. (*TM* 426)

In describing the special multiplicity that obtains in the repeated proclamation of the event of the original Word's redemptive act, Gadamer emphasizes the impossibility of separating, by a reflective act, meaning from the event of utterance. Drawing on an example that Geoffrey Hartman also uses to make a similar point in *Saving the Text* and elsewhere, Gadamer likens this utterance to a curse: "*Being an event is a characteristic belonging to the meaning itself.* It is like a curse, which obviously cannot be separated from the act of uttering it. What we understand from it is not an abstractable logical sense like that of a statement, but the actual curse that occurs in it" (*TM* 427).

Second, as Augustine points out in a passage that foreshadows the familiar Romantic analogy between divine and human creativity, both divine and human words effect action, and though we can have language without action, all action depends on language: "As it is said of that Word, 'All things were made by Him,' where God is declared to have made the universe by his only-begotten Son, so there are no works of man that are not first spoken in his heart" (*On the Holy Trinity* 210). According to Bultmann, this principle of word as action—translated from Word as Son of God to the actual word of preaching—is manifested concretely in Paul, who historicized eschatology by "conceiving the time for the Messiah's reign as the time between Christ's resurrection and parousia—i.e., as the Now in which the proclamation is sounding forth (1 Cor. 15:23–28)." This means that "the proclaimed word is neither an enlightening *Weltanschauung* flowing out in general truths, nor a merely historical account which, like a reporter's story, reminds a public of important but by-gone facts. Rather, it is *kerygma*—herald's service—in the literal sense—authorized, plenipotent proclamation, edict from a sovereign" (Bultmann, *Theology of the New Testament*, 1:307). Walter J. Ong, emphasizing the priority of the spoken word, generalizes this principle:

> Words in an oral-aural culture are inseparable from action for they are always sounds. Thus they appear of a piece with other actions, including even grossly physical actions. The Hebrew use of the word *dabar* to mean both word and event is, as Barr would have it, probably not so distinctive a phenomenon as it has been made out to be. But, however common the usage may or may not be, this sense is perfectly consistent not only with the oral-aural state of mind but with the very nature of words themselves. For every word even today in its primary state of existence, which is its spoken state, is indeed an event. (*The Presence of the Word* 112–13)

Incarnational language effects action rather than stating general truths or representing specific facts.

It may look like a long stretch from Augustine's inner word to the concrete Wordsworthian language of incarnation. Though the link is complex, it is also close.[18] First of all, there is a slippery continuity between the pre-incarnate and Incarnate Word as far back as the prologue in John's gospel; Bultmann notes "the old dispute of the exegetes: how far does the Prologue speak of the preexistent Logos, and from which verse does it begin to speak of his appearance in the flesh?" (*The Gospel of John* 16). Augustine insists, as does Gadamer and, in my view, Wordsworth, that the Incarnation itself provides for an "inner word" (Augustine) or "thought" (Wordsworth) "becoming" materially existent without being "changed into" something else:

> And as our word [the inner word] becomes an articulate sound, yet is not changed into one; so the Word of God becomes flesh, but far be it from us to say He was changed into flesh. For both that word of ours became an articulate sound, and that other Word became flesh, by assuming it, not by consuming itself so as to be changed into it. (*On the Holy Trinity* 209)

Despite these continuities between inner and outer word, and despite the processual nature of even the inner word—all factors that can help us understand the nonrepresentational event of language as incarnation in Wordsworth—Augustine's "inner word" could not survive intact in a post-Lockean and post-Kantian world. Even though Wordsworth's incarnational language resisted the Lockean notion of words as conventional signs, Locke's separation of word from idea, making words conventional signs for ideas, made it impossible to return to the Johannine/Augustinian near-equation of thought and inner language. Also, in denying access to things-in-themselves, Kant has prohibited us from simply implementing what Augustine called "a true word concerning a true thing" (212) in "knowledge ... spoken inwardly according as it really is" (210). Language and thought can now only be reunited at the opposite end of the spectrum, in post-Romantic notions (anticipated by Wordsworth's fear of language dominating thought as "counter-spirit") of concepts being determined by language.

Where Augustine had revitalized language and linked it to the concept of the Incarnation by means of the inner word, Wordsworth, true to his empiricist heritage and mindful of the Kantian dilemma, revitalized it by seeing language incarnated as "living thing," as part of the animated material world I discussed above. In the note to "The Thorn," Wordsworth called for words to be of interest "not only as symbols of the passion, but as *things,* active and efficient, which are of themselves part of the passion" (*Poetical Works* 2:513), and Coleridge stated in a letter to William Godwin that he "would endeavor to destroy the old antithesis of *Words* and *Things,* elevating, as it were, words into Things, and living

Things too" (*Collected Letters* 1:625–26). The link to a vital, divinely derived source that Augustine had sought in the concept of the inner word is preserved, but this foundational principle of incarnational thought is moved from Augustine's interior world to the world as a whole, with the strong materiality that British empiricism had brought to consciousness. Of course, this is not to deny the concomitant influence of what Taylor calls "Augustinian inwardness"; as I noted above, Taylor emphasizes the oft-made point that in Romanticism we gain access to this larger order of nature through an interior route. But by however interior a route we get there, the bedrock of incarnational thought can no longer be simply located in the mind's inner word.

The importance of this conceptual shift for our understanding of Wordsworth is that it makes his incarnational theory of language, because of its foundation in the material world, even more oriented toward process, event, and materiality (rather than representation of presence) than its Augustinian precedent. Where Augustine's theory engaged the incarnational event of thought's entrance into historical, processual language but backed away from the world into the isolated safety of the inner word, Wordsworth's presentation of incarnational language has no choice but to remain in the often frightening contingency of the material world. One concrete manifestation of this shift is a reversal in the priority of sight and hearing as hermeneutically primary senses. For Augustine, drawing on the Johannine image of God as light, the inner word is *seen* whereas the lesser outer word is *heard:* in imagery that is emphasized consistently throughout his discussion, Augustine says, "Accordingly, the word that sounds outwardly is the sign of the word that gives light inwardly; which latter has the greater claim to be called a word" (*On the Holy Trinity* 209). Wordsworth reverses this hierarchy as he complains of a time when

> the eye was master of the heart,
> When that which is in every stage of life
> The most despotic of our senses gained
> Such strength in me as often held my mind
> In absolute dominion.
> (*The Prelude* 11.172–76)

In "Tintern Abbey" he denigrates as immature the state that had no "interest / Unborrowed from the eye" (82–83), and elevates the life that hears the "still, sad music of humanity" (91). With the disappearance of an inner word to be "seen" as a true whole, sight becomes a faculty that may arrest rather than see into the stream of animated nature to which the incarnational focus has turned. In order to "see into the life of things" (49) the "eye" needs to be "made quiet by" an aural "power / Of Harmony" (47–48).

The hermeneutic priority of hearing continues as a basic assumption for twentieth-century thinkers such as Ong and Gadamer. Perhaps as the definition of "life" moves from Augustine's inward link to God to the biological and material in post-seventeenth-century thought, the concept of "light" shifts from an inward illumination with an external (divine) source to the lesser, material light of day, and "sound," secondary in Augustine's scheme precisely because it is biologically more inward, and thus more human than divine, comes to the fore as inwardness becomes valued for its own sake even as it is situated in a more material concept of life.

Wordsworth seems almost explicitly to be lamenting the absence of an Augustinian inner word when he complains about language as "shrines so frail" (48) at the beginning of book 5 of *The Prelude:*

> Oh, why hath not the mind
> Some element to stamp her image on
> In nature somewhat nearer to her own?
> (5.44–46)

Augustine's inner word, "begotten from the knowledge that continues in the mind," would provide just such an element. Still, Wordsworth's own more material incarnational rhetoric enables him to say, by the end of the same book,

> Visionary power
> Attends upon the motion of the winds
> Embodied in the mystery of words.
> (5.619–21)

The incarnational analogy, made material by the loss of the inner word, combines the celebratory force of Augustine's sense of the Johannine Word with the threat implicit in a life that is no longer an immortally guaranteed inward vision, but is rather a very mortal existence in a world in which vision threatens to contract to sight. This reminds us of something that Augustine does not emphasize in his discussion of incarnational language, but which permeates Wordsworth's incarnational rhetoric: the strong sense of mortality (the death of Jesus) present in the original Incarnation. Mortality also receives more emphasis in Wordsworth's attitude toward representational thought. Both Wordsworth and Augustine use the incarnational interaction between thought and language to attack a representational or semiotic separation of one from the other, but for Augustine, to see the Johannine Word as representational is to be guilty of subordinationism—to deny the consubstantiality of the Word with God and the human inner word with thought. For Wordsworth, to see language as representational clothing instead of incarnation is to provoke the "counter-spirit" latent in the tendency of words to dominate and, in his own imagery, murder thought.

In addition to this historical difference conditioning the possibilities for thinking through the incarnational analogy, we must consider the difference between Augustine's use of the linguistic incarnational analogy as an extension of theology, and Wordsworth's use of the analogy as an explanation for poetry. The incarnational analogy retains a strong theological content for Wordsworth—it is not a simple "secularization" of a theological idea—but poetry is not the same as theology. Wordsworth suggests a way to think about this relation in the 1815 "Essay, Supplementary to the Preface," when he notes a specific link between the theological and the poetic versions of the problem of how to negotiate the relation between the infinite or transcendental on one hand, and the finite or sensuous on the other.

> The commerce between Man and his Maker cannot be carried on but by a process where much is represented in little, and the Infinite Being accommodates himself to a finite capacity. In all this may be perceived the affinity between religion and poetry; . . . between religion—whose element is infinitude, and whose ultimate trust is the supreme of things, submitting herself to circumscription, and reconciled to substitutions; and poetry—ethereal and transcendent, yet incapable to sustain her existence without sensuous incarnation. (*PrW* 3:65)[19]

In both religion and poetry, the problem is not how to represent or gain access to the transcendental—its existence and limited accessibility to man are pretty much taken for granted—but rather how to negotiate the interdependence between our finite, sensuous world and the world beyond, an interdependence both emphasized and problematized by Kant. The affinity between religion and poetry Wordsworth points to still contains some significant differences. Religion "submit[s] herself" to "substitutions" and "circumscriptions"; poetry is unable to exist without "sensuous incarnation." Those differences reflect an implicit trade-off. Because religion originates in infinitude, the infinite can *choose* to circumscribe itself. If this circumscription is voluntary, we can assume it could be revoked; thus the infinite is only temporarily dependent on the finite. Still, what the infinite submits itself to clearly reduces it and veils it in mere representation, in "circumscriptions," which suggest enclosure and limitation, and in "substitutions," which suggest the kind of binary representation in which there is no necessary connection between the signifying element and the referent. Conversely, poetry is lower in origin—"ethical and transcendent" rather than "infinite"—and therefore "incapable to sustain her existence" without a dependency on the sensuous that is, however, expressed in richly incarnational terms ("sensuous incarnation") rather than in terms of limitation and representation.

In poetry, as Wordsworth's incarnational poetics will demonstrate, we surrender the infinity of divine origins in exchange for an improved situation on the level of the material and finite: "sensuous incarnation" is a better deal than submission to "circumscription" and reconciliation to "substitutions." Furthermore, "incarnation" is mentioned in the context of poetry, not religion; *poetry* is the ultimate beneficiary of the originally theological incarnational process, whereas religion must settle for the rhetoric of substitution. The suggestion is that incarnational thought actually works *better* in poetry than in its native theology, perhaps because the spiritual and material poles are closer together in humanly produced poetry than in divinely originating religion.

On the divine side of the comparison, there is an important difference between the theologically "infinite" and the poetically "transcendent," however complexly these categories may be intertwined for Wordsworth. The poetic version of theological infinitude is most emphatically described in the context of the sudden appearance of Imagination in book 6 of *The Prelude*:

> Our destiny, our nature, and our home
> Is with infinitude—and only there;
> With hope it is, hope that can never die,
> Effort, and expectation, and desire,
> And something evermore about to be.
> (6.538–42)

This possibility of our being "with" infinitude depends on a definition of infinitude as the infinite potential of the finite (an idea carried to its logical extreme in Blake's "human form divine"). This *poetic* infinitude is not a transcendental other, like the Jewish God described by Hegel or the "supreme of things" noted by Wordsworth. Instead, it is like what Gadamer sees as the infinite potential of possible interpretation, the "whole" of language to which events of utterance are "parts":

> Every word causes the whole of the language to which it belongs to resonate and the whole worldview that underlies it to appear. Thus every word, as the event of a moment, carries with it the unsaid, to which it is related by responding and summoning.... All human speaking is finite in such a way that there is laid up within it an infinity of meaning to be explicated and laid out. (*TM* 458)[20]

Thus, when in the incarnational analogy, the transformation of God to Man becomes the transformation of thought to language, words become the incarnation not of a pure onto-theological presence, but of the infinity of possible interpretation, that is, of the process of "thought" taken (in a way that is not, of course, possible for us) as a "whole."

I do not mean to suggest that we can sharply differentiate the theological from the poetic versions of incarnational thought. As we have seen, the passage from the 1815 essay presents a complex combination of affinity and difference between religion and poetry. Furthemore, such a sharp difference would be anti-incarnational; if the analogy is working "incarnationally," the spiritual version of incarnational thought becomes historicized as an "event" of poetic incarnation; it is not simply translated to a lower and separate rung on the ladder of representation.

INCARNATION AND REPRESENTATION

One reason we find it so difficult to appreciate the complexity of the incarnational analogy, and so easy to read it as an interesting but ultimately "blind" (in de Man's sense) misreading of how language works, is that we are tied to the post-Saussurean notion of the sign.[21] Thus it is difficult for us to understand how the doctrine of incarnation does *not* presume the distinction between body and spirit that is retranslated in both Enlightenment and modern thought into a conventional relationship between two isolable units that can be labeled *sign* and *idea* (Locke) or *signifier* and *signified* (Saussure). Furthermore, the complex historical relationship among Enlightenment sign theory, Romantic incarnational theory, and modern or postmodern sign theory is a potential source of both terminological and conceptual confusion.

The failure of some recent critics, influenced (even at the distance staked out by Derrida) by Saussurean linguistics, to recognize their contingent place in this history (their participation in Gadamer's *wirkungsgeschichtliches Bewußtsein*) has resulted in three related problems. The first is the elevation of the Saussurean sign (whether intact or deconstructed) to an unquestioned and unquestionable foundation for meaning. The second is the consequent blurring of the historical differences between the Enlightenment sign and the post-Saussurean sign. The third is the polarization of incarnational and sign-based meaning into purely oppositional categories, when in fact they have a complex historical relationship.

As an illustration of the first problem, Gadamer critiques how both the Enlightenment and the twentieth century reduce the function of language to a system of instrumental, arbitrary signs:

> The exclusion of what a language "is" beyond its efficient functioning as sign-material—i.e., the self-conquest of language by a system of artificial, unambiguously defined symbols—this ideal of the eighteenth- and twentieth-century Enlightenments, represents the ideal language, because to it would correspond the totality of the knowable: Being as absolutely available objectivity. (*TM* 414)

Though Gadamer tends to caricature both positions, it can still be argued that Enlightenment rationality and modern science, as well as much recent literary criticism, do at least start from the premise of a code model. As Manfred Frank points out, elucidating Gadamer's position, "The minimal consensus of all linguistic theories that work on the basis of the code-model . . . rests on an interest that can be characterized as scientific: In order scientifically to achieve their capacity to control their object, language, they must unavoidably presuppose that linguistic events follow a certain lawfulness" ("Limits of the Human Control of Language," in Michelfelder and Palmer, eds., *Dialogue and Deconstruction*, 155).[22] As I have argued elsewhere,[23] even poststructuralist theories that place the sign in crisis still operate from the premise of the sign as the fulcrum of meaning. This has resulted in readings of Romanticism that miss a good deal because they cannot escape the very sign-based, representational model of meaning that is part of what Romanticism itself set out to critique. For example, Paul de Man's readings of Rousseau emphasize the violent relation between grammar and event in law, but retain the inflexibility of a structural "grammar" as a starting point, and his readings of the early English Romantics read the Romantic symbol back into the sign systems of allegory, replacing the eighteenth-century allegory to which Wordsworth and Coleridge objected with a postmodern notion of allegory.[24]

The second and third problems are inextricably entwined: a historical view of the development of the sign will reveal both the differences between the Enlightenment and the post-Saussurean sign (the second problem) and how the Romantic incarnational view of meaning helps to effect a transition from one to the other (part of the third problem). On the one hand, as I have suggested above, by moving straight from Enlightenment sign theory to modern or postmodern semiology, we fail to move outside of the realm of the sign. We thus prevent ourselves from appreciating the fact that Wordsworth offers an alternative to semiotic representation, not, as many recent critics have claimed, a fundamentally semiotic theory of representational adequacy. On the other hand, that same ahistorical view prevents us from seeing the role of incarnational theory in the history of the sign. It is in part this incarnational alternative to the sign, because it potentially dispenses with the universality of a trans-temporal code and ties itself at a very deep level to human mortality, that paves the way for the modern conception of the sign. Strangely enough, seeing how Wordsworth's incarnational language is antisemiotic may help us to see how that language looked forward to the modern conception of the sign. This idea will be developed in Chapter 2.

The relevant history of the sign inherited by Wordsworth is the history of the relationship between words and things. As suggested above, the desire that language should be an incarnation of thought is, as a version of Romantic animism, closely related to the desire that words be living things.[25] The statements that language should be an incarnation of thought and that words should be living things must be read in the context of a history that had irrevocably split the unity of word and thing; this is why for Wordsworth to want to animate the materiality of language is not simply for him to call for a restoration of the Adamic unity of language and the world, which Hans Aarsleff credits Locke with destroying.[26] Locke's separation of word and thing could not be erased, though it paved the way for a system, objectionable to Wordsworth, of detached, conventional signs to represent things or ideas.

Wordsworth was not objecting to the word-thing split so much as he was objecting to Enlightenment attempts to compensate for the split. The Enlightenment thinking that split word from thing also grounded the epistemological stability of that split by means of divine fiat, a system of laws, or a controlling subject. Locke's statements about the insufficiency of language rest on a faith, as Aarsleff says, "that God had willed man to possess sufficient powers to learn and know what was necessary for this life" (*From Locke to Saussure* 26). The shift in priority from thought to language undertaken by Etienne Bonnot de Condillac and Horne Tooke also did little to release language from its epistemological fixity. Tooke's contention that, in Aarsleff's words, "all the operations of thought reside in language alone" (*The Study of Language in England* 53) rests on a rigid system of "abbreviations," or words standing for other words. The disengagement of language from the world makes possible, for Dugald Stewart, a "theoretical history" based on system, not event:

> In examining the history of mankind, as well as in examining the phenomena of the material world, when we cannot trace the process by which an event *has been* produced, it is often of importance to be able to show how it *may have been* produced by natural causes. Thus, in the instance which has suggested these remarks, although it is impossible to determine with certainty what the steps were by which any particular language was formed, yet if we can shew, from the known principles of human nature, how all its various parts might gradually have arisen, the mind is not only to a certain degree satisfied, but a check is given to that indolent philosophy, which refers to a miracle, whatever appearances, both in the natural and moral worlds, it is unable to explain. ("Account of Adam Smith" 293)

The systematization of "the known principles of human nature" thus frees the philosopher from dependence on either divine guarantees or historical facts, enabling such statements as Rousseau's famous dismissal of "facts" from the *Second Discourse*.[27] The freedom in this possibility of synthesizing a history directly out of the "known principles of human nature" without recourse to empirical fact is echoed in Romantic syntheses such as Blake's, Coleridge's, and even Shelley's attempts at comprehensive philosophies.

Wordsworth certainly assumes the existence of such foundational "principles of human nature" to be revealed through and in a dialectical relation to empirical reality. In fact, the freedom of Romantic hermeneutics as a whole can be traced in part, paradoxically, both to its acceptance of the freedom from God and empirical nature described by Dugald Stewart and to its rejection of the systematization of history, which he sees that freedom as enabling. Wordsworth objects to the radical dissociation of system from events since, even though he cannot repair the word/thing split, he wants to see words as incarnational events. To take the most obvious example, the potential exemplary role of the dialogue between Wordsworth and Coleridge described at the end of *The Prelude*—"what we have loved / Others will love, and we may teach them how" (13.444–45)—suggests that autobiographical events can illustrate the kind of fundamental principles from which Stewart derives his theoretical history. Still, those principles cannot be arrived at except through the very real events of autobiographical language.

Even more important, or at least more complex, the Enlightenment notion of a controlling subject holds the separated word and thing in systematic tension. This is not the full-fledged "self" with which the Romantics have been burdened throughout their critical history, but rather what Charles Taylor calls the "punctual self," Locke's development of the Cartesian detached subject:

> The developing power of disengaged, self-responsible reason tended to credit a view of the subject as an unsituated, even punctual self. This ... involves reading the stance of disengagement, whereby we objectify facets of our own being, into the ontology of the subject, as though we were by nature an agency separable from everything merely given in us—a disembodied soul (Descartes), or a punctual power of self-remaking (Locke), or a pure rational being (Kant). The stance is thereby given the strongest ontological warrant, as it were. (*Sources of the Self* 514)

Condillac points out that our ability to compare three different perceptions depends on a unitary subject: "We must therefore admit of a point of re-union, a substance which at the same time shall be a simple indivisible subject of these three perceptions; consequently distinct from the body; in one word, a soul" (*An Essay on the Origin of Human Knowledge* 16). According to Louis Marin, the Eucharistic consecration grounded one of the most important Enlightenment theories of representation (in the *Logic of Port-Royal* and the theological elaborations added to it in 1683) because it enabled an authority, such as a priest or a king, to legislate a sign system by means of an utterance based on the formula "This is my body": "The eucharistic body turns out to be the matrix of all signs ... but only as a result of the uttering of the proposition that integrates signs into the unity of a sentence" (Marin, *Food for Thought*, 25). On the level of the structure of the Eucharistic utterance, the (Protestant) critique that it involves an illegitimate referential shift by which "this" in the sentence refers successively to "bread" and "my body" is solved, according to Marin, by means of the subjective "my," which links bread and body in a present moment of utterance, though that subjective fiat is presented in the guise of third-person objective reality (17–18).

This subjective guarantee of a system of arbitrary representation is crucial, because when we return in this century to a notion of language as a system of arbitrary signs, it is a very different kind of arbitrariness, partly thanks to the insights of Romanticism, and one in which the role of the subject has switched from that of master to that of victim. As David Wellbery points out, "precisely the element of free choice, which Saussure eliminates from his definition [of the sign], is central to the eighteenth-century sign concept" (*Lessing's "Laocoon"* 17–18). Whereas the movement in eighteenth-century semiotics was to locate rational and empirical guarantees for the newly discovered arbitrariness of language's relation to the world, the thrust of post-Saussurean thought has been to mistrust or at least qualify those same guarantees. The concept of the arbitrary sign as articulated by Saussure and as radicalized by Derrida, Lacan, Baudrillard, and others sees the self not as a user of arbitrary signs in the Lockean sense but as a being constituted by the play of arbitrary signs.

I should make it clear that I do not promote this polarization of the subject as in control in the Enlightenment and absent in postmodernism as a simple historical truth, because this polarization is itself partly a result of the same post-Saussurean generalizations to which I object. In discussing "Saussure's privileging of the code over the individual" (and affiliating it with Romantic thought), Charles Taylor points out the uselessness of such extreme polarization:

> This makes just as much sense as, and no more than, the equal and opposite error of Humpty Dumpty subjectivism. A position like this can only make itself remotely plausible by claiming that the only alternative to it is some such wildly extreme subjectivism. And so it has a vested interest in muddying the waters, and obscuring all the interesting insights which must necessarily lie in the space between these two absurd theses. (*Human Agency and Language* 11)

Nevertheless, as I will attempt to show in Chapter 2, the alleged "death" of the self into the system of arbitrary signification is anticipated by Wordsworth's struggles with signs, things, and a very literal sense of mortality. In this sense the notion of incarnational thought as an alternative to semiotic representation is inseparable from the notion of incarnational thought as leading toward the modern conception of the sign. On the one hand, to allow words to be incarnated as living things is to give them mortality as well as life; as Wordsworth complains at the beginning of book 5 of *The Prelude,* we are entrusting our being to "frail shrines" even more mortal than we are. On the other hand, the only answer to that problem is to give those "frail shrines" a power that is not simply the strength of adequate representation, but is the "Visionary Power" that "attends upon the motions of the winds / Embodied in the mystery of words" (5.619–21). This power, developed rhetorically in book 5 through a series of death scenes including the dream of world destruction, the drowned man of Esthwaite, and the death of the Boy of Winander, is unleashed in the world to compete with, and perhaps to kill, the very life it set out to affirm. Cavell's notion of animism as entailing jealousy and murder is clearly relevant here.

EPISTEMOLOGY AND ETHICS

An important goal of this book, pursued most explicitly in Chapter 2's discussion of the Lucy poems and in Chapter 4's discussion of *The Excursion,* is to explore the relationship between ethical positions, what Wordsworth would call the "affective" relation between man and the world, society and God, and epistemology in a way that neither polarizes them into a conflict between inflexible terms such as "ideology" and "history" nor reduces one to the other, as when the ethical dimension is seen as a problem of representation, or when systems of knowledge are seen as mere expressions of power.

On the one hand, the incarnational generation of meaning does not place meaning and historical process into a simple binary opposition: thought's incarnation into meaningful language is a series of events, not (until it is reified into a system of signs) the creation of an ahistorical system. It follows that the ethical is not in any simple way detachable from the epistemological: ethical positions are not simply results of systems of knowledge, as Kant's categorical imperative would have it; nor are systems of knowledge simply results of conscious or unconscious ethical attitudes, as many post-Marxist theorists of ideology would have it. To "know" something, to be able to represent it and discuss it, is to incarnate thought into words that are, as Coleridge hoped, "living things," which is to generate events, attitudes, and ethical positions.[28]

On the other hand, the complex history that followed Kant's attempt to ground the ethical in the rational—culminating in recent critiques of universal grounds for morality by thinkers such as Martha Nussbaum, Richard Rorty, Jean-François Lyotard, and Alasdair MacIntyre—suggests a progressive split between epistemology and ethics, as ethical judgments are less and less satisfactorily grounded in universal systems of knowledge. Wordsworth's incarnational thought works against the split, but often by transferring the very energy of that dichotomy to its own ends, as when the Lucy poems build an incarnational ethics and epistemology out of the very real conflict between knowledge and action.

Taylor, Cavell, and Emmanuel Levinas provide a convenient combination of perspectives by means of which I can pursue this question of the relation between the ethical and the epistemological in Wordsworth's incarnational thought. One way to address the combination of the ethical and the epistemological is through Cavell's theory of "acknowledgment." In Chapter 1 I invoke his argument that both skepticism (the impossibility of true knowledge) and antiskepticism (the need for a relationship to the object of what we would like to be knowledge) are necessary. Therefore it makes more sense to think of our "knowledge" of that object as "*acknowledgment*": a recognition both of the object's otherness and of our relationship to it. This thought is related to the notion of animism discussed above: it turns our relationship to the object into something that resembles a relationship to another person, a relationship that turns on, among other things, the possibility of the loss and death of that person. For my purposes, this is valuable because it restores epistemological skepticism to its larger, earlier context as a way of life, rather than a position articulable within an instrumental, detached concept of reason.[29]

As Gerald Bruns has pointed out, there is a connection between Cavell's notion of "acknowledgment" and Emmanuel Levinas's idea of the "first philosophy" as an ethical responsibility for the other, rather than a knowledge based on a detached self-consciousness;[30] in fact, Levinas will help provide some positive substance to what in Cavell is a primarily negative definition of the relation to the other. Levinas also helps connect the problem of ethics to the problem of language in Wordsworth's incarnational thought. How incarnation breaks out of systematized representation by means of a movement from spirit to event based on God's entrance into human history can be illuminated by Levinas's notion, developed in his early *Totality and Infinity*, of "infinity" as an ethical breach of the "totality" by which ontology reduces the relation to the other to an "adequate idea." The idea of "infinity" is achieved by contact with an other whose exteriority is so absolute that the relation to him cannot be contained in any ontological "totality" that can be systematized in representational structures; the relationship disrupts the process of "thematization," or the understanding of the other "as" something in a concept, and instead becomes a relationship of *conversation:*

> The face of the Other at each moment destroys and overflows the plastic image it leaves me, the idea existing to my own measure and to the measure of its *ideatum*—the adequate idea.... The face brings a notion of truth which, in contradistinction to contemporary ontology, is not the disclosure of an impersonal Neuter, but *expression:* the existent breaks through all the envelopings and generalities of Being to spread out in its "form" the totality of its "content," finally abolishing the distinction between form and content. This is not achieved by some sort of modification of the knowledge that thematizes, but precisely by "thematization" turning into conversation.... To approach the Other in conversation is to welcome his expression, in which at each instant he overflows the idea a thought would carry away from it. It is therefore to *receive* from the Other beyond the capacity of the I, which means exactly: to have the idea of infinity. (*TI* 50–51)

The conversation with the other that constitutes infinity is precisely the realm of the ethical, as opposed to the "totality" of the theoretical: "The idea of totality and the idea of infinity differ precisely in that the first is purely theoretical, while the second is moral" (83). This ethical realm of infinity is generated through language: "This discourse is therefore not the unfolding of a prefabricated internal logic, but the constitution of truth in a struggle between thinkers, with all the risks of freedom.... [L]anguage is spoken where community between the terms of the relationship is wanting, where the common plane is wanting or is yet to be constituted" (73).[31] In the later *Otherwise Than Being,* which is perhaps more sensitive to the problems of language and metaphysics raised by philosophers such as Derrida,[32] this realm of the ethical is a "saying" prior to but intimately connected with the totalization of the "said": "Antecedent to the verbal signs it conjugates, to the linguistic systems and the semantic glitterings, a foreword preceding languages, [saying] is the proximity of one to the other, the commitment of an approach, the one for the other, the very signifyingness of signification" (*OTB* 5). Still, this original, infinite expression must be translated into the "said" of statements: "The correlation of the saying and the said, that is, the subordination of the saying to the said, to the linguistic system and to ontology, is the price that manifestation demands. . . . Language is ancillary and thus indispensable" (6). This thematization of the "saying" is not a "fall" into the "said"; saying *must* be said: "Ethics itself, in its saying which is a responsibility, requires this hold" (44).

Because the ethical realm of "infinity" is a disruption of "totality" (and not a transcendental concept) or, in the later terminology, because "saying" disrupts the "said," and because this disruptive process of signification is constituted in the relation of proximity to and responsibility for the flesh-and-blood other, the psyche for Levinas is constituted as an incarnation:

> In the form of responsibility, the psyche in the soul is the other in me, a malady of identity, both accused and *self,* the same for the other, the same by the other. Qui pro quo, it is a substitution, extraordinary. It is neither a deception nor truth, but the preliminary intelligibility of signification. But it is an overwhelming of the order of the thematizable being in the said, of the simultaneity and reciprocity of the order of the thematizable being in the said, of the simultaneity and reciprocity of the relations said. Such a signification is only possible as an incarnation. The animation, the very pneuma of the psyche, alterity in identity, is the identity of a body exposed to the other, becoming "for the other," the possibility of giving. (*OTB* 69)

Though Levinas's theological roots are in Judaic rather than Christian thought, his discussion of incarnation will help us maintain the double perspective required by Wordsworth's incarnational thought. On the one hand, the event of God's entry into human history presents a primordially ethical, preontological and preepistemological event, and this provides a model for an incarnational discourse that occurs in the realm of an ethical, infinite encounter with the other, not in the realm of sign systems. In the language of *Totality and Infinity,* "Expression does not manifest the presence of being by referring from the sign to the signified; it presents the signifier. The signifier, he who gives the sign, is not signified" (182).[33] We do not represent the other in this incarnational process, but take responsibility for him: "the face with which the Other turns to me is not reabsorbed in a representation of the face. To hear his destitution which cries out for justice is not to represent an image to oneself, but is to posit oneself as responsible" (215). This presentation of the other as both a principle of infinity (because this ethical relation always transcends any attempt at appropriation of the other to the same in a totalized system) and as a direct, responsible human contact with a destitute mortal accords with the Incarnation's manifestation of infinite spirit as human mortality, with the traditional reading of the life of Jesus as a history of that manifestation, and consequently with the Romantic notion of an incarnational discourse.

On the other hand, this incarnational discourse is in a necessary relation of interdependence with totalizing representational structures. As the early Hegel recognized, Christianity's relation to Christ is situated ambiguously between an infinite relation of love and a systematic institutionalization. For Levinas, particularly in *Otherwise Than Being,* the "saying" is not simply expressed, but is necessarily given by the "said": we cannot help but see the world in terms of meaningful entities, and "entities . . . are not first given and thematized, and then receive a meaning; they are given by the meaning they have" (36). The saying, as the realm of the infinite, goes beyond the said, but also dies into the said: "Language has been in operation, and the saying that bore this said, but goes further, was absorbed in and died in the said, was inscribed" (*OTB* 36). Consciousness entails death as the brute facticity of proximity to the other is lost in conceptual universality: "Consciousness is perhaps the very locus of the reverting of the facticity of individuation into a concept of an individual, and thus into consciousness of its death, in which its singularity is lost in its universality" (*OTB* 83). This is also the dark underside of the Christian incarnation: God became man, the infinite entered the finite, but he had to die in the process, and Wordsworth's incarnational language involves not only a living connection to the infinite but also the death of the infinite in the finite, of thought in language. But this "death" into language must be distinguished from a "fall" into language as if from a paradisiacal prelinguistic state. Levinas makes the need for this distinction clear in his discussion of the dependence of the saying on the said, and the Christian tradition makes it clear by the fact that Jesus' death is part of the redemptive process.

Wordsworth also treats infinity in the incarnational process as both absolutely other to and inevitably dependent upon theoretical and representational structures. Insofar as it points to an ethical relation to the infinite, Wordsworth's incarnational discourse, including its emphasis on epitaphs and death, stands in positive opposition to and transgresses the bounds of totalizing representational structures. But insofar as it recognizes its dependency on those structures into which thought must "die," incarnational discourse entails mortality in a more negative sense, in the subjection of the infinite to the mortality of the finite. Both sides of death are present in the Christian tradition: Jesus' death is both a subjection to the mortal and a salvific route to the infinite. Both sides are also present in Wordsworth: the spots of time present restorative images of death and Mont Blanc presents the kind of death by which a "soulless image" can usurp a "living thought / That never more could be" (*The Prelude* 6.455–56). Incarnational discourse thus stands in ethical opposition to representational thought, but it also depends on that same representational thought, and we will see images of death and violence on both sides of both relationships. To some extent this is a progressive development in both Levinas and Wordsworth. I would not carry this parallel too far, but it may help explain the relation I am trying to establish between *The Prelude* and *The Excursion*. In *Totality and Infinity,* Levinas suggests that the confrontation with infinity in the face of the other can transgress the bounds of totality, and in *The Prelude* Wordsworth shows an incarnational discourse emerging from the destruction of representational figures. In *Otherwise Than Being,* Levinas emphasizes more the interdependence of the infinite saying and the totalized said, and Wordsworth's incarnational discourse in *The Excursion,* because it is being theorized by the Wanderer, is similarly tied to the very representational discourse to which it is fundamentally opposed.

In the work of both Cavell and Levinas, we are prevented from seeing our relationship to the world as one in which we play the role of detached subjects, defined by self-consciousness and freedom, using thought as a "tool" with which to reach or appropriate a detached subject. Cavell's attitude of "acknowledgment" prohibits a subject from withdrawing behind a body of knowledge separable from the claim of the other, and Levinas's "infinity" is precisely a critique of the autonomy of a subject defined by spontaneous freedom: "Infinity, overflowing the idea of infinity, puts the spontaneous freedom within us into question. It commands and judges it and brings it to its truth" (*TI* 51). Charles Taylor, in *Sources of the Self,* sees the history of philosophy as a series of attempts to narrate our orientation toward the good. Though this position is diametrically opposed to Cavell's skepticism toward precisely what Taylor emphasizes as "constitutive goods," and though it presents an idea of the ethical very different from Levinas's, it nonetheless shares the claim that the self is not, in Taylor's words, "punctual" in the Lockean sense of a free agent defined in abstraction: Human persons "are not neutral, punctual objects; they exist only in a certain space of questions, through certain constitutive concerns. The questions or concerns touch on the nature of the good that I orient myself by and on the way I am placed in relation to it" (50). Taylor shares Hans-Georg Gadamer's insights that the horizons determined by human questioning are prior to the "subject" that post-Enlightenment thought has tended to place over against the world as a primary category.

It may sound odd to evoke these critiques of the autonomous subject in a discussion of a poet often accused of having helped invent the modern version of that subject. However, an important assumption behind my argument is that, in seeing Romanticism, particularly English Romanticism, as the poetry and thought of self-consciousness, is to continue the somewhat fearful Victorian response to what is perceived as the excesses of "self" in the Romantics.[34] Our focus, whether positive or negative, on Romantic self-consciousness—from Arnold's horror at the idea that "an allegory of the state of one's own mind" would be seen as "the highest problem of an art which imitates actions" ("Preface to *Poems*" [1853], in *Poetry and Criticism* 209) all the way up to Geoffrey Hartman's analysis of Wordsworth's own fears of the autonomous imagination, de Man's analyses of self-consciousness as a blindness to allegory, and Allen Liu's recent discussion of Wordsworth's "denial of history" whose goal is to "carve the 'self' out of history" (*Wordsworth: The Sense of History* 4–5)—has blinded us to the Romantic effort to reattach that detached self to an ethical context, to replace an instrumental theory of reason, implying a detached self who knows the world through a system of signs, with a mode of thought that places such knowledge within an ethical context that at least implicitly questions the primacy of an isolable epistemology employed by an isolable subject.

This ethical context does not erase the subject in the wholesale sense claimed by early versions of poststructuralism; rather, it provides for a new definition of the subject that preserves the uniqueness of the individual human even as it rejects the ontological totalization of a self based on concepts such as freedom or self-identity. This synthesis has important connections to the history of poststructuralist thought. (I say connections, not parallels, because poststructuralist thought, in a heightened process of *wirkungsgeschichtliches Bewußtsein,* is always defining itself in terms of and against writers such as Wordsworth.) As Charles Altieri points out, "By 1980 most of the major poststructuralist thinkers had radically recast their fundamental projects to address the very issues of subjectivity they had systematically banished in order to set their antihumanist programs in motion" (*Canons and Consequences* 193). In critiquing the efforts of Barthes, Derrida, and Foucault to reconstitute the postmodern subject, and drawing on thinkers as diverse as Kant,

Wittgenstein, and Nelson Goodman, Altieri attempts to resituate that subject in a meaningful ethical context without resorting to a totalizing grammar of rationality or self-consciousness:

> A language of response and responsibility better attuned to what we might call a pragmatics of difference, [will, he hopes,] supplement poststructural theory by showing how singular agents become articulate and responsible members of communities by accepting certain principles of judgment and by learning to negotiate competing interests. (222–23)

The ethical context that I see Wordsworth engaging is less overtly sociological and pragmatic than the model Altieri proposes, but Altieri's formulation of an ethical subject that cannot be derived from rational categories will prove a useful touchstone at several points in this book.

For my purposes, Levinas provides one of the most useful models of nontotalized, ethical subjectivity. He emphasizes the individual and the personal, and unabashedly provides a foundation for a kind of subjectivity. In arguing against idealist unifications of will and reason, he states emphatically:

> The individual and the personal count and act independently of the universal, which would mould them.... *The individual and the personal are necessary for Infinity to be able to be produced as infinite.* (*TI* 218)

Still, the uniqueness of that individual resides precisely in the irreducibility of the human subject to an ontological concept of "being,"[35] in the one's noncoincidence with itself and openness to the other, rather than in a Hegelian dialectic of self-consciousness:

> The psyche is the form of a peculiar dephasing, a loosening-up or unclamping of identity: the same prevented from coinciding with itself, torn up from its rest.... The subject called incarnate does not result from a materialization, an entry into space and into relations of contact and money which would have been realized by a consciousness, that is, self-consciousness.... Incarnation is not a transcendental operation of a subject that is situated in the midst of the world it represents to itself; the sensible experience of the body is already and from the start incarnate. The sensible— maternity, vulnerability, apprehension—binds the node of incarna-

tion into a plot larger than the apperception of self. In this plot I am bound to others before being tied to my body. (*OTB* 68, 72, 76)

As Levinas shows with his emphasis on the individual's relation to the other, and as Taylor shows with his emphasis on expressive interior routes to moral ontologies that are not primarily subjective, we can reinsert the Enlightenment punctual self or even the fuller "Romantic" self into a trans-subjective ethical context—"a plot larger than the apperception of self"—without giving up the strong sense of the human individual or even certain kinds of interiority. The point here is only partly that which Philippe Lacoue-Labarthe and Jean-Luc Nancy find in the Schlegels, that Romanticism develops out of the *crisis* of the subject brought about by Kant, rather than an exaltation of the subject:

> What had heretofore ensured the philosophical itself disappears. As a result, all that remains of the subject is the "I" as an "empty form" (a pure logical necessity, said Kant; a grammatical exigency, Nietzsche will say) that "accompanies my representations." ... As is well known, the Kantian "cogito" is empty. (*The Literary Absolute* 30)

Even more important for my purposes, Wordsworth dealt with that crisis, not so much by promoting the ontology or ideology of the self for which he has been blamed by critics from Arnold to Liu, but by using the mortally human, ethical energy in incarnational discourse to generate (particularly in *The Prelude*) a temporal *Bildung* that undoes epistemological totalization but preserves the irreducibility of the incarnational subject. The ethical intrudes into epistemology, breaking open its figural structures (such as the ontology of the ego) to constitute an incarnated self characterized not by an autonomous self-consciousness, but by openness to the other, an openness whose absolute alterity characterizes the uniqueness of the individual.

For many reasons, Wordsworth is uniquely situated for a discussion of the relationship between epistemology and ethics. He saw himself as fighting against a tradition of epistemologically centered but ethically impoverished thought. The contrast he drew between language as the incarnation of thought and as merely clothing for thought provides a fundamental Romantic metaphor for how to link ethical and epistemological positions. He stands at an early point within a tradition to which the philosophers now concerned with this issue (particularly Cavell) return: the origin of the modern conception of the subject.

In "Wordsworth and the Victorians," Paul de Man points out that questions about Wordsworth's relation to philosophy have moved from his role as a moral philosopher for the nineteenth century to his role as a philosopher of consciousness for the twentieth: "Wordsworth becomes, in the twentieth century, a poet of the self-reflecting consciousness rather than a moralist" (*The Rhetoric of Romanticism* 86). De Man himself acknowledges the ethical dimension in Wordsworth, but only in the rather thin sense of that which is hidden by, and thus ultimately dependent on, the failure of what de Man sees as Wordsworth's totalizing philosophy of consciousness: "The work of Wordsworth is moral or religious only on the level of a surface which it prohibits us from finding" (92). In one sense de Man is absolutely right in a way that he may or may not have intended with that rather cryptic and isolated statement: it is often in struggles with the problems of consciousness's attempts to figure the world—an epistemological effort—that the ethical issues break through. I argue in Chapter 3 that Wordsworth's notion of language as "incarnation," as rooted in theological and ethical existence, rather than in representational thought, rises in *The Prelude* out of the ashes of a succession of failed attempts to "figure" consciousness. Still, the twentieth-century tendency to focus on Wordsworth as a philosopher of consciousness or, later (as de Man and others moved out of phenomenological problems into representational ones) a philosopher of representation, forces us to subordinate the ethical problems to the representational. I argue that we should redress the balance, not, of course, by returning to the Victorian notion of Wordsworth as moral teacher,[36] but by considering the representational questions in their ethical dimension, rather than seeing the ethical dimension as a byproduct of representational inadequacy. This fresh look does involve taking Wordsworth's explicit and implicit moral positions very seriously, but it also involves facing up to the detailed representational problems illuminated by recent criticism.

THE ARGUMENT

So far, I have tried to explain some of the premises that inform my argument as a whole. The detailed argument will begin with Chapter 1's examination of Hegel's early essay, "The Spirit of Christianity," in which the incarnational "problem" is a tension between the materiality of that which must incarnate thought or spirit (words, the bread of the Eucharist, Jesus' own body) and the effacement of that materiality in the process of representation (the disappearance of words into thought, the disappearance of Jesus into the Father, the effacement of the transubstantiated bread in its consumption by the communicant). In order to expose the fear lurking behind this tension I invoke, with some qualification, René Girard's theory that Christianity implicitly reveals rather than conceals the violence that is at the foundation of society. I argue that in both Hegel's early view of Christianity and in the premises of Wordsworth's incarnational poetics, the unity that seems to be the goal of representation, the effacement of the material before the spiritual, is related to the potential violence of undifferentiated chaos.

In Chapter 2, I explore the specific problem of the relation between materiality and its effacement in Wordsworth's treatment of words as "living things" and in his representations of death. The statement that words should be living things is problematic precisely because such things die; in line with incarnation's connection to mortality, exemplary "thingness" is achieved on the way to death. To die is also to be separated from one's life-sustaining source; thus the word, which is living and therefore mortal, has a complex relation to its source in speaker or meaning. Although the "death" of the word is thus involved with the materiality of language, that death is also the word's self-effacement before the meaning for which it is a sign; this returns us to the problem cited by Hegel, and provides a link to the complex relationship between incarnational and representational thought. The "life" of the word-thing is also problematic in that language becomes, not a tool, but a life-force on the same ontological plane with our own lives; here I invoke Cavell on the relationship between skepticism and animism. I use book 5 of *The Prelude* to show how Wordsworth places these problems into a narrative context. I use the Lucy poems to expand my focus to death's role in the relationship between epistemology and ethics. Heidegger, Cavell, Levinas, and Gadamer provide ways to approach the "unthinkability" of Lucy's death from an incarnational and ethical rather than a representational and epistemological standpoint.

In Chapter 3 I trace Wordsworth's use of the flexible concept of incarnation as a solution to the problem of finding a rhetoric to end his autobiography. The final books of *The Prelude* narrate a process by which the figural grammar that has hitherto structured the poem dissolves into a language of performative divergence from that grammar. The recuperation of the poet in the "spots of time" and Mount Snowdon episodes arises directly out of this primarily deconstructive process. This recuperation can be seen more profitably, however, in terms of the rhetoric of incarnation, which enables a complex performative language in which meaning is achieved through a process of emanation and a dialogue in which the memorialization of death accounts for historical and ontological difference. By associating himself with the transcendental side of incarnation, and invoking the incarnational rhetoric of dialogue and gift, the poet is able in book 13 to stage a bridging of the gap between his fragmentary, textually incarnated self and the source of that incarnation outside the text.

I devote Chapter 4 to Wordsworth's *Excursion*. I am not attempting to salvage this poem from years of deserved disrepute, but my philosophical interests in Wordsworth seem to demand an extended treatment of his most sustained attempt to write a philosophical poem. Its very unworkability as poetry or philosophy is what makes it interesting for my purposes: Wordsworth confronts the problem of presenting a *theory* of what in *The Prelude* had been played out as a *rhetoric* of incarnation. The problem arises because of the incompatibility of theory, which entails binary systems of signs and an instrumental concept of epistemology as something detachable from living subjects, and incarnation, a concrete mode of thought bound up with living dialogue. This makes both the figure of the Wanderer—Wordsworth's chief theoretical spokesman—and the text of the poem function within a new version of the relationship between self-effacing sign and living thing: both text and speaker must efface themselves before a "meaning" while at the same time embodying the contrary principle of incarnational materiality and life. (Here I draw on Gadamer's distinction between the self-originating life of a literary text and the self-effacing quality of a theoretical text.) The relation between theory and incarnation is further developed in the relation between ethics and representation. On one level, the ethical is seen as preferable to the representational: ethical truth is better than representational accuracy. On another level, the ethical and the representational are united from the start, in that moral law is the ground for representation: literally, the laws of conscience are the image of God. An examination of the role of law in mediating between the theoretical and the incarnational reveals that law functions both as a representational code—a fixed "theory"—and as a hermeneutically open-ended, incarnational interaction between the concrete and the general. This is related to the Christian theological controversy between law as a system of representation and law as a moral imperative. I invoke René Girard to show that, as incarnational thought faces up to its formulation within the differentiated structure of theory, that structure both conceals and reveals violence. The violence is located both in the dominating power of the theoretical language and in the incarnational rhetoric itself, whose foundation in the sacrificial death of Jesus is, at the end of *The Excursion*, explicitly contrasted with pre-Christian sacrifice.

1

Hegel and the Problem of Jesus

> Thus we must keep the dignity of the thing and the referentiality of language free from the prejudice originating in the ontology of the present-at-hand as well as the concept of objectivity.
>
> Our starting point is that verbally constituted experience of the world expresses not what is present-at-hand, that which is calculated or measured, but what exists, what man recognizes as existent and significant.
>
> —Hans-Georg Gadamer, *Truth and Method*

Though I will argue later that Wordsworth ultimately saw the incarnational analogy for language as a solution to the problems of engendering meaning in poetry, in this chapter I focus on some specific problems that the Christian incarnation itself, particularly as manifested in the Eucharist, presents for the early Hegel—problems that involve words as both signs and things. The root of many such problems is the inevitable conflict between a signifying object's function as a thing in the world, exerting a force that affects other things, and a sign, effacing itself before that to which it points. This is a problem that appears paradigmatically in the Eucharist, as well as one that the Eucharist and the Incarnation are invoked to solve. The problem is that the bread and wine are things resting on the table, yet through transubstantiation they become *signs* of a divine presence and disappear as mere *things.* Louis Marin analyzes this process as it informs the *Port-Royal Logic,* a 1662 French treatise on human reason which had a significant influence, largely through John Locke and David Hume, on English as well as French Enlightenment thought. Seen representationally this combination of unity (the bread and body are one entity) and difference (the bread represents the body) requires a double process of splitting that can only be resolved in the structure of a secret:

> The identity of the thing is split twice. The first time, it divides into a thing and a sign; the second time, the nature of the sign requires a distinction between the thing that does the representing and the thing that is represented, even as the thing being divided is suppposed to remain what it is. Moreover, the aporia—constituted by an absolute difference within an absolutely maintained identity—can only be overcome by modeling the structure of the sign-representation on that of the secret: something is indeed hidden, but not totally, for then the secret would disappear. (Louis Marin, *Food for Thought*, 11)

That is to say, the bread must divide itself between being bread (a thing) and being a sign of divine presence, but then as a sign it must embody a second distinction between two things: the representing bread and the represented body of Christ. The structure of the secret is necessary because things hide whereas signs reveal: "Since a thing can be at once a thing and a sign (two different states), it can hide the very thing that it reveals in the form of a sign" (10). Thus, insofar as the bread remains a thing, it hides the body of Christ, covering it up by the materiality of the bread. Insofar as it becomes a sign, it reveals the body of Christ, effacing itself as a thing.

Gadamer notes a similar situation applying to the picture, which is neither a sign, whose own existence is effaced before that to which it points, nor a symbol, which is revered as a tangible thing as it replaces that to which it refers: "A picture is situated halfway between a sign and a symbol. Its representing is neither a pure pointing-to-something nor a pure taking-the-place-of-something. It is this intermediate position that raises it to a unique ontological status" (*TM* 154). In the title essay to *The Relevance of the Beautiful* he points out, following Heidegger, that art's facticity combines revealing and concealing:

> Alongside and inseparable from this unconcealing, there also stands the shrouding and concealing that belongs to our human finitude.... This fact that [the work of art] exists, its facticity, represents an insurmountable resistance against any superior presumption that we can make sense of it all. (*The Relevance of the Beautiful* 34)

As I demonstrate in Chapter 2, Wordsworth encounters a similar problem when words gain the "facticity" of "living things," and thus become unable to function as transparent signs.

From Marin's semiotic perspective, this situation presents a problem that is "solved" only by the subjective sleight-of-hand of the Eucharistic utterance. The enunciation of the consecrational sentence, "This is my body," by a subject capable of saying (in Christ's place) "my" effects the shift in the referent of "this" from bread as material thing to bread as sign of divine presence. From Gadamer's hermeneutic perspective—at home with dialectic and already infused with the Incarnation's combination of historical manifestation (word as event) and spiritual connection (word as *spirit* become event)—this situation is less an aporia than an explanation of the nonrepresentational "event" of meaning. For the late-Romantic, antisemiotic Gadamer,[1] the Incarnation is a solution to the problem of meaning because it allows language to appear in its concrete historicity as event rather than mere sign. For the Enlightenment Port-Royal logicians, as seen by a twentieth-century semiotician, the Eucharistic repetition of the Incarnation is also a solution, but only as it smuggles in the present "I" of the celebrant to link the bread and body. If the Port-Royal solution is an example of the Enlightenment situation inherited by Wordsworth, as I described it in the previous chapter—the stabilization of the word-thing split by means of a subjective fiat or Taylor's "punctual self"—and if Gadamer's incarnational hermeneutics is what Wordsworth's incarnational poetics looks forward to, then Hegel's early post-Enlightenment struggles with the hermeneutic consequences of the Incarnation's presentation of sign and thing will provide a useful philosophical context for some of the problems that incarnational thought implicitly presents for Wordsworth.

For Hegel, the contradiction noted by Marin between the substantiality of the word-as-thing and the self-effacement of the word-as-sign reappears in the problematic status of the objective as that which must be both posited and transcended. By the time of the *Phenomenology of Spirit* (1807), the powerful mechanism of *Aufhebung* had expanded the terms of Hegel's argument to accommodate all problems in the relationship between spirit and the world, and the Incarnation was effectively employed in the service of that mechanism. Hegel used the Incarnation as the pinnacle of his dialectic of religion in order to help ground a system of representation based not on the rational correspondence between signs and things, but on the journey of consciousness toward absolute Spirit. The complete unification of the infinite and the finite in the process of God becoming man is part of the final stages of this journey:

> That absolute Spirit has given itself *implicitly* the shape of self-consciousness, and therefore has also given it for its *consciousness*—this now appears as the *belief of the world* that Spirit is *immediately present* as a self-conscious Being, i.e. as an *actual man*.... [T]his God is sensuously and directly beheld as a Self, as an actual individual man; only so *is* this God self-consciousness. (*Hegel's Phenomenology of Spirit,* 459)

Colin Brown, in *Jesus in European Protestant Thought, 1778–1860,* shows how Hegel uses the Incarnation, and particularly the death of Jesus, as "the focal point (*Mittelpunkt*) of the dialectic of Spirit coming to consciousness and realizing itself in the world" (95). Brown shows how late eighteenth- and early nineteenth-century Idealism reappraised traditional Christian beliefs in terms of the idealist perception of "the world as the material outworking of a spiritual reality" (78). Wordsworth was certainly part of this movement; however, his concrete poetic consciousness could not rest easy with a simple dialectical relationship between finite and infinite. Hegel himself, in "The Spirit of Christianity and Its Fate" (ca. 1798–99), saw Christianity more as a problem than a solution, because the history of Jesus and the Church poses a relationship between objective materiality and spirit that seemingly could not be accommodated to either realm or to a meaningful relationship between them. Like Jeremiah Beaumont in Robert Penn Warren's *World Enough and Time,* Hegel is looking for a passage from the purity of love and meaning to the objective materiality of human institutions and language.

Hegel saw the history of Judaism as founded on a devastating alienation between God and men that Christianity ultimately failed to reconcile. The holy and the infinite were totally other to human existence; the Jews existed only in a relationship of opposition to other nations, guided by Mosaic law that grounded that human opposition in a relationship of opposition between the absolutely finite humans and their absolutely infinite God. Hegel defined law as "the unification of opposites in a *concept,* which leaves them as opposites while it exists itself in opposition to reality" ("The Spirit of Christianity and Its Fate," in *Early Theological Writings* 209). If such a concept of law is the fundamental fact of existence, the universal and the particular will always be held apart in a relation of opposition. Thus Jesus does not (as Kant would have it, according to Hegel) simply internalize the law, because even the replacement of external law by an internal sense of duty would retain that duality. Instead, Jesus counters the restrictiveness of concept and law with existence itself: "Since the commands of duty presuppose a cleavage and since the domination of the concept declares itself in a 'thou shalt,' that which is raised above the cleavage is an 'is,' a modification of life" (212), which is restricted only in that it is directed toward particular objects, but not restricted in itself.

The problem here is that the division between universal and particular in law, to which Jesus opposes a principle of unmediated human need and love, is, in Hegel's view, basic to reflection itself and the act of naming: there seems to be a basic conflict between Christian love and reflective language:

> It is a sort of dishonor to love when it is commanded; i.e., when love, something living, a spirit, is called by name. To name it is to reflect on it, and its name or the utterance of its name is not spirit, not its essence, but something opposed to that.... [Love] is no universal opposed to a particular, no unity of the concept, but a unity of spirit, a divinity. (247)

As Christianity becomes a religion, it is faced with the contradiction between the fundamental principle of unmediated, nonreflective love and religion's need for mediation, reflection, and objectification.

This conflict is brought out in the "love-feast" of the Last Supper, whose representational structure baffles Hegel. The presence of an internal spiritual connection expressed in an act of common eating and drinking means that the Last Supper is not conventionally symbolic, in which "symbol and symbolized are strangers to one another, and their connection lies outside them in a third thing" (248). (This kind of "symbol" is of course what Coleridge calls "allegory," in opposition to his own theologically grounded concept of a closer "symbolic" connection between symbol and symbolized.) Still, the objective religious symbolism of the Eucharistic utterance pushes it toward the symbolic, which seems to be in a strange conflict with the mystical, nonobjectified union inhering in the act. Hegel discovers that this manifestation of incarnation confounds the oppositional categories available to his thought:

> Love is less than religion, and this meal, too, therefore is not strictly a religious action, for only a unification in love, made objective by imagination, can be the object of religious veneration. In a love-feast, however, love itself lives and is expressed,

> and every action in connection with it is simply an expression of love. Love itself is present only as an emotion, not as an image also. The feeling and the representation of the feeling are not unified by fancy. Yet in the love-feast there is also something objective in evidence, to which feeling is linked but to which it is not united in an image. Hence this eating hovers between a common table of friendship and a religious act, and this hovering makes difficult the clear interpretation of its spirit. (248)

The love feast can be assimilated into neither a pure expression of love, as in "a common table of friendship," nor "a religious act," in which feeling and image are objectified according to a symbolic law.

The eating of the consecrated bread suggests a problematic objectification that then returns to the subjective: "Yet the love made objective, this subjective element becomes a *thing*, reverts once more to its nature, becomes subjective again in the eating" (250). He cannot, of course, resolve that vacillation in the temporality of a subjective utterance, as the authors of the *Port-Royal Logic* did, according to Marin, but we see a similar problem, now made more complex by the additional consideration of the eating of the consecrated bread. The nonmaterial subjectivity of Jesus' love, expressed in the act of consecration and then entering into the hearer's own subjectivity when he consumes the bread, is something that is precisely *not* a "thing," and before which any representing thing must efface itself. As a religious act, however, this love feast depends on its objectification of love in "things" such as bread and wine. We sense in Hegel's problem a hint of the interplay between subjective and objective that will provide such an important foundation for the *Phenomenology*, but here he can only emphasize the contradiction: the very act that makes this a pure expression of Christian love—the complete subjective consumption of the objective bread—annuls the objective form required by religion, and thus makes the act "less" than a religious act. Jesus founded a religion based on love and human need rather than conceptual, legal objectification, but the human *religious* need is precisely for such objectification.

This contradiction between the purity of love that rejects objectification and religion's need for objectification is expressed in an analogy whose most interesting feature is that it does not work: the consumption of the bread is like reading, except that the words do not disappear:

> This return [of the objective to the subjective] may perhaps in this respect be compared with the thought which in the written

word becomes a thing and which recaptures its subjectivity out of an object, out of something lifeless, when we read. The simile would be more striking if the written word were read away, if by being understood it vanished as a thing, just as in the enjoyment of bread and wine not only is a feeling for these mystical objects aroused, not only is the spirit made alive, but the objects vanish as objects. Thus the action seems purer, more appropriate to its end, in so far as it affords spirit only, feeling only, and robs the intellect of its own, i.e., destroys the matter, the soulless.... But what prevents the action [of eating and drinking] from becoming a religious one is just the fact that the kind of objectivity here in question is totally annulled, while feeling remains, the fact that there is a sort of confusion between subject and object rather than a unification, the fact that love here becomes visible in and attached to something which is to be destroyed. (251)[2]

Like Wordsworth, Hegel sees a problematic analogy between incarnation, seen here in its Eucharistic manifestation, and the transformation of thought into language. Both reading and religion are less pure forms of eating, for in eating the objective element is completely assimilated into the subjective (as a word would ideally be effaced before thought), but in reading words remain problematically "there" even after we read them (to be read and misread and altered by others, for example), and in religion the material permanence of its objective structures prevents any assimilation into subjectivity.

On the one hand, the simile would be better ("more striking") if in fact the understanding of words destroyed them as eating destroys food. On the other hand, in an economy of reading in which the act of reading destroyed the actual words (not just the printed word, as when a newspaper is read then thrown away, but the words themselves), the world would quickly be reduced to muteness (unless we were able to produce new words to replace those that we "ate," but that would be reintroducing the objectivity that subjective "purity" demands we reject). Thus for the simile to work would be the best argument for *preserving* the objective remainder that the simile is trying to reject in favor of pure subjective consumption. To extend the implications of Hegel's simile, we need those linguistic leftovers—the words that remain after we "consume" them—in order to keep from starving in pure subjectivity. To return to Gadamer's example of the picture, one reason that a word or a picture can be neither "pure" substitution (symbol) nor "pure" self-effacement (sign) is that neither sort of purity is possible—there is always something left over, and, like sourdough starter or a yogurt culture, this leftover portion of the same impure materiality that is effaced in the eating process is necessary to the continued production of spiritual or intellectual nourishment.

The material existence of words results in a double impurity: they are dead and soulless insofar as they cannot be taken up by subjectivity, and their material persistence prevents Hegel's analogy from working perfectly. There is a further irony here; Hegel has already pointed out that analogies and parables, joining matter and spirit by a third term rather than an intrinsic link, are highly objective: the very objective materiality that allows allegories and analogies to exist prevents this particular one from working: the form of the allegory itself prevents it from being the impossible hybrid of an allegory explaining a process by which objectivity (allegory's foundation) is denied. We see here the circular trap in which a binary system of representation is caught when confronted with the enigma of the Incarnation, a trap from which Hegel will escape by means of the *Aufhebung* and Wordsworth by means of incarnation itself.

Hegel and Marin both focus on the problem of a materiality that must be both posited and annulled, as Jesus had to enter the material world and then transcend it. In semiotic terms, this is the problem of the sign's persistence as an object in the world when it must efface itself before the thing it signifies. In terms of the early Hegel, it is the simultaneous necessity and inessentiality of the objective realm in Christianity's apparently unsuccessful attempt to assert the subjective over the objective. Nevertheless, it is not enough to see this effacement and persistence of the materiality of the word as a simple tension between theology's need to cancel the material and human language's need to preserve and use the material. Theology *and* human language need both the effacement and the preservation of the material. On the one hand, human language needs for its signs to efface themselves before their referents in order for its system to maintain some kind of instrumental detachment from the world. For example, words cannot afford to be contaminated with the world they represent each time they are used, or their meanings would constantly change. On the other hand, words depend on their origins in the material world, and the real-world tradition of their usage not only preserves them, but also "contaminates" them with vital new meanings. Theologically, Hegel shows the self-effacement occurring as a demand of pure Christian love, not of human language, yet the loss of tangible material existence (as when the host is consumed) is felt as a sadness.

In summary, both Marin and Hegel approach a pair of related problems that are fundamental to the rhetoric of incarnation:

1. The "impure" persistence of the thing, the particular, the image, the human, in tension with the desire for that realm to efface itself before thought, God the Father, infinity, etc. Hegel discusses the oppositional relations that develop when the universal is opposed to the particular, and Marin points out the tendency for a sign to veer off from its signifying function and become a concrete image that must be dealt with on its own terms.
2. The negative side of the attempted (but of course impossible) "purity" that entails the effacement of the objective realm. For Hegel this is the melancholy of the Christian who feels that "something divine was promised and it melted away in the mouth" (253), or, in other words, the melancholy of the Christian who feels the conflicting desires for both objectified religion and the object-effacing love that is supposed to be this religion's content.

One important variation of the conflict between words' materiality as impure things and their self-effacement as pure signs can be discussed fruitfully in terms of Geoffrey Hartman's distinction between "truth" and "troth," to which I alluded in the previous chapter: the difference between words as units of referentiality and words (such as Lear's to his daughters) as "essentially passwords: signs of obeisance or identity or mutual recognition" (*Saving the Text* 135). The Incarnation asks Christians to trust in a person—Jesus—and defer total understanding of the source of that incarnation; thus one consequence of the incarnation of thought into language is that language becomes a system of "troth" more than "truth," a series of "timely utterance[s]" that give relief to thoughts instead of representing their truth. The distinction is not simple, however, since language's "trustworthiness" is tied into its promises of referentiality. Hartman notes that language is untrustworthy and therefore "wounding" both because it promises referential completeness, in the fantasy of an absolutely authentic name (Hartman links this to Lacan's mirror-stage), and conversely because it is equivocal (*Saving the Text* 139).

To combine Hartman's terms with Hegel's and Marin's, one might say that as words veer away from their pure signifying function to become images in the world, or as reflective thought's need for the impure but objective realm conflicts with the purity of Christian love, words enter the world as incarnate entities that act more like other people (thus is the kind of Word Jesus was) than like soulless linguistic units. Thus the status of language rises to accord with Coleridge and Wordsworth's desire for words to achieve the status of living things. But this presents two problems. One, this objective status is "impure," tied to the messy aspects of the material world and tainted with its conflict. Two, as words escape from the control of a signifying process and enter the world, they seem to be doing this on their own, and thus they are not only objects in the world, but subjects who may or may not be trusted. This is a version of Stanley Cavell's skepticism become animism, an animism that is connected to death as well as to life, as Cavell showed in the discussion of Coleridge cited in the previous chapter, and as the anthropological implications of Hegel's argument will demonstrate here.

This tension between words' uncontrollable incarnation and their role within signifying systems also suggests Levinas's demonstration of the relationship between an incarnational "saying" that depends on living human proximity, but that is necessarily betrayed by a "said," the universality of a linguistic system into which the witness of saying disappears:

> Before putting itself at the service of life as an exchange of information through a linguistic system, saying is witness; it is saying without the said, a sign given to the other.... This witness ... is the meaning of language, before language scatters into words, into themes equal to the words and dissimulating in the said the openness of the saying exposed like a bleeding wound. (*OTB* 150–51)

As this quotation suggests, for Levinas the animation in language is not a result of the relationship between a "pure" subjectivity (such as that posited by Hegel) and the objective materiality of language. Because subjectivity for Levinas is grounded not in the ego but in the nontotalizable relation to the other, the uncontrollable life-force in language comes before, not after, words enter either systems of signification or concepts of self-consciousness, both of which are on the side of the "said." For him language's living escape from a representational system is a revelation of language's original status as a pre-representational "saying"; in Hartman's terms, the "troth" side of language interrupts "truth" by staking out its prior claim. As I suggested in the previous chapter, Levinas's way of approaching this dilemma in terms of subjectivity, but without recourse to self-consciousness as a foundational category, will help us to understand Wordsworth's incarnational hermeneutics.

There is also an anthropological sense in which the problems explored by the early Hegel may reveal, not just a problem in the relationship between subjective consciousness and the materiality of representation, but a fundamental level of violence (like Levinas's sense of the exposure of the saying as a "bleeding wound" and Hartman's sense that troth-words can wound) in the way humans signify themselves to each other. The love feast of the Last Supper as memorialized in Christian ritual, which ties the Last Supper intimately to the death of Jesus on the cross, is a *sacrificial* ritual, despite Christianity's ambivalence toward pagan as well as Judaic traditions of sacrifice. The problem of the materiality versus the spirituality of the sacrificial victim, like Hegel's problem with the host, and similarly tied to the complexities of sacrifice's negotiation between material and spiritual worlds, shows up in many sacrificial traditions. Henri Hubert and Marcel Mauss discuss the dual role of sacrificial animals in these terms:

> If on the one hand the spirit was released, if it had passed completely "behind the veil" into the world of the gods, the body of the animal on the other hand remained visible and tangible. And it too, by the fact of consecration, was filled with a sacred force that excluded it from the profane world.... What survived of the animal was attributed entirely to the sacred world, attributed entirely to the profane world, or shared between the two. (*Sacrifice: Its Nature and Functions* 35)

For Hegel, this becomes the problem of the consumption of the Host into the pure subjectivity of love versus the necessary objective materiality of the religious institution founded on this sacrificial ritual.

This problem is trickiest when it is posed in terms of language and representation; as Hegel noted, words cannot be consumed the way bread can be. Jean-Luc Nancy suggests why sacrifice must be thought of in mimetic, representational terms, and why it is thus is an even greater problem for Hegel, and for all of Western thought about sacrifice, than it might have been in other traditions (though, as Nancy stresses, we can know those other traditions only in dialectical relationship to our own). Nancy argues that in the Western tradition, as represented in the sacrificial deaths of Socrates and Jesus, and in Hegel's use of sacrifice in the dialectic of *Aufhebung,* sacrifice has become *self*-sacrifice, "willed and sought after by the entire being, by the life and the thought or message of the victims. It is, in the fullest sense of the words, and in both senses of the genitive, the sacrifice of *the subject*" ("The Unsacrificeable" 22).[3] And it is not just the sacrifice of any subject, but, particularly in the Christian tradition culminating in the Hegel of *The Phenomenology of Spirit* and later works, a unique and exemplary sacrifice, which becomes the dialectical sacrificing of the subject to universality, "a uniqueness of the life and substance in which or to which all singularity is sacrificed" (23). This process entails a sublation of the moment of sacrifice itself: "The truth of sacrifice sublates, along with 'the flesh that perishes,' the sacrificial moment of sacrifice itself" (24). In this process "sacrifice" becomes an "old" notion, taken up in a process that "claims to be both rupture with and *mimetic repetition* of sacrifice" (27); for our own ends we define non-Western sacrifice as a prefiguring of this sacrifice-transcending process of self-sacrifice: "The 'old' sacrifice is an exterior figure—vain in itself—of that truth in which the subject sacrifices itself, in spirit, to spirit" (24). Thus the early Church could object to pagan and Old Testament sacrifice as outmoded, but also as replaced and sublated by Christ's unique and universal sacrifice. We reject the old sacrifice (which we define in order to reject), but we also imitate it by seeing it as a prefiguration of the "new" universal sacrifice of Socrates, Christ, or the subject in the Hegelian *Aufhebung*.[4]

This ambivalence toward sacrifice in the Western tradition exacerbates the tension between objectivity and spirituality that we find in the early Hegel, even though he went on to formulate the classic Western statement of how that tension is dialectically resolved. It is not just that the sacrificial victim must negotiate between the material and the spiritual world, but that the notion of sacrifice itself—defined by the West as a prefiguration of the sublation of sacrifice, if we are to believe Nancy—leaves us caught between two unsatisfactory alternatives in this post-sacrificial world: mere figurative representation on the objective side (the act of consuming the host as tied to the objectivity of the Church as a representative institution, with a history tied mimetically to the "old" sacrifice) and the vacuum left by dialectical *self*-sacrifice on the subjective side (the disappearance of the host into subjective love in its being-eaten). We no longer have even the limited satisfaction of a genuine, tangible sacrificial victim situated ambiguously between the material and the spiritual worlds, but only (as Nancy says, commenting on Bataille) "a choice ... between simulacrum and nothingness; that is also to say, between the representation of the 'old' sacrifice and the postulation of self-sacrifice" ("The Unsacrificeable" 29). We will see this problem reappear at the end of Wordsworth's *Excursion*, in the complex mimetic relationship by which the Pastor pairs pre-Christian human sacrifice and salvation through the death of Christ.

The role of mimesis in Hegel's early interpretation of the Christian sacrifice can also be understood in relation to sacrifice's function as a sociological mechanism rather than a problem of transcendence. The language of infection, as well as the anthropological assumptions that

Hegel makes "The Spirit of Christianity" force us to raise the fundamental question posed by the work of René Girard: does the Christian incarnation express a fundamental unity of the finite and the infinite, restoring a unity that was lost, or does it, as Girard argues, reveal the collective violence that lies at the heart of all human activity but is simply kept under control by various systems of law and sacrifice? This is a particularly important question to explore for Wordsworth, whose recent critics assume that an incarnational poetics is a poetics of unity and adequate representation, when in fact that incarnational poetics is grounded in scenes such as the horrific murder in the first "spot of time," and, as I discuss in Chapter 4, the memory of human sacrifice at the end of the *Excursion.*

Girard's basic argument is that human society is founded on relationships of rivalry and acts of collective violence. Culture provides systems of differentiation, from sacrificial rituals to judicial systems, in order to contain that violence and to hide the violent nature of culture's origins. To see unity of self and other as a goal and difference as an impediment to that unity is a romantic illusion. The truth of the matter is that difference is the safety mechanism that keeps us from seeing the other as the Same; if self and other are identical, rivalry results, and society is reduced to its original state of reciprocal violence: "Order, peace and fecundity depend on cultural distinctions; it is not these distinctions but the loss of them that gives birth to fierce rivalries and sets members of the same family or social group at one another's throats" (*Violence and the Sacred* 49). Girard sees the Judeo-Christian scripture (though not necessarily the tradition engendered by those texts) as fundamentally different from all previous religions, because instead of hiding the fundamental violence at the heart of human relations, the story of Jesus reveals it. For example, most myths would portray the scapegoat as guilty, and only a deconstructive reading of the myth that undid its explicit mythologization would reveal that the mob had displaced its own violence onto the victim in order to set up a differential relationship between the society and the victim, a relationship that would hide the truth of the society's origins in reciprocal violence. Thus Oedipus's guilt and expulsion sets him up as other to the society, hiding the truth that Oedipus is not a guilty man but a scapegoat: behind the family structure is a structure of rivalry and violence, in which sons are the same as their fathers; the rivalry for the mother's love leads to murder.[5] In the Christian story, however, the victim is explicitly portrayed as innocent: Pilate's judicial system fails, and the mob chooses Jesus over Barabbas in a gesture that is arbitrary and violent. In his preaching, as when he accuses the Pharisees of imitating their murderous fathers as the Pharisees affirm their difference from their fathers, Jesus reveals the violence at the heart of man's institutions, and is thus violently silenced. Girard says that all religion is "organized around a more or less violent disavowal of human violence." Yet the uniqueness of the biblical account of this process is that

> by affirming this point without the least equivocation, Jesus infringes the supreme prohibition that governs all human order, and he must be reduced to silence. Those who come together against Jesus do so in order to back up the arrogant assumption that consists in saying, "if we had lived in the days of our fathers, we would not have taken part with them in shedding the blood of the prophets."
>
> The truth of the founding murder is expressed first of all in the words of Jesus, which connect the present conduct of men with the distant past, and with the near future (since they announce the Passion), and with the whole of human history. The same truth of the founding murder will also be expressed, with even greater force, in the Passion itself. (*Things Hidden* 166–67)

As Girard puts it in *The Scapegoat*, "The Bible enables us to decipher what we have actually learned to identify in persecutors' representations of persecution," that is, mythical accounts that conceal originary violence. "It teaches us to decode the whole of religion" (101).

Throughout Hegel's "Spirit of Christianity and Its Fate," we see the idea of Jesus revert to unwanted relationships of opposition, as the Christian principle of unity that Hegel seems to want to find comes close to revealing itself as the kind of precultural reciprocal violence that Girard sees the story of Jesus as unveiling. For example, Jesus attempted to institute a realm of love, but as that effort was frustrated, he accepted the domination of the state, imitating the subservient behavior he was sent to correct, and he engaged in reciprocal verbal violence with the Pharisees. Hegel tells a story of impurity and contagion (suggesting the idea of infection that Girard sees as a central metaphor for the impure contact that is related to the nondifferentiation of violence[6]) in discussing how rivalry between "pure" Christianity and "impure" Judaism threatened exactly that distinction:

> When [Jesus] and the community he founded set themselves in opposition to the corruption of their environment, the inevitable result was to give a consciousness of corruption both to this

corruption itself and to the spirit still relatively free from it, and then to set this corruption's fate at variance with itself. The struggle of the pure against the impure is a sublime sight, but it soon changes into a horrible one when holiness itself is impaired by unholiness, and when an amalgamation of the two, with the pretension of being pure, rages against fate, because in these circumstances holiness itself is caught in the fate and subject to it. ("The Spirit of Christianity," in *Early Theological Writings* 286)

Here Hegel sees the process by which the rivalry between the "pure" and the "impure" leads to a process of contagion in which both sides are reduced to near identity and the "sublime" battle of antithetical forces becomes the "horrible" chaos of nondifferentiation. Hegel sees this process as a problem with Christianity, of course, and not as the foundation of culture, but the essential point for my purposes is that he sees it as a result of the same Christian incarnation that is supposed to provide a unity of finite and infinite, not a chaotic lack of differentiation.

The point of this is not simply to show that Girard's insights are implicit in Hegel, but to show how radically the concept of incarnation points both toward wholeness and unity and toward a demythologizing revelation of culture's violent foundations. Girard, in *Things Hidden Since the Foundation of the World* and *The Scapegoat*, sees the Bible as revealing just such a demythologizing process. Still, in Hegel, and even more graphically in Wordsworth, incarnation can be seen as what Girard earlier called a process of "desymbolization," in which the differentiating structure of the symbol that *conceals* nondifferentiation (in ritual, according to Girard) can also *reveal* the process of nondifferentiation (in tragedy), which is also a destruction of the symbol's own differentiated structure (*Violence and the Sacred* 62–65). Girard's insight gives new urgency to the stakes involved when the incarnate Word, the bread in the Eucharist, and Wordsworth's incarnate words are seen as both living things that conceal and self-effacing signs that reveal: the very structures of differentiation and unity that occur in the generation of meaning, such as Marin's double splitting of the thing becoming a sign while also remaining a unity, are tied to the tension between violent nondifferentiation and regulatory differentiation at the very basis of culture. That which the bread-as-thing conceals and the bread-as-sign reveals might not be just the divine spirit revealed by Christianity, but also the precultural violence revealed in Jesus' story. The tension between unity and differentiation in the process of things becoming signs may then flip over into the tension between the violence of the Same and the cultural institution of differentiation. This reflects the general idea that, in the structure of incarnation, not only are materiality and spirit involved in an impossible relationship by which spirit is both contaminated by and dependent on materiality, but in addition that relationship threatens to become the reciprocal violence of the Same.

Much of the problematic status of incarnation can be traced to Christianity as, in the words of "Ode: Intimations of Immortality from Recollections of Early Childhood," a "faith that looks through death." As usual, Wordsworth's ambiguity is exact: on the one hand, we look through death toward something beyond; death is annulled by faith. On the other hand, we view the world through death-colored glasses: death is the necessary epistemological ground. Death alone allows for the completed representation of a human being, and thus the placement of that human being in a context beyond that of life and death. As the Priest in *The Excursion* says of the dead he is about to eulogize,

> with these
> The future cannot contradict the past:
> Mortality's last exercise and proof
> Is undergone; the transit made that shows
> The very Soul, revealed as she departs.
> (5.663–67)

Death grants closure to the endless process of interpretation, which, for example, the autobiographer must endure, but it is also the fundamental ground for philosophy and theology, the "last exercise and proof" of our mortal life, and that which more fundamentally than anything else reveals "the very Soul ... as she departs." Not only is death the ground of knowledge, but it is a knowledge *of* passing—a glimpse at one who is in the process of departing, not a set of stable truths. As Geoffrey Hartman writes, "The problem of religious thought ... was finding a positive beyond the positivity of the negative [death]," and "Philosophy's attempt to have 'nothing' as its presupposition merely veils the reality of death as the something that always precedes" (*Saving the Text* xvii). Death stops interpretation as it limits life, but also inaugurates a process of interpretation, since knowledge of death is a knowledge of a transition, a "threshold" process of knowing—to invoke Angus Fletcher's useful term[7]—that can only be interpretation and metaphor. Also, *because* death provides such absolute closure at the end of life, it provides an incentive for interpretive activity within life. As Frances Ferguson says in her discussion of *The Prelude,* death's removal of the "props of affection" "thus creates the necessity of the search for meaning in the visible world; only when 'something is wrong' can there even begin to be the creation of a myth of the fall, an explanation and/or a balm for the unhappiness" (*Wordsworth: Language as Counter-Spirit* 133).

The enigma of death, which is fully confronted in the death of Jesus, grounds all of the oppositions we have discussed so far. Like the word as thing or sign, the dying body effaces itself before whatever is beyond, but does so in the act of becoming the soulless objectivity that is left behind in the tomb as a problematic thing that is also a sign, represented by Wordsworth's favorite sign/things, tombstones. Death is the final link forging a community of the living and the dead, but it is also the reduction to dust, the chaotic Sameness that grounds and denies culture. Behind Wordsworth's argument that epitaphs represent "truth hallowed by love—the joint offspring of the worth of the dead and the affections of the living" (*PrW* 2:58) Girard would see culture's founding act of

> conjuring away man's violence by endlessly projecting it upon new victims. All cultures and all religions are built on this foundation, which they then conceal, just as the tomb is built around the dead body that it conceals. Murder calls for the tomb and the tomb is but the prolongation and perpetuation of murder. The tomb-religion amounts to nothing more or less than the becoming invisible of the foundations, of religion and culture, of their only reason for existence. (*Things Hidden* 164)

The poetics of incarnation faces the enigma of incarnation's double pull; in Wordsworth it is directed both toward the act of murderous, reciprocal violence from which the boy flees in the first "spot of time," and toward the beneficial "visionary dreariness" into which that memory feeds. Just as the notion of the Incarnation, in which God united himself with man and then died a violent death, links its restorative unity indissolubly with a revelation of violence, so is Wordsworth not doing anything as simple as constructing a "tomb religion" to conceal or domesticate the reality of death. For language to be the incarnation of thought is to open language and its speakers to the possibility of death, a death memorialized in the history of language just as Jesus' death is memorialized in the Eucharistic ritual that, as we have seen, re-presents the problematic issues of incarnational representation.

It is implicit in this double pull that our very ownership of the world is conditioned by the possibility of the death of our conception of the world. This is how Stanley Cavell interprets Coleridge's statement in the

Biographia Literaria about the reflective faculty's participation in death: "I interpret the death, of which the reflective faculty partakes, as of the world made in our image, or rather through our categories, by Kant's faculty of the Understanding, namely that very world which was meant to remove the skeptic's anxieties about the existence of objects outside us" (*In Quest of the Ordinary* 44). Cavell is developing Wittgenstein's idea that "criteria, for all their necessity, are open to our repudiation, or dissatisfaction" (*In Quest of the Ordinary* 5); thus both skepticism and its resolution are essential to the experience of human language: we need to erect criteria by which we judge the world, but in order for those criteria to be *our* criteria we need to be able to repudiate them and see them die. Cavell sees this paradox as an important part of his own philosophical program and as part of the Romantic response to the Kantian imperative, but it is also an idea with roots in the Incarnation: Christians must have a savior who will be a source of ontological, epistemological, and ethical criteria, but he can be claimed by humans as a savior because he died a human death.

We have again been thrown back into the realm of "troth" rather than "truth." As I pointed out in the previous chapter, Cavell sees skepticism (doubt of the existence of the world) turning into solipsism (doubt of the existence of other minds) and therefore expressible as an animism that is both embraced and rejected by the Romantics in the possibility that "skeptical doubt is to be interpreted as jealousy and that our relation to the world that remains is as to something that has died at our hands" (55). The world is thus seen, not simply as something to be understood, but as that which both is and is not (as the animism is embraced or parodied) a kind of living (because susceptible to death) other whose potential for death is essentially linked to its status as "our" world: it exists in our categories, and those categories are ours because we can let them die or kill them. The world becomes an other of whom we are jealous, and, if the rivalry becomes too intense, whom we will murder or who will murder us, with the potential result that difference will be reduced to the chaos of the Same. But alternatively this incarnate world may be manifested as Levinas's other whose absolute alterity provides us with a foundational sense of the infinite. In any case, the world thus conceived becomes a being who may or not be trusted, rather than a locus for the presence or absence of truth.

If words could function according to the dream of transubstantiation, and be totally transformed from things to signs—if "this" bread could become a divine "my body," effacing the conflict between those two states, there would of course be no need for skepticism; ownership of the world, of the objective by the subjective, would occur by divine or priestly fiat. But the messy objective remainder of words as things—the linguistic leftovers of the Last Supper, in Hegel's analogy—requires that the words constituting our world be encountered as objects in their own right, and even as constituting other subjects, Wordsworth and Coleridge's "living things," "incarnations" that live and die as we do. They are "our" words not so much because we control their operation as signs, as because we can use them to create inherently mortal structures in which to understand the world, structures that will die.

There are important historical ways in which those words, incarnations of thought midway between signs and things, are both ours and not-ours. For example, we struggle with a tradition-encrusted language in order to claim our categories of understanding, a claim based on the death of previous categories and, by extension, the death of our own. As Hans-Georg Gadamer points out in "The Universality of the Hermeneutical Problem," all works that claim historical objectivity, perhaps especially those that pretend to a transhistorical "truth," such as "those masterworks of historical scholarship that seem to be the very consummation of the extinguishing of the individual," will ultimately be seen as expressions of their time and place rather than as expressions of objective "truth": "We can classify these works with unfailing accuracy in terms of the political tendencies of the time in which they were written" (*Philosophical Hermeneutics* 6). The point here is not that they are "ideological," in the sense that they express a limited point of view that theoretically could be corrected by a more objective view, to be achieved in the future, but that this is how truth works, as a continuous interaction of always-limited horizons. Charles Taylor makes a similar point when he states that our act of making sense of our lives is fundamentally a *narrative* act, not the discovery of static absolutes: "Making sense of one's life as a story is also, like orientation to the good, not an optional extra.... [O]ur lives exist also in this space of questions, which only a coherent narrative can answer" (*Sources of the Self* 47).

Seen in this way, Enlightenment categories of understanding do not exist for Wordsworth as "untruths" so much as they exist as opponents who, perhaps, must be killed, and Wordsworth recognizes, if only implicitly in the rhetoric of incarnation, that the death of all concepts—like the death of his faith in the French Revolution—is part of their humanness, and essential to the nature and possibility of our "troth" in them. Just as objectivity, for Hegel, is necessary to reflection—perhaps because the "purity" of subjective unity is also the chaos of nondifferentiation—so is mortality a necessary part of our relationship to our "incarnated" thoughts. Those thoughts must be incarnated in a language that is ours and not-ours both semiotically, as words' objective materiality prevents them from effacing themselves before the pure content of our thought, and historically, as we struggle to claim ownership of words that are claimed by rival conceptual structures, some living and some dead, some that we need to kill and some that may kill us.

I argue in Chapter 3 that Wordsworth's incarnational poetics, as put into play in *The Prelude*'s rhetoric, can be a way of producing meaning that confronts exactly these problems that stem from incarnational language's double orientation toward self-effacement and thing, spirit and materiality, without sublating that doubleness, as Hegel does in his *Phenomenology of Spirit*, and without introducing a subjective fiat to ground a system of arbitrary representation, as the authors of the *Port-Royal Logic* do, according to Marin. But despite Wordsworth's qualified "success" in making his incarnational rhetoric work, he had to struggle with the fact that incarnation is precisely that which reveals his inherited representational conflicts, even as it gestures toward a route out of those conflicts. The question of whether an incarnational epistemology and poetics is grounded in a principle of unity, a principle of fundamental violence, or a seemingly impossible accommodation between the spiritual and the material must be faced by both Hegel and Wordsworth. Hegel's baffled Christian mourns the melting of the Host on his tongue, the purity of his faith demanding the disappearance of the very objective materiality that would give him access to his Savior through religion. In order to speak that faith in a viable incarnational rhetoric, one must, to paraphrase Cavell, see one's relationship to that Host as an acknowledgment of its disappearance, regaining it in its otherness *as gone* from one. The disappearance of the material aspect of the sign *is* the process of representation, though it is a process of losing the very materiality that is celebrated when words are praised as things, not simply a process of the sign disappearing before its referent.

This means that the binary sign is not simply collapsed, but is instead no longer the appropriate model for meaning. As I noted in the previous chapter, Gadamer's incarnational theory of meaning is set up in explicit opposition to the semiotic model; he claims that the dominance of the sign has led to the "ideal of the enlightenment of the eighteenth and twentieth centuries" as "the self-conquest of language by a system of artificial, unambiguously defined symbols" in which the word is not a powerfully historical, varied, and contingent producer of meaning, but "a mere tool of communication" (*TM* 414). In Wordsworth's terms, the alternative to the binary sign is to see the performative collapse of figural, semiotic structures as part of the violence occasioned by a process analogous to the Incarnation's ultimately salvific translation of spirit into event. As Cavell puts it, "Since the categories of understanding are ours, we can be understood as carrying the death of the world in us" (*In Quest of the Ordinary* 44); to acknowledge the death and violence inherent in an incarnational rhetoric, rather than "knowing" the spirit that is incarnated, is precisely the way (and perhaps the only way) in which we can "own" a language that thus teeters in the balance between spirit and event.

This turn (in Geoffrey Hartman's terms) from "truth" to "troth," is, like many Romantic tensions, made much more explicit in the next generation of poets, for example, in Arthur Hugh Clough's radically absent Power, which is unnameable but (in an appropriately negative near-rhyme with "unknown") "not unowned": "O not unowned, Thou shalt unnamed forgive" ("Qui Laborat, Orat" 17). Cavell ends his essay "The Uncanniness of the Ordinary" with a discussion of George Stevens's 1942 Hollywood film, *The Woman of the Year,* which presents marriage as a recuperated skepticism that gives up knowledge but embraces acknowledgment, "the mutual acknowledgement of separateness," in "mutual pleasure without a concept" (*In Quest of the Ordinary* 178). Clough's "Natura Naturans" (published in 1849) is based on a chance love-encounter on a train and concludes with a sentimental Edenic dream; its plot would not be out of place in the Hollywood of the forties, and it strikes a similar bargain with absence. Clough is talking of a kind of religious-sexual Being and Cavell of specifically ordinary beings, but Clough joins Cavell in seeing that, given the blank misgivings of creatures forced to move about in a world that Kant has made unrealizable, our only way of "owning" the world (in the sense of "possessing" it) is to "own" it (in the sense of "acknowledging" it) rather than to "know" it:

> We sat; while o'er and in us, more
>   And more, a power unknown prevailed,
> Inhaling, and inhaled,—and still
>   'Twas one, inhaling or inhaled.
> . . . .
> Ah no!—Yet owned we, fused in one,
>   The Power which e'en in stones and earths
> By blind elections felt, in forms
>   Organic breeds to myriad births;
> By lichen small on granite wall
>   Approved, its faintest feeblest stir

> Slow spreading, strengthening long, at last
> Vibrated full in me and her.
> ("Natura Naturans" 13–16 and 41–48)

The acknowledgment of that vibration, whether its unnameable source is in Clough's Power, or Wordsworth's light of setting suns, is the gesture enabled by the rhetoric of incarnation. This gesture is also, as in "Natura Naturans," an acknowledgment of the self's disappearance into the "blind elections" of evolutionary processes, or, as in Wordsworth, the self's constitution in the death of figures.

2

Words, Things, and Death

> Let us beware of saying that death is opposed to life. The living is merely a type of what is dead, and a very rare type.
> —Nietzsche, *The Gay Science*, no. 109

> "Being" is *not* the antithesis of non-being, appearance, nor even of the dead (for only something that can live can be dead).
> —Nietzsche, *The Will to Power*, no. 581

In the previous chapter I laid out some of the problems that the Christian Incarnation presented for Hegel as he thought through the relationship between the spiritual and the material, and it might seem at this point as if the incarnational analogy were more trouble than it is worth. I raise throughout this book the problematic aspects of incarnation as a way of thinking about thought and language, in order to correct the misperception that Wordsworth's incarnational thought merely expresses a nostalgia for representational adequacy. However, I also show how the incarnational analogy was a hermeneutically enabling concept for Wordsworth because of the non-representational way incarnational thought negotiates the relationship between spirit and event, thought and language.

As in Hegel, Wordsworth's complex attitude toward the objective materiality of language exemplifies the problematic and enabling aspects of the incarnational analogy. For Wordsworth, this materiality is very concretely envisioned in the notion, shared by Coleridge, that words should be treated as "things." The idea that words can be things has many different possible ramifications in both Romantic and contemporary theory. I further contend that the materiality of language is closely related to Gadamer's incarnational sense of language as historically contingent "event." An "event" is not exactly a "thing," but events and things share contingency, historical specificity, and effective force (the objective materiality that posed such a problem for Hegel) that are essential to Wordsworth's notion of language as incarnation. Words as things are in fact more complex than words as mere events. For J. L. Austin, words are events ("performatives") insofar as they are not descriptive or representational "statements"; however, words as things in Wordsworth's thought can be *both* something like events and also something like statements or signs. They exert a real, material force in the world, and as things, more easily than pure events, can stand in the place of other things and thus perform a semiotic representational role.

The most extreme Romantic sense in which words can be things can be found in Blake. Though Blake objected strenuously to Wordsworth's dependence on material nature,[1] Henry Crabb Robinson recalls Blake saying that "the moment I have written, I see the Words fly around the room in all directions. It is then published.—The Spirits can read and my MS: is of no further use" (*Blake's Poetry and Designs* 500). Blake's complex sense of the possibility of an unmediated incarnation of visions is of course very different from Wordsworth's highly mediated sense of the incarnational, but he nonetheless provides an important limit case for the possibility that words are things. Keats provides a muted auditory version of this when he suggests in the "Ode to a Nightingale" that "Forlorn! the very word is like a bell / To toll me back from thee to my sole self!" Wordsworth's notion of the poem as inscription or epitaph, which Geoffrey Hartman has elucidated,[2] as well as his localization of the moment of composition ("Tintern Abbey") or the poem itself ("Lines Left Upon a Seat in a Yew-Tree") contribute to our sense of the materiality of the poem as a very physical conglomeration of word-things.

The most important point here is that I emphasize the thingness of the incarnated word as a problem in its own right, not just as part of an ultimately visionary scheme. John McGowan says insightfully of the Coleridgean symbol's equation of word and thing, "Words and material things become equivalent in that both serve as symbols of something beyond themselves" (*Representation and Revelation* 15). Still, this is a negative definition of words' materiality—words are like things only in relation to something that is neither word nor thing—whereas I am attempting to formulate a positive description of words' thingness.

Modern theory provides many ways to understand the materiality of the word, some of which I draw on and none of which fits exactly my sense of Wordsworth's incarnational language. Most obvious perhaps is the poststructuralist sense of the materiality of the signifier. The efforts of Saussure and Lévi-Strauss to separate the sign into arbitrarily related material and conceptual elements ("signifier" and "signified" or "event" and "structure")[3] were followed by the efforts of Marxist, psychoanalytic, and deconstructive readers of the structural linguists and anthropologists to liberate the signifier from its logocentric and ideological ties. Writing amid the turmoil of the 1960s in France, these writers were easily led to analogies between economic and linguistic materiality as defining "things" to be liberated.[4] Though I draw on Derrida and de Man in particular, the poststructuralist reading of Saussure is too narrow both politically and linguistically. Though it seems to deconstruct the binary Saussurean sign, it remains tyrannized by it. Particularly in American readings, the material signifier is polarized as the victim to be liberated from the ideology or logocentricity of the signified, and there is no room for a more flexible—in my terms, incarnational—relation between or alternative to these poles.

The more current way to treat the materiality of the word would be through a new historical or cultural-materialist approach that would see words as things in the sense of commodities or political counters on a level with other events in history. I avoid that approach partly because, after the work done by James Chandler, Marjorie Levinson, Kurt Heinzelman, Alan Liu, Raimonda Modiano, William Keach, and others, the sense in which Romantic thought is incarnated in poetic commodities or historical dramas seems to have been pretty well covered. I also find that approach limiting, because things do not always function as commodities. In Chapters 3 and 4 I discuss the tension between the notion of a word-thing as a commodity and as a gift.

More true to Wordsworth's own sense of words' materiality, though still limited by the circularity of its own metaphoricity, is Geoffrey Hartman's notion, developed throughout his work but most insistently in *Saving the Text*, (especially 121–44) of words as containing a power that can "wound"; the sense that words' deictic or "pointing" function is to be understood almost literally, in the sense of words "poking" with their sharp "points."[5] I attempt to broaden Hartman's sense of words as powerful things by invoking not only Gadamer, but also Cavell, Levinas, and of course Heidegger, philosophical ancestor to all four. What I just disparaged as the "metaphoricity" of these approaches, however, is also the virtue of what Irving Massey calls "the ethics of particularity,"[6] that is, the emphasis on the nonrepeatable particularity of experience both in and of literature and the notion that "categories have something of the fraud about them" (34). Massey treats this as both a critical observation and a methodological principle; his examination of the particular is effected through examples rather than categorizations. This approach, which I admire, raises an insoluble methodological problem for me, as I believe it did for Wordsworth: to call a word a "thing" is to emphasize precisely its noncategorizable particularity, and thus attempts to theorize about that thingness will inevitably be contradictory and insufficient. One reason I keep returning to Gadamer for theoretical support is that his anti-"method" description of interpretation plays on its own historical contingency despite his emphasis on tradition and on interpretation's particularity. Thus my emphasis on the thingness of the incarnated word in Wordsworth is intimately related to my desire to avoid reducing this to a "theory" of incarnate materiality. I share this problematic situation with Wordsworth's Wanderer in *The Excursion*, as we shall see in Chapter 4.

In the development of the incarnational analogy in the third "Essay Upon Epitaphs," the complex role played by the body shows Wordsworth's double-sided evaluation of the materiality of language. The analogy, which is put in terms of "incarnation" and "counter-spirit" in the passage I quoted at the beginning of my first chapter, is stated a few sentences earlier as a subordinate clause, in a sentence critiquing recent epitaphs that have been stultified by the influence of Dryden and Pope:

> Energy, stillness, grandeur, tenderness, those feelings which are the pure emanations of nature, those thoughts which have the infinitude of truth, and those expressions which are not what the garb is to the body but what the body is to the soul, themselves a constituent part and power or function in the thought—all these are abandoned for their opposites,—as if our Countrymen, through successive generations, had lost the sense of solemnity and pensiveness (not to speak of deeper emotions) and resorted to the Tombs of their Forefathers and Contemporaries only to be tickled and surprized. (*PrW* 2:84)

The contrasting pairs used as analogies for the generation of meaning are soul to body (good incarnation) and body to garb (bad counter-spirit). The body is used as both a negative and a positive term in the course of this analogy, as it is alternatively the incarnation of the soul and that which is covered by clothing. The first term of each pair moves from "soul" in the good process to "body" in the bad process, implying that counter-spirit degrades thought to the degree that body is lower than spirit. In the second term of each pair, however, body is elevated over clothing: language should be "body" rather than mere "garb." Thus, if "body" ultimately stands for the materiality of incarnational language, it is a term that is both elevated and denigrated, just as the objective materiality of the word is both effaced and deemed necessary in Hegel.[7]

My point here is that, aware of the kinds of problems faced by Hegel, but also with a sense of the incarnational possibilities for poetry, Wordsworth necessarily has a very mixed attitude toward the materiality of language. His statement in the note to "The Thorn" that words are things both celebrates and indicts language, as it argues that repetition of words does not entail tautology. It begins by portraying "repetition and apparent tautology" as a function of language's inadequacy: "Now every man must know that an attempt is rarely made to communicate impassioned feelings without something of an accompanying consciousness of the inadequateness of our own powers, or the deficiencies of language." But it ends by celebrating a very different position: repetition is not tautological because words excite interest "not only as symbols of the passion, but as *things*, active and efficient, which are of themselves part of the passion" (*Poetical Works* 2:513).

THE PRELUDE, BOOK 5

Book 5 of *The Prelude* has a similar structure, beginning with a lament for language's inadequacy and ending with a celebration of language's power. This process takes on the structure of a post-Miltonic elegy, moving from an expression of grief through various strategies for "reconcilement" with the death at issue, to the placement of the death into a context that allows for a kind of cathartic celebration. It is strange that this book, whose function in the poet's autobiography is to celebrate his literary education—a fairly happy topic—should take an elegiac form, but it demonstrates the close and complex link between poetic incarnational language and human mortality. With a self-conscious sense of this paradox, the opening lines focus the poet's grief not on the "woes" that humanity "endur[es]" (5.5–6) but rather on "the honours of [its] high endowments" (5.9). The opening lamentation culminates in a complaint about the difference between the human powers of thought and language, apparent in the mortal frailty of the "things," works of human language, upon which the mind must stamp her image:

> Oh! why hath not the mind
> Some element to stamp her image on
> In nature somewhat nearer to her own?
> Why, gifted with such powers to send abroad
> Her spirit, must it lodge in shrines so frail?
> (5.44–48)

The book ends, however, by celebrating the "visionary power" of those same frail shrines:

> Visionary Power
> Attends upon the motions of the winds
> Embodied in the mystery of words.
> (5.619–21)

By examining how the poet gets from one position to the other, we shall see more clearly how a language of incarnated word-things is necessarily involved with human mortality.

On the one hand, the desire for words to be living things is a logical extension of the late eighteenth-century desire for a "natural language" in which the threat of the arbitrary but inescapable connection between signs and ideas intimated by Locke is ameliorated by the possibility that those signs themselves have, as Herder and others suggested, a natural origin. Wordsworth places this desire into the incarnational context by comparing God's creation of Nature to man's creation of works of language:

> Hitherto
> In progress through this verse my mind hath looked
> Upon the speaking face of earth and heaven
> As her prime teacher, intercourse with man
> Established by the Sovereign Intellect,
> Who through that bodily image hath diffused
> A soul divine which we participate,
> A deathless spirit. Thou also, man, hast wrought,
> For commerce of thy nature with itself,
> Things worthy of unconquerable life;
> And yet we feel—we cannot chuse but feel—
> That these must perish. Tremblings of the heart
> It gives, to think that the immortal being
> No more shall need such garments; and yet man,

> As long as he shall be the child of earth,
> Might almost 'weep to have' what he may lose—
> Nor be himself extinguished, but survive
> Abject, depressed, forlorn, disconsolate.
>
> (5.10–27)

This passage does not suggest a simple pantheism—nature as a manifestation of divine spirit—but neither can this be simply deconstructed to show, as Andrzej Warminski claims, that "God's phenomenal figure" becomes "the image of man—in fact, worse than that, an image *of* language, an image created by man's language, by man's speech" ("Facing Language" 26). This either/or approach to incarnation (fairly typical of deconstructive readings of Wordsworth), leaving no alternative between a "blind" perception of God in Nature and an "insightful" understanding of that perception as a man-made sign system, misses the complexity of the incarnational link between the divine and the human, thought and language. This passage demonstrates neither naive pantheism nor deconstructed materialism, but rather the kind of incarnational animism or humanization discussed in the first chapter: the important consequence of nature's infusion with the divine is that nature thus becomes human, and must be dealt with as such, with all the relational complexity that relations to humans entail.

The interlocking analogies give the "human" as it relates to language a very complex status here. The basic comparison is that as God created Nature, humanity creates books, and of course humanity's creations suffer by comparison because they are mortal. Still, God's creation of nature is also presented as a human incarnation of the divine: nature is, like Jesus, a "prime teacher"; it has a very human "speaking face" and is a "bodily image" with a "soul divine." As in Levinas, the infinite is associated with the nontotalizable alterity of another's face. This "deathless spirit" (reduced to a perception of "the eye of fleeting time" in the 1850 version [5.17]) in which humanity participates is the fulcrum on which this passage turns, moving from God's creation of nature to humanity's creation of books. The analogy between God and human remains intact (we humans still have our "immortal being" even at the depressing end of the passage), but partly because of this the other side of the comparison—nature and books—does not hold up. *Because* humanity is immortal, a sharp division exists between the immortal intention behind the linguistic "things worthy of unconquerable life" and their actual mortal existence as things in the world. In fact, Wordsworth uses the language that later appears in the famous comparison of the third "Essay

Upon Epitaphs": what should be *incarnations* become *garments* whose relation to "immortal" being is transitory.

Here we see what happens to a theory of natural language when it is refracted through the incarnational lens. The language in human books is "natural," but in the sense that, as God's spirit is incarnated in (a therefore humanized) nature, humanity's (divine) spirit is incarnated in mortal word-things. The problem from the point of view of the human mind is that those word-things are not human; the mind would prefer to "stamp her image on" something "in nature somewhat nearer to her own." God gets to animate nature with a human "speaking face," but in man's parallel operation the word-things he uses have an objective materiality that resists animation, and thus tends toward the "counter-spirit" of mere garments.

It is only by coming to terms with the mortality implicit in the process of incarnation that the poet will be able to reach the stage at which words can be celebrated as "visionary powers." If words are merely objective things with no life, then they will become the garments of counter-spirit, or mere "shrines," which will themselves fade like the monuments in "Hart-Leap Well." Moreover, as Hegel recognized, they will not efface themselves before a "live" meaning; the linguistic leftovers will remain as unavoidable but also—to continue the culinary analogy—"inedible" word-things. This situation is untenable, but it can be resolved only by performing an act of recognizing death as fundamental to incarnate life: much as Cavell recognizes that as skepticism toward the world becomes mistrust of a human other, that animated world becomes mortal, and the attempt to resolve skepticism becomes an act as potentially murderous as the Mariner's shooting of the albatross. For words to share human life, they must also share human death.

As the passage above suggests, Wordsworth's natural world is already infused with animism, because Nature can incarnate God. For language to incarnate thought, however, word-things must be similarly animated. The skeptical relation to those word-things, which here at the beginning of book 5 is the complaint of their difference from the mind, can only be resolved by recognizing them as living powers which retain that principle of difference and the accompanying threat of death. We can only animate word-things if we grant them the possibility of death. In that way, we do not deny our skepticism regarding language: word-things retain their impenetrable otherness, or what Gadamer calls the "facticity" that "represents an insurmountable resistance against any superior presumption that we can make sense of it all" (*The Relevance of the*

Beautiful 34). Still, we can at the same time share a life with that animated language, with all the risks attendant on sharing life with another human: both Cavell and Wordsworth naturally turn to marriage as an analogy for these processes of expression.

If, as Coleridge hoped, it is possible "to destroy the old antithesis of *Words & Things,* elevating, as it were, words into Things, & living Things too" (*Collected Letters* 625–26), then words would in fact become an element nearer to the mind's own. Wordsworth, however, was very much aware that things can be living or dead, and that if words are to become things they must confront both life and death. A passage that faces this issue specifically, rejected from the final manuscript of *The Prelude,* was originally intended to follow the ascent of Mount Snowdon in the five-book *Prelude.* The speaker sees a horse silhouetted in the moonlight:

> With one leg from the ground the creature stood,
> Insensible and still; breath, motion gone,
> Hairs, colour, all but shape and substance gone,
> Mane, ears, and tail, as lifeless as the trunk
> That had no stir of breath. We paused awhile
> In pleasure of the sight, and left him there,
> With all his functions silently sealed up,
> Like an amphibious work of Nature's hand,
> A borderer dwelling betwixt life and death,
> A living statue or a statued life.
> (MS W 64–73, in the Norton edition of *The Prelude* 498)

On one hand, to become a statue is to die; this is a reason for the horse's "amphibious" liminal position. On the other hand, a statue brings forth meaning in a process that affirms the relation between nature and the mind. To become a dead thing is to be sealed into a process that is inaccessible to articulation, as in "A Slumber Did My Spirit Seal," when Lucy achieves natural thingness as "a thing that could not feel / The touch of earthly years." Blind and deaf she is "rolled round in earth's diurnal course, / With rocks, and stones, and trees." As Dan Latimer points out, the identity promised by nature is a kind of knowledge which "is useless in human terms because it leads through the door of death. It is mute knowledge, inexpressible information" ("Real Culture and Unreal Nature" 52). Nevertheless, to attain this sort of identity is also to become the kind of "thing" to which words aspire: a natural object or a meaningful statue.[8]

For Wordsworth, exemplary "thingness" is inextricably connected to the passage between life and death—hence the paradigmatic significance of the epitaph as a model for meaning. Like the dead Lucy or the still horse, words achieve the status of things and thus become effective powers rather than transparent, arbitrary signs precisely as they are sealed off from their life source in the speaker. This process is an important part of Wordsworth's use of the image of incarnation as an analogy for the relation between language and thought. Gadamer points out that, unlike the divine Word, the human word "has left behind it the path of the thought to which alone, however, it owes its existence" (*TM* 425). Thus being cut off from its source, the spirit transformed into event, or the thought transformed into language, involves for the word a kind of "death" into the world even though this is not a simple separation, and even though the word remains an exertion of "living" power. Thus the incarnational analogy allows us to see the materiality of the human word not in Greek terms of the more or less adequate representation of a transcendental logos, but in terms of an event in history, cut off from a unifying source and informed by human mortality. For a word to be a thing is not for it to be a more or less adequate sign, but is rather for it to be an event. To enter the world as a thing is to become, not a sign of something in the world, but rather another thing in the world, contiguous with, and perhaps even in competition with, the "idea" or "thought" that originated the word.

Death has a dual role here: on the one hand, to use Levinas's terms, the movement from "saying" to "said," from an incarnational relation of proximity with the other to the sealing off of the concrete individual into a concept of universal consciousness (or even, further down the line, into a system of representation) entails the individual's "consciousness of its death, in which its singularity is lost in its universality" (*OTB* 83) as Lucy is sealed off into the diurnal course of the earth. On the other hand (and here Wordsworth's appreciation of death is closer to Heidegger's than Levinas's[9]), that same process of sealing off into a condition bounded by death can *found* the very concrete facticity that, in the process of incarnation, gives words and images an animated life that is irreducible to concepts and systems, hence the ambiguous status of the silhouetted horse and, as we shall see, the status of "Lucy" as both dead object and founder of incarnational subjectivity.

For Wordsworth, as many readers have noticed, words function much like funeral monuments, especially where memory is involved. If the preservation of meaning through word-things can be compared to the preservation of the memory of the dead by marking places of burial, then it may be helpful to note that, in the first "Essay Upon Epitaphs," the practice of marking places of burial is traced to a "twofold desire; first, to guard the remains of the deceased from irreverent approach or from savage violation: and, secondly, to preserve their memory" (*PrW* 2:49). Though intimations of immortality provide a means to resolve these "two sources of feeling" into one, it remains clear that the processes are both different and interdependent: like the "books" to be buried in the dream of the Arab Quixote in *The Prelude* the dead "thing" must be sealed off into an impregnable tomb—cut off from its source in the living world—precisely so that it can be protected, preserved, and related to (not simply represented in) the active temporality of the living world's memory. Thus it is not just that Wordsworth desires to express a relation to death, but that the notion of death is fundamental to the authentic expression of one's relation to the world. This insight, carried out in the elegiac structure of book 5 in *The Prelude*, is a significant moment in the history of the elegy as a genre: the Wordsworthian elegy is not an attempt to overcome death, as in the Christian ending of Milton's *Lycidas*, or even to acknowledge a difficult relationship to a particular death, as it will be in Shelley's *Adonais* or Tennyson's *In Memoriam*. Even Wordsworth's elegy on his own brother—"Elegiac Stanzas" on Peele Castle—presents death as a guarantee of aesthetic truth and authentic perception rather than as something to be resolved into a religious economy or a psychological structure of grief: "A deep distress hath humanized my soul."

Cavell provides a description of something like this relationship to the mortal life of the word-thing by claiming that our very ownership of the world is conditioned by the possibility of the death of our conception of it. If our linguistic relation to the world means that words become mortal living things, then our wording of that world involves seeing our relation to it as a relation to a living human other who might die. The world (which, we must remember, includes words among its things) is thus seen, not simply as something to be understood, but as that which is a living other whose mortality is essentially derived from its status as "our" world. In Wordsworth, we see this most clearly when the temporal process of memorialization (the present poet brooding over the past) is expressed as a living relationship between human beings. That which is dead is, of course, a trace of that which *was* living, but the very process of memorialization engendered by this relationship is figured in the first "Essay Upon Epitaphs" as a marriage between two living beings. We know from "Tintern Abbey" how easy it is for Wordsworth to see a female other (in that case, Dorothy) as an emblem of a past self. In the first "Essay Upon Epitaphs" we have a similar use of a male-female union to portray the generation of meaning over an unbridgeable temporal gap—not exactly the gap between autobiographical present and past, but the related gap between the living and the formerly living. A hallowed truth is born from the wedding of the living and the dead: "It is truth hallowed by love—the joint offspring of the worth of the dead and the affections of the living!" (*PrW* 2:58). An epitaph becomes a poetically effective "thing" when the affections of the living mate with the worth of the dead to produce a living—and by implication mortal—child. An epitaph is an exemplary word-become-thing because it partakes of both this foundational mortality and the related interaction with a living other: it is an inscription interacting with traveling people, expressing "truth" generated by a living relation to the dead body hidden beneath it. Death thus plays a very specific role in the generation of poetic meaning: words are incarnated as living but mortal things, and our linguistic relation to the world becomes a relation to a living other whose death is a condition of that life. The death at the center of the Lucy poems is a prime example of this situation.

These connections among incarnation, mortality, and linguistic thingness help to explain the rhetoric of book 5 of *The Prelude*, as it traces the path between the "frail shrines" and the "visionary power" of words. One of the most important accounts of death's role in this process follows the famous "Boy of Winander" passage, a paradigmatic account of the incarnational education of the voice. The Boy unwittingly finds an alternative to those Cartesian subjects who would totalize and control learning in a mechanistic way,

> Sages, who in their prescience would controul
> All accidents, and to the very road
> Which they have fashioned would confine us down
> like engines.
>
> (5.380–83)

The Boy of Winander (whose experience I have discussed elsewhere as an enactment of imagination as catachresis[10]) comes to recognize by contrast "the unreasoning progress of the world" (5.384) ignored by those sages. He first attempts a mimetic relationship to nature, engaging in a process of near-mechanical reproduction:

>   he as through an instrument,
> Blew mimic hootings to the silent owls,
> That they might answer him.
>   (5.397–99)

Of course it is in the subversion of that mimetic relationship that a precisely nonmimetic revelation occurs, and the Boy experiences the classically Wordsworthian interaction within nature, and between nature and the mind. As I will argue in Chapter 3, an important part of *The Prelude*'s rhetoric is built on the recuperation of doomed figural structures—structures of signs—into a nonsemiotic incarnational rhetoric. Here, when "pauses of deep silence mocked his skill" (5.405),

>   the visible scene
> Would enter unawares into his mind
> With all its solemn imagery, its rocks,
> Its woods, and that uncertain heaven, received
> Into the bosom of the steady lake.
>   (5.409–13)

The Boy has failed in the attempt to manufacture the owl's sound; we might say that he has failed to create an artificial sign that can be used as an arbitrary "instrument" in a communicative situation. Out of this very failure comes a transformation of spirit into event that follows the logic of the incarnation. The lake becomes a living object (it has a "bosom"), and the separation of the solidly incarnated object from its spiritual source is suggested in the difference between the "uncertain heaven" and the "steady lake."

Death enters in the lines immediately following: "This boy was taken from his mates, and died / In childhood ere he was full ten years old" (5.414–15). As Alan Bewell points out in his analysis of this episode, the development of language and the development of systems for memorializing the dead are complementary processes in Wordsworth's anthropology.[11] At first, death produces silence; the Boy's death is specifically accompanied by poetic silence, as if the sight of the grave precludes speech, when the writing poet claims to have stood *mutely* by his grave: "A full half-hour together I have stood / Mute, looking at the grave in which he lies" (5.421–22). As Dan Latimer puts it, "The death of the Winander boy is Wordsworth's own imagined death, the fate of a silence that he (Wordsworth) thankfully did not have. The muteness at the boy's grave is his response to one who accepted nature's voice into himself and never found his own" ("Real Culture and Unreal Nature" 53). The end result of the "successful" natural education of the voice is the death of that voice into nature, like the death that follows Lucy's education by nature in "Three Years She Grew," or, more enigmatically, the death-into-nature in "A Slumber Did My Spirit Seal."

The muteness does not last, of course; the Boy's death is reappropriated into the poem's living language by a complex series of rhetorical shifts:

> Even now methinks I have before my sight
> That self-same village church: I see her sit—
> The thronèd lady spoken of erewhile—
> On her green hill, forgetful of this boy
> Who slumbers at her feet, forgetful too
> Of all her silent neighborhood of graves,
> And listening only to the gladsome sounds
> That, from the rural school ascending, play
> Beneath her and about her.
> (5.423–31)

In a shift to the writing present (the moment of the actual creation of the poem's language), the syntax presents a classic Wordsworthian ambiguity: does "forgetful" in lines 426 and 427 modify "I" in line 424 or the "thronèd lady" in line 425? The context of the passage quoted here suggests that the poet is being forgetful, and then listening, but the syntax allows for both, the "thronèd lady" is closer to the first "forgetful," and the personification of the church as the one who actively beholds this scene is suggested in the following lines:

> May she long
> Behold a race of young ones like to those
> With whom I herded.
> (5.431–33)

The Boy is both objectified and forgotten by either the speaker or the personified church, "dying" a second time into the system of the "silent neighborhood of graves." His humanly active, metaphorically alive "slumbering" metonymically shifts to the silence of "graves"—inanimate memorial objects in the landscape—and this enables a shift to the living children above ground. The personified village church effects this transition from death to life by an act of forgetting—the memorializing function of the churchyard must itself "die" so that a conceptual link back to life can be made. The speaker has an ambivalent relation to this process: on one reading of the syntax he performs this act of de-animation, objectification, and self-forgetting. On the other reading, if we ascribe this forgetting to the "thronèd lady," the speaker implicitly critiques the process. For him, the narration of the church's act of forgetting is an act of remembering, an incorporation of the Boy's death into an active process of memorialization. The fact that the very syntax of the poem allows us to see the speaker as both sealing the dead Boy into a forgotten inanimate grave and as implicitly critiquing that act in a gesture toward incarnate life suggests the depth at which death plays a dual role.

The shrines of language are indeed frail when their visionary power depends on the denial of their very memorializing function; the "life" to which words aspire is truly "but a sleep and a forgetting," or a route to death: living language moves toward—and in this case through—dead objectivity because of the mortality that grounds its life. On the one hand, the Boy's death leads to the "gladsome sounds" of living play. On the other hand, the necessity of death in that process leaves the poet silently confronting the idea of the Boy's dead body as the "thing" that remains, a dead thing that must be forgotten even as it is memorialized so that we can return to the world of the living, but which, like Hegel's leftovers, cannot be forgotten because our notion of the "living" is so dependent on the idea of its death. Wordsworth's starkest portrayal of the negative side of this double notion of death is "A Slumber Did My Spirit Seal." In that poem, for Lucy to be envisioned as beyond "the touch of earthly years" requires, at least in one possible reading, that the speaker give up his humanity: "I had no human fears." To see the situation from a living human perspective entails the horrifying recognition of death as objectification of Lucy's body "rolled round . . . / With rocks, and stones, and trees."

The visionary power of the Boy of Winander is assimilated into the text through his deathly objectification and obliteration from memory; however, the drowned man of Esthwaite is assimilated through a simpler process of association with romance. This episode begins a process in book 5 that implicitly allegorizes the increasing complexity of the young poet's relationship to death, leading toward the incorporation of words' involvement with death into their possession of visionary power. He sees a heap of garments distinctly, but he misinterprets it as the sign of a temporarily absent swimmer:

> Twilight was coming on, yet through the gloom
> I saw distinctly on the opposite shore
> A heap of garments, left as I supposed,
> By one who there was bathing.
>
> (5.459–62)

Proper signification only occurs as the sign becomes distant from its referent: the longer the signifying garments are unclaimed, the clearer it becomes that they refer to a dead man: "The succeeding day, / Those unclaimed garments [tell] a plain tale" (5.466–67). Nevertheless, the discovery that the heap of garments "means" a dead man is not a source of "vulgar fear" (5.473) because, says the poet,

> my inner eye had seen
> Such sights before among the shining streams
> Of fairyland, the forests of romance—
> Thence came a spirit hallowing what I saw
> With decoration and ideal grace,
> A dignity, a smoothness, like the words
> Of Grecian art and purest poesy.
>
> (5.475–81)

Here the separation between clothing and body allow sign and referent to remain separate, arbitrarily related entities, which is exactly the relationship language and thought should *not* have, according the third "Essay Upon Epitaphs." From the point of view of Wordsworth's theory, the Popean language of clothing rather than incarnation leads to the madness and death associated with the coat of Nessus; the "ill gift" of non-incarnational language is "such a one as those poisoned vestments, read of in the stories of superstitious times, which had power to consume and to alienate from his right mind the victim who put them on" (*PrW* 2:84–85). Within the poetry of book 5 of *The Prelude*, however, the separation of sign and referent in this system means that the clothes are the language of signs, not things, and can thus be taken up into other sign systems—such as those suspiciously "Grecian" fairy tales—without concern for language's more problematic, nonsemiotic, incarnational existence as a collection of living things.

Clothes have meaning and shape not in themselves, but only as they signify an owner; thus throughout this story the young poet is concerned with the clothes not as things, but only as arbitrary signs. They are signs whose meaning can be controlled by a subject standing outside of the system, and can thus be manipulated, placed into internally coherent systems, and prevented from becoming more threatening word-things. Perhaps because of the poet's interpretive immaturity—when the Valley's "paths, its shores, / And brooks, were like a dream of novelty" to the poet's "half-infant thoughts" (5.452–54)—his self can function simply as the Lockean "punctual self": a self defined not, as the mature self will be, in terms of a complex engagement with the world, but defined instead as detached manipulator of systems. In this case, such a stance uses the resources of sign systems to escape, in the very presence of a dead body, the incarnational relationship between words and death.[12]

This immature incorporation of death into language through a series of shifting signs sets the stage for the narration of the youthful relation to literature. Entry into a more mature relation to word-things occurs when

> sober truth, experience, sympathy,
> Take stronger hold of us; and words themselves
> Move us with conscious pleasure,
> (5.566–68)

that is, when words become living things with which an affective relationship is possible. This early recognition of words appreciated "for *their own sakes*" (5.579; Wordsworth's italics) is immediately associated with their death, as the poet laments the fact that these early loved poems "are now / Dead in [his] eyes as is a theatre / Fresh emptied of spectators" (5.573–75). If the theater analogy is pressed, the poet bears some responsibility for this death; he has abandoned these works as the theater is abandoned by the spectators.

The larger context of this passage also suggests the mortality implicit in this relation to "words themselves." This state occurs midway between the childhood world of free, extravagant fictions, in which "our simple childhood, sits upon a throne / That hath more power than all the elements" (5.532–33) and the time in which "we learn to live / In reconcilement with our stinted powers" (5.540–41). The value of the "lawless tales" (5.548) of childhood lies in their reinforcement of childhood's power of autonomous subjectivity; they "make our wish our power, our thought a deed, / An empire, a possession" (5.552–53). Here, incarnation of thought into language has not yet occurred; the language of fairy tales provides a system of signs—not things—that reinforce the subjective ideality of thought by demonstrating the subject's power to manipulate those signs. The later, opposite extreme, life "in reconcilement with our stinted powers," is an effacement or at least a subjugation of that autonomously subjective realm by the objective world, a world that detaches words from their subjective sources, and reifies them into dead objects. It is midway on this route from autonomous subjectivity to dead objectivity—in a middle realm that does not permit a simple distinction between subject and object—that the incarnation of words into living things can take place, and words can be properly effective as things "for their own sakes."[13]

As I tried to suggest in my account of the poet's mourning for the Boy of Winander, words that incarnate as "things" are mortal not only because they are sealed off from their life sources; their living power has the temporal and temporary power of mortal life. Hence the "frail shrine" ("shrine" once meant "coffin") of the words that must, in the dream of the Arab Quixote, be buried like a human body in the face of "An ode in passion uttered, which foretold / Destruction to the children of the earth" (5.97–98). For words to become things is not simply for them to achieve a "natural" status that must be preceded by a kind of death, but that grants them a permanence in the face of human death; rather, the limits of mortality require that words achieve their status as living things only midway on a temporal arc that leads toward death. In terms of the rhetoric of autobiography, this death is the end the "river" of the written life avoids, "part swayed by fear to tread an onward road / That leads direct to the devouring sea" (9.3–4), and which is expressed much earlier in the poet's fear that he is "unprofitably travelling toward the grave" (1.269). In that sense this autobiography is always elegiac, particularly since *The Prelude* was not to be published until after Wordsworth's death: the celebration of visionary moments always looks forward to the "death" of the autobiography in the "devouring sea" ("ravenous sea" in the 1850 version) of the extrapoetic temporality of the poet, a temporality of his life during the poem's private circulation in 1805 and after, and of his death during the poem's public circulation after 1850.

To allow words to be incarnated as living things is to give them mortality as well as life; as Wordsworth complains at the beginning of book 5, we are entrusting our being to "frail shrines" even more mortal than we are. The only solution to that problem is to give those "frail shrines" a power other than that of adequate representation. This is one way to read the "visionary power" celebrated at the end of book 5:

> Visionary Power
> Attends upon the motions of the winds,
> Embodied in the mystery of words:
> There, darkness makes abode, and all the host
> Of shadowy things do work their changes there,

> As in a mansion like their proper home.
> Even forms and substances are circumfused
> By that transparent veil with light divine,
> And, through the intricate turnings of verse,
> Present themselves as objects recognized,
> In flashes, and with a glory scarce their own.
> (5.619–29)

Forms and substances are not "represented" by words; instead they are animated, actively "present[ing] themselves" through the dark process "embodied" or incarnated in words. This living process is, like the Incarnation, a suffusion of divine light on the earth, but it is also a process of "darkness" and "shadowy things." This force, reified into the oxymoronic "transparent veil," "circumfuse[s]" those forms and substances with "light divine," but at the same time preserves the difference between the mind and its linguistic media noted earlier: the "host / Of shadowy things" are not in their "proper home," and forms and substances, incarnated as recognizable "objects," present a "glory scarce their own" in the 1805 version, and an even further removed "glory not their own" in the 1850 text. It is part of the incarnational process that words assume visionary power, not simply by a Coleridgean conceptual, symbolic link to transcendence, and not simply by admitting their conceptual inadequacy, but by allowing themselves to be interrupted by that which is absolutely other, and therefore "infinite" in Levinas's sense. "Forms and substances" are thematized "as objects recognized," but that very reduction to a "said" is interrupted by a recognition that the transcendent is being belied. As Levinas says, "Transcendence owes it to itself to interrupt its own demonstration" by means of "an overflowing of the said itself by a rhetoric which is not only a linguistic mirage, but a surplus of meaning of which consciousness all by itself would be incapable" (*OTB* 152). Thus words, in the sense that they reduce transcendence to a "said," are "frail shrines" that memorialize, rather than animate our thoughts, but they are a living power, a "saying" or witness that is revealed in and by the interruption of the reduction of transcendence to the said. We saw this dual perspective in the memorialization of the dead Boy of Winander: his reduction to a lifeless form in a forgotten graveyard is interrupted by the poet's recognition of that as an act of forgetting and objectification. The very same words in that narrative which are a "said"—a thematization and conceptualization—from the point of view of the "thronèd lady" are a "saying" (a nonconceptual, incarnational witness) from the point of view of the poet, who implicitly breaks up the unity of that said. The ambiguity of the syntax indicates how closely intertwined these processes are.

Human monuments, words that become memorial things, undergo their own death in a process that itself memorializes human mortality. That is the message of "Hart-Leap Well," in which Nature

> leaves these objects to a slow decay
> That what we are, and have been, may be known;
> But, at the coming of the milder day,
> These monuments shall all be overgrown.
> (169–72)

One of effects of the mortality of the incarnated word-thing is that, when word-things die, they decay into mere signs, as Sir Walter's constructions fade into a testimony to human vanity and mortality in "Hart-Leap Well," and as *The Prelude* dies into the extratextual life. Unlike a word that persists as a living thing, a sign has achieved its goal when it dies, or effaces itself before its referent, as these monuments will ultimately do.[14] The clothes of the drowned man of Esthwaite, for example, are not important in themselves as living things, but are "dead" signs pointing to the dead man; their significance ceases once their signifying function is complete. Though the Boy of Winander moved from a user of signs to a vehicle for incarnational rhetoric, the death and self-effacement entailed in that process is also, at least from the point of view of the "thronèd lady," a move back to the mere referentiality of signs, as evidenced by the *dead* Boy's involvement in the complex referential structure of the graveyard and the church. As the Pastor says in book 5 of *The Excursion*, death has a

> two-fold aspect! wintry—one
> Cold, sullen, blank, from hope and joy shut out;
> The other, which the ray divine hath touched,
> Replete with vivid promise, bright as spring.
> (5.554–57)

This is the twofold aspect of language as living but mortal "thing." In order to see the incarnated poetic word as "replete with vivid promise," one has to see it die into a sign effacing itself before its referent. The alternative is to preserve its existence as a thing to be buried and preserved, as in the drama of the Arab Quixote, but that entails the "cold, sullen, blank" state of the forgotten Boy of Winander and the "statued life" of the horse; either way, the living thing must die.

This is not to deny the power of the word as thing; on the contrary, the Romantic effort to admit words to the arena of living things was perhaps to condemn the self to a slow death at the powerful hand of that "living" language. Wordsworth's desire for a language of incarnated things, and his recognition of the necessary relation to death in that desire, enable him to carve out a unique space on the boundary of the Enlightenment and the modern conception of the sign. He wanted a workable alternative to the Lockean sign, which he viewed as an unsatisfactory tool to be applied to ideas arbitrarily and willfully. What made that system of language both so usable and, to Wordsworth, so cheap, was its insistence on language's separation from the human subjective life that claimed to be able to control it, as it were, from the outside, as the "sages" would "controul / All accidents." The reanimation of the word through the rhetoric of incarnation allowed words and human beings to share a common ground as living things, and seemed to counter both the reduction of language to arbitrary signs by Locke and Pope and the reduction of the self to perceptions and then categories by Hume and Kant.

Still, to allow words and beings to operate on the same level, especially when the mortality of each is clearly in view, is to look forward to the death of the very Romantic self mirrored in those living words. When we return in this century to a notion of language as a system of arbitrary signs, it is a very different kind of arbitrariness, thanks partly to the insights of Romanticism. If the arbitrary system of signs becomes a factor that determines us, instead of a system over which we exercise choice and control, then the Romantic lesson that beings and words are on the same ontological plane becomes, not an elevation of words to life, but a reduction of life to words. Wordsworth recognized that words "hold above all other external powers a dominion over thoughts" (*PrW* 2:84), an insight that would reappear in Nietzsche and again in Derrida. These thinkers will suggest that words as living "things" have, like Victor Frankenstein's creature, turned on their creator as a result of the very shared life they have been granted, and now they determine his existence.

FACING DEATH IN THE LUCY POEMS

So far I have discussed death as a problem of language; but for Wordsworth death is not simply an analogy for the mortality of language in poems. On an even more fundamental level, it is related to the problem of the relationship between epistemology and ethics: the problem of how our ways of knowing affect our moral orientation and action in the world. The Lucy poems face this issue directly in their treatment of our relationship to death. Epistemological questions have haunted interpretations of these poems from the early biographical speculation on Lucy's identity, to recent assertions such as that of Frances Ferguson: "A radical ambiguity about the status of the object of poetic representation underlies these lyrics on the most basic level" (*Language as Counter-Spirit* 174–75).

The 1802 sonnet "Methought I Saw the Footsteps of a Throne" is an almost trite lesson that death is to be considered in the context of incarnate human events, and not in the abstraction of representation:

> Methought I saw the footsteps of a throne
> Which mists and vapours from mine eyes did shroud,
> Nor view of him who sate thereon allow'd;
> But all the steps and ground about were strown
> With sights the ruefullest that flesh and bone
> Ever put on; a miserable crowd,
> Sick, hale, old, young, who cried before that cloud,
> "Thou art our king, O Death! to thee we groan."
> I seem'd to mount those steps; the vapours gave
> Smooth way; and I beheld the face of one
> Sleeping alone within a mossy cave,
> With her face up to heaven; that seemed to have
> Pleasing remembrance of a thought foregone;
> A lovely Beauty in a summer grave!
>   (*Poems, in Two Volumes*)

The terrible situation in the octave was created by thinking of Death as an abstract and inaccessible object of representational knowledge: no "view" is allowed, and the result is that the people below are tyrannized by this unseen presence. Once the poet, in the sestet, climbs the stairs, he learns that there is no "Death" in the abstract as an object of knowledge; there are only dead people, who are, even in death, part of an incarnational process of life that involves a natural setting and the residue of active human memory.

This lesson can be extended, though it becomes much more complex in the process, to the problem of thinking of even dead individuals in representational terms. To discuss Lucy as "present" or "absent" is to reduce the question to the tyranny of representational one-dimensionality. Of course she is representationally absent, partly because, as Heidegger points out, death is precisely that which is so absolutely one's own that it admits no representational substitutions:

> This possibility of representing breaks down completely if the issue is one of representing that possibility-of-Being which makes up Dasein's coming to an end, and which, as such, gives to it its wholeness. *No one can take the Other's dying away from him.* . . . In "ending," and in Dasein's Being-a-whole, for which such ending is constitutive, there is by its very essence, no representing. (*Being and Time* 284)[15]

Wordsworth himself, in the note to "Ode: Intimations of Immortality," acknowledges how difficult it is to "admit the notion of death as a state applicable" to his own being (*Poetical Works* 4:463).

Heidegger points out that the route toward an authentic relationship to death lies partly in looking at the back side of the inauthentic one: "Our everyday falling evasion *in the face of* death is an *inauthentic* Being-*towards*-death. But inauthenticity is based on the possibility of authenticity" (303). Part of this is because death's absolute individual "ownness"—that which makes it impossible to substitute anything else for it—means that our existential certainty of death will always run ahead of any evidential or experiential statement we can make about death: "In anticipation [*vorlaufen*, Heidegger's term for how we comport our whole Dasein toward death as a possibility] Dasein can first make certain of its own inmost Being in its totality—a totality which is not to be outstripped. Therefore the evidential character which belongs to the immediate givenness of Experiences, of the 'I,' or of consciousness, must necessarily lag behind the certainty which anticipation includes" (*Being and Time* 310).

In the Lucy poems, this means that death's unrepresentability, the tragic awareness that Lucy's death is not something the poet can "know" or "represent," is a basic premise for these poems, not an interpretive conclusion. Death is the most certain thing we have, but "knowledge" does not reflect that certainty because the anticipatory certainty of death is way ahead of and incompatible with our usual sense of experiential knowledge. The route to an authentic relation to death must begin (as does "Methought I Saw the Footsteps of a Throne") with the inauthenticity of a representational relation, but it cannot end there. In Cavell's terms, the poet must find a way to "acknowledge" her death (or acknowledge her as dead) in a way that unites the impossibility of a nonskeptical knowledge with the human desire for an affective link to that which cannot be "known." This affective link must be ethical rather than epistemological, a way of living rather than a way of knowing, and therefore we must look behind the epistemological problems to their ethical backgrounds. Charles Taylor points out that, especially after the Enlightenment turn from theology to scientific reasoning, moral grounds for epistemological positions are largely unarticulated (*Sources of the Self* 337–40); one of Wordsworth's concerns in the Lucy poems is to reset epistemological questions in their ethical contexts.

Ferguson points out that these poems are in a mixed genre: "part love-poem, part epitaph" (*Language as Counter-Spirit* 176). That mixture suggests Wordsworth's concern for this connection between the epistemological knowledge conveyed in an epitaph (though for Wordsworth the epitaph is itself a mixed genre) and the ethical relationship established in a love poem. "She Dwelt Among the Untrodden Ways" presents the confrontation between an epistemological act of knowing and an ethical act of acknowledging an affective relationship most directly. The poem builds on a contrast between the absence of *knowledge* about the deceased and the presence of "the difference to me." There were "none to praise her"—her qualities were not fixed in linguistic representations—and there were "very few to love" her. The second stanza connects her hiddenness and her beauty: the image of the half-hidden violet becomes the beauty of a star that is unique—"when only one / Is shining in the sky"—as if she is fair precisely because she is not encoded within a social system of identification in which she is "known" to many people. In the third stanza, the absence of knowledge of her life becomes an absence of knowledge of her death: "She lived unknown, and few could know / When Lucy ceased to be."

The unknown Lucy is complemented in "I Travelled Among Unknown Men," in which the private difference of Lucy's death becomes the public difference of "unknown men"; this allows the public (England) to memorialize the private (Lucy who "lived unknown"). The "unknowns"—from the private Lucy to the public men—which border and define experience unite across the boundaries of public and private in order to allow the public to memorialize the private. This doubling of the "unknown" allows the lyric to become a public declaration of something that looks like knowledge: only in "I Travelled Among Unknown Men" is an addressee found, and that addressee is England, the political entity that not only memorializes Lucy, but provides a partner in dialogue that defines the poet himself. Such is the kind of epistemological, representational knowledge sought and problematized.

Still, in "She Dwelt Among the Untrodden Ways," it is precisely in the *cessation* of her existence that Lucy is finally "known" as an entity; in a line that echoes the end of "Strange Fits" (" 'If Lucy should be dead!' "), her name does not appear in "She Dwelt" until it is associated with the fact of her death: "when Lucy ceased to be." Revisions of the manuscript are largely efforts to remove the specifics of Lucy's life, as if Wordsworth was consciously excising the possibility of an epistemological approach to Lucy. To "name" Lucy at the end, then, is, paradoxically, both to locate her epistemologically, more or less for the first time in the poem, and to face (as opposed to "know")—in an ethical act of self-orientation—the fact of her death. That naming in conjunction with the cessation of being is turned in the next line to a positive, albeit affectively neutral statement about her place. "But she is in her grave" becomes a statement not only about where she is, but about the fact that she "is" in this way: She "is" or exists only in the grave. This is not an existence that can be known as a "presence-to-hand," as Heidegger would say, through any simple epistemology, but is rather an existence to be acknowledged through the mediation of our representational systems of graves and memorializations—the metonymies and substitutions that fill graveyards. The last line is an exclamation of feeling (prefaced by "oh," a purely affective word with no representational content) based on a felt "difference" to "me," the final word in rhyming opposition to the opening "She."

This last stanza has thus gone from cessation and naming, to the body memorialized in the grave, to a difference-to-the-poet.[16] That is, from the impossible but inevitable interrelation of known, named being ("Lucy") and the ethical fact of its cessation, to the neutral fact of the grave as her place in nature and in human systems of signification, to the essential, affective fact of difference. One could say that we have moved from the problem of ethical relations in confrontation with epistemology, through the fact of mediated representation (a disappointing epistemology), to a recognition of the ethical basis to the entire issue. "Difference" resonates with classic Wordsworthian polyvalence: a difference between the speaker and those to whom Lucy is unknown (her death made a difference to him, not to them), a difference and an interruption within the speaker's life caused by her death, and perhaps an even more universal sense of "difference" within life as a whole caused by her death.

The progress through these three stages represents the translation of an epistemological/ethical dilemma—the confrontation of the name (an epistemological fact) and the cessation of life (an ethical fact)—into a statement of felt "difference," where "difference" expresses a positively ethical, responsibility-laden, strongly experienced event instead of just a negative quality of differentiation. The resonance of "difference" here comes partly out of the epistemological problem of Lucy's death's (or any death's) unrepresentability, but that premise of unrepresentability is placed into the framework of a strong ethical evaluation. In the poet's response to her death, it is almost as if he is following Emmanuel Levinas's rewriting of Heidegger's individual being-toward-death as the responsibility for the death of the other:[17] to "face" Lucy's death is to acknowledge responsibility for that glance between them—an idea that could be explored in terms of the shadowy connection between Lucy and Dorothy, whose "wild eyes" are such an evocative image for the poet of "Tintern Abbey."

If that is claiming too much (one could also argue that Wordsworth habitually avoids such responsibility), Wordsworth is at least performing a Cavellian acknowledgment of the other in this poem that recognizes the impossibility of an epistemological knowledge, even as it values the acknowledgment that one "owns" the other constitutively by means of the fact that the other can be lost. Thus the attempt to "know" the other—the epistemological problem—is irreducibly tied to the ethical problem of our having and losing the other.

"Strange Fits of Passion" demonstrates how this acknowledgment works according to a rhetoric of interruption; it is through the interruption of representational structures that an ethical relation to nonrepresentable death is glimpsed. The moon on which the speaker focuses his gaze in that poem is a uniquely Wordsworthian trope. Not a "sign" of anything, it is an image that links the poet to his lover by functioning as a natural object (with a long rhetorical history) that can take on the movement of the approaching poet. The moon-trope "fails," interrupting the natural dream by falling behind the cottage, precisely when the poet gets too close for poetry, when his relationship to the lover will be extrapoetic intersubjectivity, instead of a relationship mediated by the poetic trope of the moon. (Poet and lover literally meet "outside" the poem, in the canceled final stanza in which the poet tells his lover of his dream.) The moon goes out with a revelatory flash (like the Imagination in book 6 of *The Prelude*), becoming "bright" whereas in previous stanzas it had been merely "sinking" and "descending." Its revelation is an intimation of mortality, a dream interrupted by another dream of death, stated as a self-divisive internal dialogue on the improbable but terrible: " 'O mercy!' to myself I cried, / 'If Lucy should be dead!' "

Here the interruption occurs on the "safe" side of image and dream rather than life: the moon's light is only a reflection, after all, and although it is involved in diurnal change, it only produces "wayward thoughts"; Lucy is not yet absorbed into "earth's diurnal course." Still, that disruption is significant both as a *strange* fit, a disruption of the normal that replaces representational structures with ethical positions, and as a disruption that defines the normal. That disruption *is* the conversation that incarnates meaning and inaugurates the lyric cycle of the Lucy poems (though the poems are ordered differently in Wordsworth's editions, this poem is always placed first[18]). Just as death is the final, unrepresentable interruption that defines mortality, the interruption of the moon's imaginative work defines and grounds that work. Behind the dismissive tone of "fond and wayward thoughts" is a fundamental relationship between life and poetry, a relationship highlighted by and founded upon this essential relation of interruption between life and death: to write, that is, to live in a world of life-sustaining, connecting images like the moon, is to live in relation to a living lover, but that life is defined by the possibility of its loss: to lose those connecting images is to face the possibility of the other's death. That possibility of loss exposes the ethical basis of those representational images.

Interruption takes a more serious turn in "Three Years She Grew," when nature does not lend the "gentlest boon" of a dream-language to the poet, but instead forcibly takes Lucy out of the poet's language into its own. Lucy's death is figured by the voice of nature as it interrupts the poet's voice. The poet has only a single line—"Three years she grew in sun and shower"—before nature appropriates both Lucy and the rest of the poem. Nature's voice requires a different verse form; the traditional ballad stanza of a tetrameter line followed by a trimeter line is replaced by an asymmetrical pattern of two tetrameters followed by a trimeter. This confrontation of multiple lyric voices rehearses a variation of Wordsworth's rhetoric of incarnation: human death is incarnated into natural life. Nature herself is highly vocal (even verbose by the standards of these brief poems) and dominating: "Myself will to my darling be / Both law and impulse." But in both supplying and limiting natural energy ("To kindle or restrain"), nature's voice places Lucy in a world in which voices are either silent, as in "the silence and the calm / Of mute insensate things," or inarticulate until translated into *visual* beauty: "Beauty born of murmuring sound / Shall pass into her face." Herein lies the paradox of the "natural voice": it is the main voice of the poem, but as it speaks loudly to the poet and reader it silences the poem's (formerly) human referent. "A Slumber" completes this process of appropriation by the voice of nature, and the poet is reduced to sealing himself within a slumber from which he can intimate the nonhuman ("I had no human fears"), nontemporal ("She seemed a thing that could not feel / The touch of earthly years"), motionless ("No motion has she now") circularity ("Rolled round") of Lucy's human death/natural life. This is not quite the "faith that looks through death" of the "Ode," nor is the poet "laid asleep / In body" so as to "become a living soul" as in "Tintern Abbey." Instead the lyric voice is brought to the verge of sleep so that the inarticulate noise of that which is beyond sleep—death—can be dimly heard. The incarnation of Voice into voices in Wordsworth always depends on the presence of death at the outer limits of voice, since to live is to be mortal and thus look forward to death, but here the muteness of death is itself brought into the voice of the poem as the nearly silent echo of garrulous Nature.

As Alan Bewell points out in regard to the second quatrain of "A Slumber Did My Spirit Seal," "the narrator's vision of the afterlife... could hardly be cruder, or more marvelously strange and terrible.... What has been immortalized is not a spirit, but the body, which rolls interminably, as a 'thing,' hardly different from 'rocks and stones and trees'" (*Wordsworth and the Enlightenment* 203). As Hartman points out, however, the second quatrain is an afterimage of the first;[19] her absolute thingness in the second reflects the slumberous state of sealed-over affections in the first. This is terrifying precisely in its denial of "human fears," part of the ethical relations of human existence. The transcendence of the first thought—the idea that she is above "earthly years" and "human fears"—is counterbalanced by the equally extreme naturalism of the second thought. Between these extremes, in the space between the two stanzas, the poem becomes a treatise on the unthinkability of death.

As Gadamer notes in his essay "Der Tod als Frage" (in *Neuere Philosophie II*), our very freedom to think transcendentally, to have intimations of immortality, prevents us from thinking of ourselves as not being.[20] The paradoxical result of this is that we *acknowledge* death's *unthinkability,* and our ability to do that is a constitutive human characteristic. (Gadamer comes very close to Cavell in this development of Heidegger's notion of being-toward-death.) Wordsworth notes in the first "Essay Upon Epitaphs" that feelings of death are early and naturally associated with feelings of immortality (*PrW* 2:51); the Lucy poems, and particularly "A Slumber," work out the consequences of that combination for the problems of facing and representing death. Earlier in the Gadamer essay, whose basic question is whether our ways of thinking about death are really ways of hiding death, Gadamer points out that a classic means of this avoidance is to place the irreducibly unique event of death into a context of repetition, such as that of dreaming or sleeping and reawakening (166), which is certainly what the second quatrain of "A Slumber" does by locating Lucy in a grim natural cycle. Thus the poem is both crude, in the sense that it performs this classic act of avoidance through a myth of repetition, and terrifying, in that this brutally natural cycle is so clearly *not* an intimation of immortality. In this sense, "A Slumber" can be read as a backhanded recognition that our freedom to transcend ourselves and hide death (whether in transcendental slumbers or natural cycles) is our way of acknowledging—placing ourselves in an ethical orientation toward—the fact of death's necessity and unthinkability. Thus with "A Slumber" we move far out of the universe of epistemology. Knowledge is either not available, absurdly transcendental, or absurdly naturalistic. What remains is the acknowledgment of an ethical relation to a death that we cannot know.

Though "A Slumber" at least partially subverts the incarnational acknowledgment of death by hiding it in a mythical structure of repetition, there is another, more authentically incarnational kind of repetition to consider. As I pointed out above, Wordsworth's note to "The Thorn" argues that repetition which appears to be tautological can be justified by an appeal to words as things: "There are also various other reasons why repetition and apparent tautology are frequently beauties of the highest kind. Among the chief of these reasons is the interest which the mind attaches to words, not only as symbols of the passion, but as *things*, active and efficient, which are of themselves part of the passion" (*Poetical Works* 2:513). That which appears tautological from the point of view of words as representational symbols (repeated representations of the same referent are redundant) can be "beaut[y] of the highest kind" from incarnational point of view, in which the incarnated materiality of the word itself repeats previous occurrences of the word, but also presents a new manifestation of meaning.

This kind of repetition is an important part of the theology of the Incarnation. There is an element of repetition in typological relations between the Old and New Testaments, in the Son's relation to the Father, but most important for our purposes, in the Eucharist's repetition of Christ's action at the Last Supper, an action that preceded and presaged his death. The celebration of the Eucharist is not simply a representation of Christ's action, but a repetition of that event, with an efficaciousness of its own, in which God is not represented but presented.[21] Gadamer suggests a paradigm for this kind of repetition in the idea of the festival:

> It is in the nature of periodic festivals, at least, to be repeated. We call that the return of the festival. But the festival that comes round again is neither another festival nor a mere remembrance of the one that was originally celebrated.... As a festival it is not an identity like a historical event, but neither is it determined by its origin so that there was once the "real" festival—as distinct from the way in which it later came to be celebrated. From its inception—whether instituted in a single act or instituted gradually—the nature of a festival is to be celebrated regularly. Thus its own original essence is always to be something different (even when celebrated in exactly the same way). (*TM* 122–23)

This is a sense of repetition which works incarnationally rather than representationally; rather than totalizing language in a representational cycle of repetition, as the dead Lucy is "represented" in the diurnal natural cycle, this kind of repetition does give us a context for understanding events, but also allows each "event," the repetition of the festival, the celebration of the Eucharist, and the repetition of the word as thing, to generate a nonrepresentational manifestation of meaning that acknowledges difference to be a part of its original essence.[22] This incarnational repetition consists in repeated acts of acknowledgment rather than a systematic assertion of knowledge. We see this in the repeated acknowledgment of an ethical relation to Lucy's death in the Lucy poems as a whole, or the retelling of the narrative "in the Lover's ear alone" in "Strange Fits" (repeated more emphatically in the canceled final stanza)—a repetition of the story which is also an act of love.

Implicit in the rhetoric of interruption and repetition that pervades the Lucy poems is a critique of the autonomous subject, and a presentation of the kind of incarnational subjectivity that I discussed in the introduction. Particularly "A Slumber" and "Strange Fits" narrate complex stories of self-enclosed subjects who experience what Levinas calls the "coring out" of the ego (*OTB* 64, 180–81), the incarnational experience of "the non-coinciding of the ego with itself" (*OTB* 64). In tracing the history of interpretation of "A Slumber," Brian Caraher notes the ambiguity of the reference of "she" in the first stanza. Conventionally, "she" is taken to refer to Lucy, but Hugh Sykes Davies argues that "she" refers to "my spirit," which would turn the poem into a private death fantasy rather than an elegy:

> In following out the logic of Davies's line of interpretation, the poem can become a private death fantasy; that is to say, it becomes for the speaker a vicarious experiencing of his own final and complete slumber. The narrator would seem to be a very self-involved, perhaps an even morbidly isolated solipsist. (*Wordsworth's "Slumber"* 55)

The conventional line of interpretation—in which "she" refers to Lucy—presents the speaker as still solipsistic, but as awakening to a recognition of lost love rather than as fantasizing his own death: "Examined in the light of the conventional line of interpretation, the speaker—while still solipsistically self-involved—seems only imperceptive and insensitive" (55). Caraher suggests a third line of interpretation that incorporates this ambivalence as it conflates "the morbidity and inhumanity of the speaker of the one interpretation" with "the imperceptivity and insensitivity of the second" (56). This third line of interpretation turns on the syntactical ambiguity of the first line: "A slumber did my spirit seal" can mean both "a slumber sealed my spirit" and "my spirit sealed a slumber." As the reader proceeds to this third interpretation, he sees the speaker in an even crueler light:

> If "my spirit" "did ... seal" "a slumber," then the speaker seems by no means slumberous, insensitive, and imperceptive. He marks, closes, impresses, or enforces a slumber, though the passive recipient of this action is yet undeclared. The speaker now appears to be an active agent, an executor of deeds, rather than a passive undergoer of his own vicarious death fantasy or an insensitive and belated mourner of lost love. "My spirit" sealed "a slumber"; "I had no human fears:" The agent appears cold-blooded, as if inhuman. The colon then directs us into the reason why the speaker had no such fears: She, a woman, appeared to him to be a thing untouchable by age or mortality or perhaps even by blemish or change.... Now, in the present and separated by some undisclosed amount of time from the past moment of the first stanza, the woman has no motion or force, no life or mortality. She is left ruthlessly and shockingly a corpse among the things of a landscape denuded of their own relations to human life and livelihood. The speaker

chillingly confesses a murder; the slumber that his spirit has sealed is the murder of a woman. (45–46)

The point of Caraher's narration of these three stages of interpretation enabled by the poem's ambivalence is to argue that the poem, rather than simply expressing a solipsistic death fantasy, engages in "a creative inquiry into and cultural critique of a Romantic death fantasy" (61). In following the solipsism of the first two readings and confronting their incompatibility, the reader "break[s] through to the third way of reading 'A Slumber' " (62) and comes to this critical recognition of the speaker as a murderer.

The ambivalence of the speaker in "A Slumber" parallels the syntactical and thematic ambivalence of the speaker who mourns the dead Boy of Winander in book 5 of *The Prelude*. In both cases, the lines can be seen as both expressing and critiquing a stance of autonomous self-involvement. In book 5, the speaker himself can be seen on the one hand as forgetting about the Boy, sealing him into a system of graves in a gesture that permits the speaker to turn to "a race of young ones like to those / With whom I herded" (5.432–33), children that reflect his own life, and on the other hand as implicitly critiquing the "thronèd lady" for just such forgetfulness. Similarly, "A Slumber" both enacts and critiques a death fantasy.

This interruption of the autonomous subject is not, for Wordsworth, simply a negative moment in a dialect that moves toward a higher self-consciousness, but is rather an implicit recognition of what Levinas calls an incarnational subjectivity: a subjectivity in which the intentionality that would appropriate or exclude the other is interrupted by a "saying" that "approaches the other by breaking through the noema involved in intentionality, turning inside out, 'like a cloak,' consciousness which by itself would have remained for-itself even in its intentional aims" (*OTB* 48). The autonomous intentionality of the solipsistic speaker of "A Slumber," or of the forgetful mourner in book 5 of *The Prelude*, is interrupted by an ambivalence that threatens such autonomy and forces an acknowledgment of the other—the dead Boy or the dead Lucy—as someone who cannot be so easily forgotten or murdered. "Strange Fits" presents an almost parodic version of this process, since the illusion of autonomy is revealed from the start as a "strange fit." The self-involvement of the speaker in his illusory perception of the moon's progress leads to a fantasy of his lover's death, but in recognizing that fantasy *as* a fantasy, the subject is thrown back into living relation to the other: the demystified narrative of the illusion is told "in the Lover's ear alone," and in the canceled final stanza she responds with "laughter light."

This process must involve "strange fits," "fond and wayward thoughts," and even ambiguous syntax, because, according to Levinas, since intelligibility depends on thematization in a "said," the eruption of incarnational subjectivity in "saying" can only be seen in the language of the "said" (the language of thematization and concepts) as unintelligibility or nonsense:

> Signification ... where the other is not assumed by the one, presupposes the possibility of pure non-sense invading and threatening signification. Without this folly at the confines of reason, the one would take hold of itself, and, in the heart of its passion, recommence essence. (*OTB* 50)

This unintelligibility is not simply a para-deconstructive displacement or ironization of the autonomous subject, because rather than revealing absence, it shadows forth the very concrete human, communal temporality that precedes and breaks through the possibility of conceptual intelligibility. It is a trace of the putting-out-of-phase that constitutes incarnational subjectivity:

> What will show itself in a theme said is the unintelligibility of incarnation, the "I think" separated from extension, the *cogito* separated from the body. But this impossibility of being together is the trace of the diachrony of the-one-for-the-other. (*OTB* 79)

Through conceptual unintelligibility we see traces of the diachrony of incarnational subjectivity: one "unintelligible" sentence or line in a poem such as "A Slumber" forces us, in Caraher's terms, into successive, mutually exclusive interpretations that break up the autonomous subject and present it in a nontotalizing, temporal relationship with living or dead others. The temporality is manifested both in the irreconcilable stages the speaker goes through in the course of a Lucy poem or *The Prelude* and in the interpretive process forced on the reader. Death is treated in fantasies of murder or one's own death, as in the variant interpretations of "A Slumber," but human subjectivity's ability to incorporate dual points of view—in Wordsworth's case, the enactment and critique of death fantasies—manifests a preconceptual, incarnate, even physiological temporality that both confronts and postpones death. As Levinas says in *Totality and Infinity*,

> The originality of the body consists of the coinciding of two points of view. This is the paradox and the essence of time itself proceeding unto death, where the will is affected as a thing by the things—by the point of steel or by the chemistry of the tissues (due to a murderer or to the impotency of the doctors)—but gives itself a reprieve and postpones the contact by the against-death of postponement. (229)

This postponement of death is an essential part of the rhetoric of *The Prelude*; at the outset of book 9 the poet is "part swayed by fear to tread an onward road / That leads direct to the devouring sea" (9.3–4), and earlier he fears he may be "unprofitably travelling towards the grave" (1.269). *The Prelude* is Wordsworth's most ambitious attempt to create an incarnational, nonrepresentational subjectivity as "saying," an act of retelling that becomes a living thing and a performative act of love, but must emerge from and interrupt the "said" of representational structures.

3
Ending *The Prelude*: Incarnation and the Autobiographical Exit

> [O]ften do I seem
> Two consciousnesses, conscious of myself
> And of some other Being.
> —*The Prelude* (1850) 2.31–33

Autobiography is a natural field in which to pursue many of the issues discussed in the previous chapters: what better way to see the phenomenal world of word-things as a mortal other to be elegiacally acknowledged but not known, than by exploring the other of one's own life? The living unity (or life-and-death combination) of skepticism and anti-skepticism discussed by Stanley Cavell is essential to autobiography: Cavell points out that the Romantic project to replace religion with an interaction between philosophy and poetry was accompanied "with the disreputable sense that the fate of the contest is bound up in one's own writing, and moreover with the conviction that the autobiographical is a method of thought wherein such a connection can find a useful field" (*In Quest of the Ordinary* 43). Wordsworth constructed his written life as a series of conceptual or figural programs that become his "own" past exactly to the extent that they die into subsequent figures. In this chapter I hope to show how a non-semiotic, incarnational rhetoric emerges from the collapse of the figural systems in which the autobiographer has conceptualized his past life, and how the temporality of that process suggests an incarnational subjectivity manifested as a "coring out" of the autonomous ego rather than a dialectic of self-consciousness. I focus on the final books of *The Prelude* because it is there that the representational issues become most acute: there the boundary of the text needs to be finally established, and there the relationship between the publicly written, exemplary "poet's mind" and the invisible private self that exists before, beneath, and after the written self can be tested against the complex rhetoric of autobiographical figuration that has emerged in the course of the poem.

The first eight books of *The Prelude* develop an evolving and constantly challenged figural rhetoric in which the present enunciation of discourse (Wordsworth's poetic argument to Coleridge) is figured by a narrative oriented exclusively toward the past. In book 1, the narrative of the poet's life emerged as a provisionally unitary figure for the discourse of the presently writing poet. Already in book 2, the stability of the autobiographical figure is threatened by the poet's recognition that he sometimes seems to be "two consciousnesses," an insight allegorized in the assembly-room episode (2.31–47). In book 3, the world of Cambridge, "a privileged world / Within a world, a midway residence / With all its intervenient imagery" (3.553–55), injects a principle of mediation that permits a more flexible relation between narrative and discourse to be explored in book 4. The digressive refinement of the poem's rhetoric in book 5 in specifically literary terms paves the way for the climactic fusion of narrative and discourse in the "Imagination" episode of book 6.[1]

THE COLLAPSE OF GRAMMAR

Most of the poetry in books 7 through 9 of *The Prelude* is overshadowed by the autobiographical narrative's inability to stand as a figure for what the discursive poet wants to say. As Paul D. Sheats says of the later books, "Wordsworth gives up the attempt to construe the past as a continuous ascent toward a naturalistic consummation" ("Wordsworth's Retrogrades" 481). In book 7 Wordsworth, echoing Milton, attempts a second beginning, but the echo of book 1's "glad preamble" initiates a process by which, in books 7 and 8, the autobiography is, like the second half of *Don Quixote,* sustained more by reference to the past *text* than to the past *life* of the poet.[2] This move is partly necessitated by the otherness of London, which cannot be readily assimilated into Wordsworth's discourse. This highly textual self is allegorized in the "Blind Beggar" episode, in which the blind man "propped against a wall" wearing his autobiographical text becomes an "emblem of the utmost that we know, / Both of ourselves and of the universe" (7.618–20). The discursive "I" becomes more and more a textual artifact instead of a referent outside of the text, and the narrated events present a reality that cannot be appropriated by the figural structure of the text.

In book 9, the figural grammar of the poem begins a process of collapse into tropological performance. Paul de Man uses these terms to characterize the text of Rousseau's *Social Contract*. A legal system or text is "grammatical" insofar as it is a general, self-sufficient, systematic code indifferent to the specific events of its application, even though the need for such specific application itself generates the grammar: "Just as no text is conceivable without grammar, no grammar is conceivable without the suspension of referential meaning. Just as no law can ever be written unless one suspends any consideration of applicability to a particular entity ... grammatical logic can function only if its referential consequences are disregarded" ("Political Allegory" 668). In short, a body of law must treat every case before it with equal indifference if it is to remain consistent with itself.

The discourse/narrative structure of *The Prelude* is a grammar insofar as it encodes the relationship between the discursive "I" and his narrative past, placing them into a pattern of opposition whose always questionable stability depends, it can be argued, on a suspension of reference to the particular encounters with the past that tend to subvert the figural model. Of course, these "referential consequences" assert themselves even as the grammatical level of the text attempts to ignore them. According to de Man, "The logic of grammar generates texts only in the absence of referential meaning, but every text generates a referent that subverts the grammatical principle to which it owed its constitution" ("Political Allegory" 669). That is, each individual application of the law threatens the self-sufficiency of the system, because it forces the generality of the law to confront the specificity of the individual referent—the specific case to be adjudicated—of the law. De Man translates this into textual terms by proposing that "the divergence between grammar and referential meaning is what we call the figural dimension of language" ("Political Allegory" 669). What in legal terms is the conflict between "the State as a defined entity ... and the State as a principle of action" is in linguistic terms the conflict between "the constative and the performative function of language." ("Political Allegory" 670). In *The Prelude,* this can be seen as a conflict between the structural "figure" of autobiography, in which the narrated life is expected to "represent" the present, discursive "I," and which tends toward hypostasis, and the *performatively* figural dimension, in which the grammar of the figure is subverted.³

The language of incarnation provides a medium for analyzing the recuperation at the end of *The Prelude*. In books 9 and 10, however, de Man's discussion of the tension between grammar and performance remains an appropriate framework for reading the rhetoric of *The Prelude*. The grammar of the poem's figural rhetoric is indeed subverted, particularly in the crisis surrounding the French Revolution, and we witness a collapse into a text negatively characterized by loss and divergence. The events in France begin by providing the poet with a new grammar, a figural structure in which the progress toward political liberty is an image of progress toward personal and universal liberty. The belief that "there was one, / And only one solicitude for all" (10.227–28) turns the French struggle into a synechdoche for universal liberty. The poet's personal education in nature made the French Revolution seem a natural reflection of the liberty on which he had been nursed and which *The Prelude* has been describing:

> It could not be
> But that one tutored thus, who had been formed
> To thought and moral feeling in the way
> This story hath described, should look with awe
> Upon the faculties of man, receive
> Gladly the highest promises, and hail
> As best the government of equal rights
> And individual worth.
>
> (9.242–49)

It is significant that the word "formed" should be used here, and that the project of the poet's formation should be intimately connected in the next two lines with its poetic representation in *The Prelude*. The crucial Romantic concept of *Bildung* or formation gestures toward both the process of formation and its culmination in a form and figure that partakes of the universality of self-consciousness. As Gadamer points out, the concept of *Bildung* is complicated further in that the German word *Bild* "comprehends both Nachbild (image, copy) and Vorbild (model)" (*TM* 11).⁴ Wordsworth uses the resonances of this concept of complete self-formation to develop a figure in which his "gebildet" narrated life has the triply figurative sense of a life informed by the process of Bildung, a life that is a copied image in a poem, and a life that stands as a figural model. This complex figure is metaphorically connected to a concept of democratic liberty that is still operative even in the 1850 *Prelude*. Thus a grammar is generated within which the attractiveness of the Revolution can be read.

This figural grammar of liberty, however, is intimately connected with its subversion, not only because we know that the poet will be disillusioned, but also because this grammar, like the one identified by de Man in Rousseau, is so clearly dependent on the exclusion of its constitutive referents. For example, the natural correspondence between the poet's formation in liberty and the French struggle is admittedly premised on an ignorance of history: the poet valued "the historian's tale ... but little otherwise than I prized / Tales of the poets," which is to say according to a standard of fanciful excitement, "as it made my heart / Beat high and filled my fancy with fair forms" (9.207–10). The identification of his personal history with that of France is just such a poetic interpretation of history, a reading of events that can remain within the grammar of poetry only by suppressing the historical events (of both France and the poet's formation) that make the identification possible. Similarly, the attractive perception of Beaupuy, who wanders through the events "as through a book, an old romance, or tale" (9.307), has for the poet, almost like the experience of the drowned man of Esthwaite in book 5, the specifically literary unity of a romance, grammatically self-consistent precisely because it suppresses the particularities of historical events. Just as in book 5 death was immaturely accommodated within the attractively coherent sign systems of fairy tales, here the violence of the Revolution is suppressed by recourse to the grammar of romance.

The poet not only organizes his attention to the events in France in the grammar of romance, but actually replaces that attention with romance, when he substitutes the allegorical story of Vadracour and Julia for the discussion of the "ever-varying wind" (9.548) of particular, changing events that cannot be assimilated by the grammar which figurally pairs individual and political liberty. The tale will have the self-consistency of a tragic narrative, operating on a general level precisely because of its poetic distance from specific referents. The story of Vadracour and Julia achieves this grammatical generality as an allegory that refers to, but is distanced from, both the individual pole (Wordsworth's affair with Annette Vallon) and the political pole (the subversion of natural law by class-based social law) of the figure.[5] In this narration of the process by which a figural grammar reaches its limits, the divergence between the grammatical structure (the figural identity of personal and political liberty) and its referents (the actual events in France and in the poet's life) becomes so great that the autobiographical text trails off into an allegory whose significant relation to events is that of distance.

As the narrative veers off from a course that can effectively represent the "argument" Wordsworth claims for his poem, or as the grammar of the poetic discourse is disturbed by narrative events that do not fit the pattern, Wordsworth faces the possibility that an autobiographical narrative may ultimately be incapable of representing the self that necessarily precedes and outlives the written life story. In terms of the complex river imagery with which book 9 opens, the poem continues to make rhetorical "motions retrograde" (9.8) so as to defer the "devouring sea" of the extratextual life into which the autobiographical narrative must ultimately drain, but the grammatical banks of the poem are finding it increasingly difficult to contain the narrative. It is even suggested that, instead of the autobiographical narrative flowing into the extratextual life, we might have been faced with a death that would prevent both the continuation of life that would give the autobiography a point, and the writing of the poem (or any poem) itself. He would have "haply perished ... to the breast of Nature have gone back ... a poet only to [him]-self" (10.195–99).

In book 10 the subversion of grammar implied by the infrastructure of the poem's rhetoric becomes open conflict as the figural grammar of liberty dissolves into the performance of a personal revolution. Until "the strength of Britain was put forth" (10.229) against France, destroying the equilibrium of Wordsworth's identification of personal and political liberty, he "had thought / Of general interests only, beyond this / Had never foretasted the event" (10.247–49). That is, he had considered the grammar of liberty on its own general level only, and had not considered the event that would signal the subversion of that system. That event incited the only true "revolution" in *The Prelude*'s terms: that within the poet: "no shock" had he known "that might be named / A revolution" (10.233, 236–37) until this final subversion of the figural grammar of liberty.

"Figure" is no longer the appropriate term for the poem's rhetoric at this point. In its Greek, Latin, and modern senses, "figure" emphasizes a form or outline that in some sense transcends the temporality of its production. It is a teleological structure: the end result or final form of a figural transposition is valued over the act of making the transposition. This leaves out the possibility that such an act may stem from an efficient cause, without a figural end product in view. The word "trope," however, originally meaning "to turn," emphasizes the act rather than the end of the figural process. "Trope" allows us to speak of the figural dimension of language as a turning away, a divergence from some initial point, rather than a movement toward a "figure."[6] Tropological activity entails a "beginning," in Edward Said's sense[7] of a movement that is related to what has gone before by a complex network of discontinuity, continuity, divergence, and mimesis, but does not entail an end or a circular return to an origin.[8] "Trope" is thus a more appropriate word for the nontotalizable—because always historicized—process of incarnational interpretive activity that Gadamer sees as an alternative to Greek modes of representational thought, and that Levinas sees as constituting incarnational subjectivity.

In the narration of the young poet's disillusionment, attention is shifted from the erection of figural structures—the establishment of grammars—to the tropological activity involved in the decay of such structures and to the "turn" involved in the subversion of grammars. The sequential narrative, despite its many turns, until now has been pulled along and directed by the "final cause" of the present "I"; the poem has narrated a "progress on the self-same path / On which with a diversity of pace" the poet "had been travelling" (10.238–40). Suddenly that path becomes a specifically antiteleological turn away from the line, "a stride at once / Into another region" (10.240–41).[9] From this new position the poet objects to those who see substitution, a primary characteristic of tropological activity, within a false teleology of "higher" positivities, such as occur in putatively "completed" figural structures. "Apostacy from ancient faith" is not seen by such people for what it is, divergence from truth, but is teleologically misread as "conversion to a higher creed" (10.284–85).

The figure that had paired individual and political liberty is divided and turned against itself along every possible axis. On the political side, the split between England and France divides what was once a united pair of metaphors for liberty. On the individual side, a divisive "treachery and desertion" is found in the poet's "own soul" (10.379–80). And of course the individual pole of the figure is separated from the political: Wordsworth leaves France, but feels like an "uninvited guest" (10.272) in an English church. Liberty is no longer the core of a figural grammar within which the poet can read his individual and political existence. "Her blessed name" (10.350) still functions in an authoritative figural grammar—"all beneath / Her innocent authority was wrought" (10.349–50)—but her authority is invoked without meaning; the grammar is completely opposed by its referents.

As the narrative turns away from the figural identification of individual and political liberty, its status can best be summarized in reference to the passage that describes the rise and fall of revolutionary France in an extended solar metaphor. The poet speaks of Nature's permanent assistance in the face of this catastrophe:

> And lastly, Nature's self, by human love
> Assisted, through the weary labyrinth
> Conducted me again to open day,
> Revived the feelings of my earlier life,
> Gave me that strength and knowledge full of peace,
> Enlarged, and never more to be disturbed,
> Which through the steps of our degeneracy,
> All degradation of this age, hath still
> Upheld me, and upholds me at this day
> In the catastrophe (for so they dream,
> And nothing less), when, finally to close
> And rivet up the gains of France, a Pope
> Is summoned in to crown an Emperor—
> This last opprobrium, when we see the dog
> Returning to his vomit, when the sun
> That rose in splendour, was alive, and moved
> In exultation among living clouds,
> Hath put his function and his glory off,
> And, turned into a gewgaw, a machine,
> Sets like an Opera phantom.
> (10.921–40)

I quote at length because the structure of this entire passage exhibits a strange kind of "turn" that mirrors its function as an exposition of tropological divergence. The elaborate metaphor in which the natural sun becomes artificial is clearly the poetic climax of this passage, but that importance contrasts sharply with the image's syntactic position. The main clause of this second half of a long compound sentence speaks of nature's permanence, conducting the poet to "open day." The solar metaphor is only part of a series of subordinate images describing the crowning of Napoleon, with which the nature-given "strength and knowledge" successfully contends. That success, however, is accompanied by and perhaps even achieved through a *divergence* from the sun's proper role as the source of the revivifying "open day" and that which "was alive, and moved / In exultation among living clouds." This sentence about nature's permanence turns into an image of nature becoming artificial (the sun becoming a gewgaw) in a subversion of the sentence's "grammar"—in both the special and the common senses—by the specifics of its concrete images.

The sun is a problematic image in any case; as Derrida has noted, it represents both the "natural" and the introduction of the "metaphorical" in the language of philosophy.[10] Wordsworth's image is similarly paradoxical. The natural, life-giving sun leads the poet toward the Platonic "open day" in order to oppose a sun that has become an artificial "gewgaw"; however, that natural sun is also the metaphorical *source* of the artificiality, as the sun turns into an "opera phantom" whose presence in these lines in fact outshines the first, "real" sun. The controlling image of the sentence diverges from its grammatical meaning, and the image is itself one of divergence. The natural rising and setting of the sun becomes a transition away from the natural: the sun rises full of the life of nature and sets as a device that proclaims itself as a flagrantly inadequate metaphor.

Just as the sun has become an artificial self-parody, the young poet's changing intellectual affiliations present a series of exaggerated grammars that, from the older poet's perspective, parody the possibility of a universal grammar in which one's life can be read. He seeks a succession of systems, the purity of whose self-consistency is paid for by the passions' alienation from their own appearance in the event of language; one such system would fix the hopes of man "for ever in a purer element" in which "passions had the privilege to work, / And never hear the sound of their own names" (10.812–13). This parodic decay of the figural system manifests itself as autobiographical alienation:

> Thus strangely did I war against myself;
> A bigot to a new idolatry,
> Did like a monk who hath forsworn the world
> Zealously labour to cut off my heart
> From all the sources of her former strength.
> (11.74–78)

Thus, the subversion of grammar is not simply a movement that occurs within the narrative of the poet's various disillusionments; it has also disrupted the figural grammar, which had held narrative and discourse meaningfully apart. The discursive "I" criticizes, opposes, and actively interrogates the narrative plot of his life. As the events subvert the grammar, the relationship between discourse and narrative ceases to be a figural structure within which the poet's life can be read.

In terms of the poet's life, there was in the war between France and Britain

> not, as hitherto,
> A swallowing up of lesser things in great,
> But change of them into their opposites,
> And thus a way was opened for mistakes
> And false conclusions of the intellect,
> As gross in their degree, and in their kind
> Far, far more dangerous. What had been a pride
> Was now a shame; my likings and my loves
> Ran in new channels, leaving old ones dry.
> (10.762–70)

The events in the poet's psychological history no longer form a teleological chain of supersession, "a swallowing up of lesser things in great," but have become a "change of them into their opposites" (10.763–64). As Charles Taylor implies in his discussion of the importance of self-narration for human identity, the replacement of one narrative by another is not necessarily teleological in the modern world. Without the resources of ready-made religious or political narrative structures in which to shape our life stories, the meaning of life must be seen both as "the causal consequence of what has transpired earlier" and as "something that unfolds through the events" (*Sources of the Self* 289). The latter suggests that the narrative discloses a meaning already latent in the events, whereas the former suggests that the particular sequence of events actually causes the meaning to exist. The radical implications of the idea that the events produce rather than disclose life's meaning include a strong sense of the self's contingency: we cannot guarantee that our "story" will have a foreordained narrative coherence even of a teleology of consciousness, much less a traditional structure of, for example, religious coherence. As a whole, *The Prelude* is situated between traditional Augustinian narratives of conversion—in which events disclose the latent "truth" of authentic religious experience toward which the narrative leads—and modern narratives in which the "self" is the non-unified product of a series of contingent historical events. In a recognition of this modern side of narrative as identity, the poem's familiar river image now presents the narrative as a divergence from the line that, running "in new channels, leaving old ones dry," destroys the line itself.

INCARNATIONAL RECOVERY

Perhaps the most important thing about the image of the sun becoming "a gewgaw, a machine" (10.939) is that the movement away from the natural occurs within a natural movement: this process of divergence from the natural *is* the natural rising and setting of the sun. This is not a substitution of an artificial grammar for a natural one; the events are not simply to be read by artificial light, as in an opera house, but instead by natural light "among the living clouds." If the "natural" course of events is a movement away from the natural, then events must be read in terms of tropological divergence instead of figural grammar. This signals a major change in the structural principles of *The Prelude*. No longer (until the very end, in a modified way) will the narrative seek its authority in figural pairs such as narrative and discourse or individual freedom and political liberty. Instead, the poem will build on its own tropological activity, its narration of acts of interpretation that involve divergence from the grammar of totalizing figures. In order to account for that tropological activity, we must shift our critical terminology. The language of de Man and Derrida is certainly appropriate to describe the breakdown of figural structures in books 9 and 10, but such terms fail to characterize adequately the recuperative efforts of books 11 through 13. The notion of incarnation helps define how tropological divergence can lead to a rhetorical recuperation that reformulates rather than denies that divergence.

If we are to see Wordsworth's figural language along the lines of incarnation rather than counter-spirit, we must be able to see the relationship between grammar and its performative subversion in terms other than the absolute difference posited by de Man. As noted above, de Man sees a clear conflict between the need for coherence in a legal system and the subversion of the system in the application of the legal grammar to an individual case. It is possible, however, to see the performative figurality that emerges from the interaction between grammar and individual case in terms of a productive incarnation of meaning, instead of a subversion of grammar. Gadamer sees legal hermeneutics as exemplary precisely because of the mutually productive relationship between the law transmitted from the past and its application to the present instance:

> Legal hermeneutics serves to remind us what the real procedure of the human sciences is. Here we have the model for the relation-

> ship between the past and present that we are seeking. The judge who adapts the transmitted law to the needs of the present is undoubtedly seeking to perform a practical task, but his interpretation of the law is by no means merely for that reason an arbitrary revision.... The judge seeks to be in accord with the "legal idea" in mediating it with the present. (*TM* 327–28)

In more general terms, "our knowledge of law and morality is always supplemented by the individual case, even productively determined by it. The judge not only applies the law in concreto, but contributes through his very judgment to developing the law ('judge-made law')" (*TM* 38). From this perspective, we can see the difference between grammar and event not as a subversion of grammar, but instead as the production of meaning.[11] This is implicit in de Man's argument, when he equates the subversion of grammar with the realm of figural language; the difference is that Gadamer sees the interaction between the law and its specific application as prior to either term, and thus constitutive of meaning, whereas de Man sees the tropological interaction as the result of the violence done to the grammar of law. (This is not to say that the incarnational position evades violence; we will see in the next chapter how, in both Hegel and Wordsworth, the priority of the incarnational to the legal can reveal a foundational violence.)

Gadamer's reading of the relationship between legal system and the concrete event of application as productive of meaning allows us to retain de Man's insight into the constitutive difference between grammar and event, without forcing us to view that difference and the resultant activity simply as a breakdown of systems or an ideological displacement.[12] Similarly, the notion of incarnation (encompassing the Word becoming Flesh, the memorialization of that event in the Eucharist, and the long tradition in which, by analogy, language is seen as an incarnation of meaning) preserves the complex differences between meaning—divine or human—and its incarnation, but allows us to speak of the productive role of those differences.

According to Herbert Schneidau, folllowing Rudolf Bultmann and others, biblical history as a whole is a critical discourse of demythologization, a subversion, by the event of prophetic utterance, of the grammars within which the culture desired to read itself. The prophets adopted a critical, rather than a mythologizing relationship to their culture. In contrast to the classical world's "cybernetic" feedback loop of continuous reaffirmation in myth, biblical thought presents us with the *kerygma* of the Word's utterance. "The kerygmatic logos ... disconfirms structure.

The very event is itself the message, a performative utterance in the fullest sense" (*Sacred Discontent* 10–12, 295–96). In a similar vein Gadamer points out that the Incarnation is not the denial of history, but rather its founding:

> If the Word became flesh and if it is only in the incarnation that spirit is fully realized, then the logos is freed from its spirituality.... The uniqueness of the redemptive event introduces the essence of history into Western thought, brings the phenomenon of language out of its immersion in the ideality of meaning, and offers it to philosophical reflection. For in contrast to the Greek logos, the word is pure event. (*TM* 419)

Levinas pushes the notion of incarnation even further away from the totalization of a structure by defining the incarnational subject as a preconceptual, existentially basic exposure to the other that overwhelms and critiques the totalization enacted by the conceptual structures of the "said":

> It is an overwhelming of the order of the thematizable being in the said, of the simultaneity and reciprocity of the relations said. Such a signification is only possible as an incarnation.... It is because subjectivity is sensibility—an exposure to others, a vulnerability and a responsibility in the proximity of the others, the one-for-the-other, that is, signification—and because matter is the very locus of the for-the-other, the way that signification signifies before showing itself as a said in the system of synchronism, the linguistic system, that a subject is of flesh and blood, a man that is hungry and eats, entrails in a skin, and thus capable of giving the bread out of his mouth, or giving his skin. (*OTB* 69, 77)

Despite the differences between Gadamer and Levinas—such as the priority of a radically existential subjectivity founded on absolute alterity in Levinas, which denies the priority of a mutually comprehensible arena of conversational reciprocity so important to Gadamer—the notion of incarnation in both allows us to see the human word not in Greek terms of the more or less (usually less) adequate representation of a transcendental logos, but in terms of an event in history, with all the temporal difference that implies. Angus Fletcher notes Coleridge's insight "that incarnation is a relativistic concept and that, with it in mind, the philosophic poet can introduce relativity—in the form of causal conditions—into the otherwise absolute and timeless mysteries of a Platonic system" (" 'Positive Negation' " 144). The Incarnation can be read as the "performative utterance" of Jesus' becoming human, in which he brought to fulfillment the prophetic role of the critical relationship between man and God while at the same time bringing God into human history and grounding the new relationship in the affective sphere of human proximity and love.[13] Similarly, in the tropological subversion of grammar in *The Prelude,* we witness a critical relationship between mythological human grammars and the events that subvert grammar in a process that creates incarnational rather than simply representational meaning. The performative subversion of grammar—in Levinas's terms, the overwhelming of the thematizable "said" by the existential fact of human relations—is the negative statement of the rhetoric of incarnation.

This production of meaning through incarnation does not signal a return to an ahistoric union of word and meaning; on the contrary, it is profoundly historical. Wordsworth's own interpretation of the "spots of time," written in 1804, shows how the establishment of the autobiographical self is both incarnational and historical:

> The days gone by
> Come back upon me from the dawn almost
> Of life; the hiding-places of my power
> Seem open, I approach, and then they close;
> I see by glimpses now, when age comes on
> May scarcely see at all; and I would give
> While yet we may, as far as words can give,
> A substance and a life to what I feel:
> I would enshrine the spirit of the past
> For future restoration.
> (*The Prelude* 11.333–42)

In giving his feelings "a substance and a life," the poet is incarnating his thoughts in the living materiality of language. The dialogue with his past is here a dialogue between the substance the poet desires to confer on feeling and the unapproachable origins of feelings ("the hiding-places of my power / Seem open, I approach, and then they close").

This relationship between language and meaning is as complex as the incarnational relationship between the Son and the Father. Just as in the "Imagination" episode in book 6, when the poet's experience of the imagination's power is also the experience of self-loss, Jesus' individuality is grounded in his total dependence on God the Father. The Dutch theologian Frans Jozef van Beeck, whose book on the rhetoric of Christology is influenced by Romantic hermeneutics, and even by Wordsworth, states the relationship this way:

> While living in total dependence on, total familiarity with, and total orientation to God, the man Jesus Christ is himself in a way no self-affirmation could ever hope to produce. (*Christ Proclaimed* 424)

Thus the Incarnation provides a model of subjectivity that accommodates the assertion of the absolute individual in Wordsworth as well as the complete dependence of that self on inaccessible sources. As Levinas explains it, the uniqueness of the incarnational self, as well as its connection to an inaccessible past, resides not in its participation in concepts such as self-consciousness, but in an absolute facticity that precedes all such conceptualization of self-identity: "The oneself comes from a past that could not be remembered, not because it is situated very far behind, but because the oneself, incommensurable with consciousness, which is always equal to itself, is not 'made' for the present" (*OTB* 107). That absolute subjectivity is also absolute dependence; because it has not become totalized in a concept of being that would allow it to appropriate its relations to others in a system (for example, a system that would allow it to understand itself and others according to a concept of self-consciousness), the incarnational subject must accept others in their absolute alterity. If the universe of others cannot be appropriated in a conceptual system, it presses on one with a force of command and a relationship characterized by primal responsibility:

> The self is a *sub-jectum;* it is under the weight of the universe, responsible for everything. The unity of the universe is not what my gaze embraces in its unity of apperception, but what is incumbent on me from all sides, regards me in the two senses of the term, accuses me, is my affair. (*OTB* 116)

For Wordsworth, an active historical process, rather than a desire for representational presence, is invoked in the desire for the "spirit of the past" to be enshrined in such a way that it can effect "future restoration." The poet's past is "approach[ed]" with trepidation: faced in a way that precedes understanding and conceptualization, and that accommodates both unique individuality and absolute dependence on hidden sources of power. The "spirit of the past" is "enshrine[d]": memorialized in the concrete incarnational process that is discussed in the "Essays Upon Epitaphs" and suggested by the burying of the books in the dream of the Arab Quixote. This memorialization occurs in the service of the temporally divided subject's absolute responsibility—in this case, the responsibility for "future restoration" (of himself and others, as the ending of *The Prelude* will stress)—not in the service of self-identical autonomy.

The "spots of time" themselves present a version of tropological divergence in which the failure of reading, closely connected to mortality, is recuperated through an incarnational rhetoric. In the first spot (*The Prelude* 11.278–327), the "monumental writing" seen by the boy near the sight of the execution is not exactly "read" at all; it is not interpreted within a grammar that can provide a systematic code of signification leading to knowledge. As Thomas Weiskel points out, the letters are in the "liminal space where the signifier appears but is not yet fully— consciously—read" (*The Romantic Sublime* 184–85). This grammar does not enable a reading despite (or perhaps because of) the fact that the actual history of the death echoes a highly grammatical, closed, and violent legal system in which crime (murder) and punishment (execution) have a relation of pure reciprocity. The inscription of this event, instead of producing a grammatical "reading" of itself, leads to a literal avoidance of reading: a tropological divergence from and resistance to this violent grammar. The 1850 version brings this resistance out more clearly than the 1805 text: "A casual glance had shown them, and I fled, / Faltering and faint, and ignorant of the road (*The Prelude* [1850] 12.246–47). The boy is ignorant even of the divergent direction in which he veers away from the written characters. This tropological act—the turn away from grammatical reading in flight up the hill— initiates the perception of "visionary dreariness," forcing the reader to "read" the scene in tropological, rather than grammatical terms.

The words that are thus "read" are very much things rather than signs. Their materiality is emphasized by the local citizens' ritual clearing of the grass; their action gives reverence to the actual letters carved into the ground, which are preserved and not allowed to disappear before their meaning as signs would. Hegel's dilemma reappears here: in order for the words to be read at all, they must be preserved in their materiality, but that objective preservation gives them a historical effect (involved with the ritualistic clearing as well as the young poet's unique reaction) that diverges from their original signifying function of naming the hanged murderer. We not only join the boy in his flight up the hill, away from the reading of the inscription, but we are also prohibited from seeing the "visionary dreariness" in terms of a fixed, grammatically determined image. Our sense of the visionary does not come directly from the image of the girl, the beacon, and the pool, but from the boy's faltering trek up the hill (reflected, perhaps, as Weiskel points out, in the girl's struggle against the wind); the *passage* from reading to vision (*The Romantic Sublime* 179–80).

This vision, which gives the "spot" its actively meaningful role in *The Prelude*, is achievable only by a rhetoric that can incorporate death and grammatical unreadability. The lost boy witnesses a death scene in which the implements of death are in ruin or absent ("The gibbet-mast was mouldered down, the bones / And iron case were gone"), but in which the death is revealed in an anonymous inscription, preserved from nature's encroachment by human effort, as the grass is cleared away each year by the local residents. Thanks to the ritualistic clearing away of the grass, that inaccessible death is reinscribed into the temporality of a very human language whose meaning is in turn grounded in that death. According to a representational rhetoric that meaning is certainly unearned, resting as it does on a series of displacements that lead back to death and absence. According to an incarnational rhetoric, however, meaning enters language (as Jesus is said to have entered the world) precisely by a very human act of clearing-away-to-reveal, an act which is at the same time an insertion of the human into nature and an openness to that which is beyond the horizon of any concept of human temporality, to that whose proper representation would demand "colours and words that are unknown to man" (11.309), a horizon bounded by signs of death. As Levinas would have it, for the incarnate human subject infinity resides, not beyond the human, but in the irreducible alterity of the human other. The experience of the second "spot of time" (11.344–88), to be discussed in more detail below, takes place "one Christmas-time," we told at the outset; the theological Incarnation is thus an explicit presence here. Again meaning is achieved through mortality; this time it is the much more personal death of the poet's father.

Though Frances Ferguson contrasts linguistic incarnation with the "de-incarnation" of death (*Language as Counter-Spirit* 34), the notion of incarnation is itself intimately connected not only with death, but also with criminal judgment. Jesus is a criminal from the state's viewpoint, and Judas is a criminal from the Christian viewpoint. Jesus' greatest act of both autonomy and obedience as the incarnate God was the sacrifice of his death. The Incarnation's repetition in the founding of the Eucharist is closely linked to Jesus' betrayal and death; in the three Gospel accounts that narrate the Last Supper, the transubstantiation at the Last Supper is preceded by a recognition of Judas' upcoming betrayal and followed by an acknowledgment that this was to be Jesus' last meal before his death.[14] The transubstantiation of the wine is recognized by Jesus as the blood that will be shed: "This is my blood of the covenant, which is poured out for many for the forgiveness of sins" (Matt. 26:28). It is thus no surprise that Wordsworth's statement on the need for an incarnation-based linguistic model should occur in an essay about how the dead should be represented, and that the notion of self-sacrifice should help to inform the interpretation of the "spots of time": "From thyself it is that thou must give, / Else never canst receive" (11.332–33). From early on in *The Prelude,* the Wordsworthian subject develops in the context of judgment by a living other infinitely impervious to assimilation by the subject, as when "huge and mighty forms, that do not live / Like living men" (1.424–25) haunt the mind of the boy whose stolen boat is stalked, paradoxically, by a "huge cliff," which "with measured motion, *like* a living thing / Strode after me" (1.409–12; emphasis added). As in the process described by Levinas, one becomes a subject characterized by the ability to give and sacrifice by being open to the accusation, judgment, and even persecution of the humanly infinite other: "The psyche in the soul is the other in me, a malady of identity, both accused and *self,* the same for the other, the same by the other" (*OTB* 69). The subject exists in putting itself into question by taking responsibility for the other's persecuting approach: "The subjectivity of a subject is responsibility of being-in-question in the form of the total exposure to offense in the cheek offered to the smiter" (*OTB* 111). This "becoming 'for the other' " is "the possibility of giving" (*OTB* 69) in a very concrete transcendence in which communication is founded on sacrifice:

> Communication with the other can be transcendent only as a dangerous life, a fine risk to be run. These words take on their strong sense when, instead of only designating the lack of certainty, they express the gratuity of sacrifice. (*OTB* 120)

This "fine risk" can be run by the Wordsworthian subject because the notion of incarnation allows that judgment and sacrifice to constitute, rather than simply threaten the infinitely grounded subject.

In the specifically Christian tradition inherited by Wordsworth, in which death plays a somewhat different and more fundamental role than in the existential-phenomenological process elaborated by Levinas, incarnational language locates an important part of its meaning in the distantly past death of Jesus, which is repeatedly memorialized in the culturally preservative ritual of the Eucharist. This is reflected in *The Prelude* when a scene of reinscribed death attains its restorative value as it is revisited and can be read by the light of a "radiance more divine" that stems "from these remembrances, and from the power / They left behind" (11.324–25). That divine radiance stems from an incarnation of meaning: a restorative relationship in which, as in the Incarnation, thought becomes human, and gains its energy from the remembering of a death that is involved in the demythologizing temporality of tropological divergence.

This restorative process is not only the "via naturaliter negativa" described by Hartman in *Wordsworth's Poetry* (31–69), according to which the failure of vision leads dialectically to self-consciousness; death is here reinscribed within consciousness, not simply transcended. Though the final result of both theological and Wordsworthian incarnation is positive, Wordsworth's poetry (if not his prose) refuses to deny the violence and terror associated with thought's incarnation into language. According to Irving Massey, the religious memorialization of the Resurrection involves the experience of "a panic, a madness, an ecstasy, a breathtaking thing-about-to-be that has already taken place" (*Find You the Virtue* 137). In addition to the Incarnation's incomprehensibility, however, the requirement to believe in this impossible event leads to the possibility of violence associated with judgment: "To question is to be turned into Pentheus, crazed to witness by one's own disbelief, negative testimony to what can be described only through that which is not: finally, to be destroyed by the believers" (Massey, *Find You the Virtue*, 137).[15] The violence implicit in the incarnation's sacrificial aspect, intimated by Hegel, will become explicit in Wordsworth at the end of *The Excursion* (see Chapter 4), when pre-Christian and Christian notions of sacrifice are compared.

In this sense the rhetoric of the Incarnation is closely related to the aesthetics of the sublime, by which man desires to, in Schiller's words, "overcome the concept of violence" (*On the Sublime* 194) as he (in Weiskel's generalization of Kant's definition) regards the mind's "inability to grasp wholly the object as a symbol of the mind's relation to a transcendent order" (*The Romantic Sublime* 23). The believer in the Incarnation must, if he is to escape the predicament Massey describes, be able to turn the event's incomprehensibility into a transcendental relationship. Similarly, the Wordsworthian language of incarnation attempts to elide the violence of "those poisoned vestments... which had power to consume and to alienate from his right mind the victim who put them on" (*PrW* 2:84–85), but in a way that pays tribute to the violence and judgment that is implied by incarnation.

The scene viewed from atop Mount Snowdon in book 13 of *The Prelude* presents a climactic version of the conflict between figural structures and incarnational rhetoric:

> I looked about, and lo,
> The moon stood naked in the heavens at height
> Immense above my head, and on the shore
> I found myself of a huge sea of mist,
> Which meek and silent rested at my feet.
> A hundred hills their dusky backs upheaved
> All over this still ocean, and beyond,
> Far, far beyond, the vapours shot themselves
> In headlands, tongues, and promontory shapes,
> Into the sea, the real sea, that seemed
> To dwindle and give up its majesty,
> Usurped upon as far as sight could reach.
> Meanwhile, the moon looked down upon this shew
> In single glory, and we stood, the mist
> Touching our very feet; and from the shore
> At distance not the third part of a mile
> Was a blue chasm, a fracture in the vapour,
> A deep and gloomy breathing-place, through which
> Mounted the roar of waters, torrents, streams
> Innumerable, roaring with one voice.
> The universal spectacle throughout
> Was shaped for admiration and delight,
> Grand in itself alone, but in that breach
> Through which the homeless voice of waters rose,
> That dark deep thoroughfare, had Nature lodged
> The soul, the imagination of the whole.
>
> (13.40–65)

The scene starts out from within a figural grammar, then reveals its "soul" in the usurpation of that figural structure by truly tropological activity. The initial "sea of mist" is a figure of the sea, a representation of the "real sea," which will later reveal itself. A "still ocean," this figural sea is "meek and silent," subject to the control of the viewer, because it resides in a controllable figural grammar. It can be unproblematically identified as part of a systematic relationship in the manner of the Enlightenment in that the figurative seas are paired with real seas and the figural is subordinated to the real. The tropological divergence from this situation begins when the sea of mist breaks out of its figural mold. No longer "meek and silent," it usurps the real sea "as far as sight could reach." In a sharp turn away from its original figural grammar, the mist metamorphoses into a series of figures of land—"headlands, tongues, and promontory shapes"—whose middle term figurally echoes the organ of speech, looking forward to the "voice of waters." The mist thus changes from that which veils but images the sea to that which encroaches on the sea. Thus the vapours shoot themselves "into the sea, the real sea, that seemed / To dwindle and give up its majesty." Finally the figural relationship between sea and mist dissolves altogether, and the mist is fractured, revealing "a deep and gloomy breathing-place." The description of that unapproachable place emphasizes the homelessness of the voice, which, despite its totalization in the similes that follow, is emphatically an absolute interruption of the figural scene. This place is a "soul," not, like the murderer's writing or the father's death, tied to an event in human history, and it is therefore not susceptible to simple reinscription in human temporality. As Hartman says in "The Poetics of Prophecy," "should a God-Word precede in Wordsworth, it is rarely foregrounded, but tends to be part of the poem's ground as an inarticulate, homeless or ghostly, sound" (in *The Unremarkable Wordsworth* 179). It is, in Hartman's classic formulation, an "omphalos," a "place of places," which is "at once breach and nexus, a breach in nature and a nexus for it and a different world" (*Wordsworth's Poetry* 122).

As he envisions himself standing above the scene and invokes the Miltonic description of creation,[16] the poet places himself closer to the transcendental source of incarnation than to the human event of incarnation. The analogical emphasis is now not so much on God becoming a historical event as on the incarnate God pointing back to his inaccessible origin in the Father. If Wordsworth thus adopts the pose of the Miltonic Creator, he has some right: the origin of the autobiographical incarnation is the self of the poet that exists outside of the text, like the Father outside of his creation, as its source, and as the poem nears its end the poet depicts himself in such extratextual postures even within autobiographical episodes such as the ascent of Mount Snowdon. The movement we have been following from figural grammar to tropological performance, and from the negative subversion of grammar to the positive terms of incarnation, is written along the contours of a line curving out of the text into this extratextual self. The line of the withdrawal from the written "I" into a pre-textual "I" reaches the border of the text at infinity, since the withdrawal from the autobiographical text cannot actually occur within the text. In this sense, despite the traditional theological-conceptual language that Wordsworth invokes, the voice of this pre-textual "I" is like Levinas's "saying": its trace is audible in the "said" of the autobiographical text, which is its necessary thematization, but the pre-textual "I" is a fundamental temporality and infinite alterity, a subjectivity always "out of phase," which precedes any thematization.

Because of the elusiveness of the pre-textual "I," which can be understood as this kind of nonthematized infinity, but which is also expressed in Judeo-Christian theological language, the transcendental side of the incarnation presents more radical problems for poetic language than the side which emphasizes the transition from God to man. Wordsworth lacks the Miltonic theological and philosophical machinery that could provide a representational framework for this mystery; in *Paradise Lost*, the visible Son represented the invisible Father in an understandable system. For Wordsworth, the language of incarnation cannot be articulated in such structures; that is precisely why he opposes the notion of incarnation to the notion of a binary opposition between language and thought. The language of incarnation in *The Prelude*, as we have seen, is the language of *event*, of divergence from totalizing grammatical structures. Without the support of such structures except as a point of departure (as the Snowdon scene departs from its figural beginning, or as Wordsworth departs from Pope, or as language-as-incarnation departs from language-as-dress), language's only options seem to be to veil meaning, calling attention to itself as it conceals its transcendental source, or to disappear into meaning, revealing, as Gadamer says with reference to language's relation to the Trinity, that "it has its being in its revealing" (*TM* 421).

Theologically, this dissolution of the word into its source is Jesus' return to the Father, but in the incarnation of meaning in *The Prelude*, it is the dissolving of the language of autobiographical narrative into the silence of that language's source in the extratextual self of the poet. This is problematic for autobiographical language, however, just as it was for Hegel's language-as-food in Chapter 1 and for Wordsworth's words as self-effacing signs or persistent things in Chapter 2. If words disappear into meaning as into "streams / Innumerable, roaring with one voice" (13.58–59), they become unintelligible or silent, in contrast to the single winding stream of the autobiographical narrative with which book 9 opened, or even the river from whose progress one can draw "the feeling of life endless, the one thought / By which we live, infinity and God" (13.183–84).

Wordsworth's language, of course, does not yet disappear; the Snowdon episode is contained in a complex rhetoric that allows this transcendental side of the language of incarnation to be read. Whereas in book 10 the poet had pictured himself as "a clouded ... moon" (917), here he says that the moon, which illuminates the landscape of the imagination, "stood naked in the heavens at height / Immense above my head," and later that "the moon looked down upon this shew / In single glory." The moon guarantees and legitimizes the poet's Godlike position above this scene, so that he experiences, as Hartman notes in "The Poetics of Prophecy," "the 'timely utterance' with which Genesis begins—the very harmony between cause and effect, between fiat and actualizing response" (in *The Unremarkable Wordsworth* 173).[17] Here, in a situation unlike that of the "spots of time," we are presented with a vision *of,* not *in* tropological activity, totalized into a figure when the poet claims that the scene "appeared to me / The perfect image of a mighty mind, / Of one that feeds upon infinity" (13.68–70). The "spots of time" presented "unreadable" events that, because they were events, could be memorialized fruitfully and reinscribed into temporality. In the Snowdon episode, the disappearance of language into the "deep and gloomy breathing place" should be even less readable, but through the miracle of reflection (in both the thinking and the mirroring senses of that word) the scene is completely readable. The sun, which the travelers anticipated (and which illuminated the similar scene described in *Descriptive Sketches* 492–505), is displaced by the reflected light from the moon, which first appears reflected again as "a light upon the turf." Reflection is raised to a second power when the scene is interpreted as a natural analogy—specifically, a "counterpart"—to the interactive power of the mind (13.84–119).

Philippe Lacoue-Labarthe and Jean-Luc Nancy, in *The Literary Absolute,* argue that Romanticism, working uneasily between the Kantian emptying of the subject and the Hegelian or Fichtean positing of absolute self-consciousness, saw the desired "auto-production" of the subject-as-work in terms of "reflection" on several levels. The "hiatus introduced at the heart of the subject" (*The Literary Absolute* 32) by Kant is both acknowledged and resolved by means of the mirror of irony as well as the completion of poetic autoproduction through the reflective task of criticism. Recalling Walter Benjamin, Lacoue-Labarthe and Nancy say that "the systematic vision of the absolute and the absolute vision of the system face each other, stare at each other, and in a certain sense disfigure each other in the same satire of the work, in what amounts to a double parody of theory—or of religion—in the Work" (*The Literary Absolute* 80).

As the poetic voice of *The Prelude* prepares to withdraw from the text into the silence of the pre- and post-textual poet (the life *The Prelude* looks to as its origin and the projected life of the poet of *The Recluse*, which will supposedly validate *The Prelude*), we are presented with this kind of figural, reflective structure in which nature and mind can mirror each other. This is in one sense a return to "grammar," but a grammar in which the performative subversion of earlier grammars is inscribed. As the autobiographical figure is rounded off and completed—as *Bildung* resolves itself into a *Bild* of the poet's self—the outlines of the figure must be blurred: the final *Bild* must be an image of the tropological process of *Bildung*, and thus not a grammatical, systematic *Bild*. The mutual reflection of these two movements is precisely the constitution of autobiographical self. To adapt Lacoue-Labarthe and Nancy's terms, the analogy with nature provides a "systematic vision of the absolute" poetic subject. At the same time, we are presented with an "absolute vision of the system"[18] of tropological interaction, precisely *not* subject to appropriation within human, grammatical systems, in that the analogy between mind and nature is at the same time an interaction: It is the "power . . . which Nature thus / Thrusts forth upon the senses," which is the "genuine counterpart . . . of the glorious faculty / Which higher minds bear with them as their own." This power is "the very spirit in which they deal / With all the objects of the universe" (13.84–92). Nature's intrusion on the senses is reflected in the mind's creative/receptive relation to the world. Through a complex sequence of interlocking reflections, the mind and nature are in the same gesture bound to the poles of a figural system and engaged in an interpretive interaction. In the rejected lines from MS. W,[19] several more scenes "embody / This pleasing argument" of the analogy between mind and nature, including the horse, discussed in Chapter 2, that is "a borderer dwelling betwixt life and death" (MS. W 72), which can be viewed as a "living statue or a statued life" (MS. W 73), an animated monument or a life that is becoming its own memorial.

The conflicting desires thus awakened by the approach of the autobiographical end involve the sort of eschatology of time that Hartman defines in "The Poetics of Prophecy" as "apocalyptic": "An anticipatory, proleptic relation to time, intensified to the point where there is at once desire for and dread of the end being hastened. There is a potential inner turning against time, and against nature insofar as it participates in the temporal order" (*The Unremarkable Wordsworth* 167). The end is desired insofar as incarnate language desires to dissolve into its meaning, and *The Prelude* desires to be made subordinate to *The Recluse*, dissolving into the framework of life and life-work outside *The Prelude*. The end is dreaded because the completion of the autobiography is the point at which the stream of autobiographical narrative dissolves into the "devouring sea" (*The Prelude* 9.4) of the chaos that surrounds the created text.

Within the poem, this double movement appears as the oft-noted disturbance of the poem's temporality in the final books. The poet himself admits that since he "withdrew unwillingly from France, / The story hath demanded less regard / To time and place" (13.334–36). Restoration occurs, not as the telos of a process, at the "end" of the autobiography, but in the internal reworking of autobiographical temporality. That is, the "spots of time" and the Snowdon episode had been in the poem's plan all along, but their restorative power is felt only when they can be put into the performative context of a narrative that in fact diverges from the figural grammar of a linear temporality. Thus the poet recognizes that the process of human consciousness, which the Augustinian tradition of autobiography as the exemplary story of "conversion" desires to see within the figure of a teleological progression of temporal change, is, as Gadamer puts it, "not a temporal relation... but a mental process" of internal dialogue. The restorative language of incarnation does not describe afterward, but is coeval with, the events of thought. "The word is not formed [*gebildet*] only after the act of knowledge has been completed... but it is the act of knowledge itself. Thus the word is simultaneous with this [*Bildung*] (*formatio*) of the intellect" (*TM* 423–24).

FRAGMENTS AND DIALOGUE: THE POST-TEXTUAL POET

This relationship of simultaneity between word and thought is conditioned, however, by some important differences between divine language and human language, between the Word and the word. Following Aquinas, Gadamer describes the human word as

> like a mirror in which the object is seen. The curious thing about this mirror, however, is that it nowhere extends beyond the image of the thing.... What is remarkable about this metaphor is that the word is understood here entirely as the perfect reflection of the thing—i.e., as the expression of the thing—and has left behind it the path of the thought to which alone, however, it owes its existence. This does not happen with the divine mind. (*TM* 425)

In contrast with the unitary divine Word, we have only diverse human words, each expressing its object but leaving behind its source in thought. There is of course a dialectical relationship between the unity of divine Word and the multiplicity of the human word—a dialectic expressed by the event of the Incarnation—but the problem of difference remains. This limitation of the human word is comparable to the limitation of an autobiography in relation to the life it expresses. Like the word cut off from its source in thought, the autobiographical self is cut off from the extratextual life to which it owes its existence.

The autobiography is literally a fragment, which is how De Quincey described *The Prelude*: "The Prelude therefore, complete as it is with regard to a brief period of the poet's life, is only a fragment, and one more example of the many which the last generation could produce of the uncertainty of human projects and of the contrast between the promise of youth and the accomplishment of manhood."[20] Fragmentariness is in a close and complex relation to totality: according to Lacoue-Labarthe and Nancy, writing about the Schlegels, "The empty place that a garland of fragments surrounds is a precise drawing of the contours of the Work" (*The Literary Absolute* 47). The absolute incompletion of the fragment indicates its detached individuality as well as the totality beyond it:

> Each fragment stands for itself and for that from which it is detached. Totality is the fragment itself in its completed individuality. It is thus identically the plural totality of fragments, which does not make up a whole (in, say, a mathematical mode) but replicates the whole, the fragmentary itself, in each fragment. (*The Literary Absolute* 43)

Unlike the Schlegels' *Athenaeum* fragments, *The Prelude* is not self-consciously structured as a fragment, but it certainly partakes of some of the logic of the fragment. Its contours, as we have seen, cannot be traced in terms of a totalizing grammar, but only in a performative tropology, which plays out the fragmentation of grammar through events—themselves fragmentary—such as the "spots of time" and the ascent of Snowdon. Vision is a process of seeing by fragmentary and temporary "glimpses": "I see by glimpses now, when age comes on / May scarcely see at all" (11.337–38). The "soul" and the "imagination" of the Snowdon scene reside in the fractured "breach / Through which the homeless voice of waters rose" (13.62–63); fragmentation is the expression of imaginative totality. *The Prelude* is, on the one hand, a fragmentary piece of the poet's life, which, the poet has painfully discovered, is like the "fragment-project" that "does not operate as a program or prospectus but as the *immediate* projection of what it nonetheless incompletes" (*The Literary Absolute* 43). That is, the life story does not proceed according to a plan, despite Wordsworth's desire for it to be seen as representing a growth toward poetic maturity, but instead it projects its own incompleteness, which *is* its completion. It is, to return to Gadamer's Thomistic description of the human word, a perfectly formed mirror of a fragment, but the perfection of its mirroring lies in its performance of the act of fragmentary perception, because that is the locus of the poetic existence that *The Prelude* intends to portray.

Because Wordsworth is trying *not* to write a fragment, though his project becomes more and more fragmentary, he must find a way to exit *The Prelude,* a "ruse of writing," to use Louis Marin's term,[21] which will attempt to bridge the gap between the life inside and outside of the autobiographical text. This "ruse of writing" must also account for the strange reversal of the event of incarnation that occurs as the poet begins to identify himself with the transcendental source of incarnation rather than with the event of its occurrence.

The poem's exit strategy begins with the allegorization of the poet's withdrawal from the text. Only when he rises above the scene, with the mist at his feet instead of around him as he struggles to climb the mountain, can the poet interpret the scene as visionary and translate it into a figure of the mind, moving from the ego caught in the struggle of existence to the effortless realm of the view from on high.[22] The "I," having literally risen above the scene of tropological activity, which it is then able to totalize as other to itself, now asserts itself as a "post-textual" reader of the preceding text.[23] This turn is a complex rhetorical act that subtly begs the essential autobiographical question. The poet's right to step from behind the curtain of his text can only be gained via a fiction of that text's completeness and his own position "above" it. Thus he describes himself as a lark soaring above the textual "world" of his autobiographical self:

> Anon I rose
> As if on wings, and saw beneath me stretched
> Vast prospect of the world which I had been
> And was; and hence this song, which like a lark
> I have protracted, in the unwearied heavens
> Singing, and often with more plaintive voice
> Attempered to the sorrows of the earth—

> Yet centring all in love, and in the end
> All gratulant, if rightly understood.
>
> (13.377–85)

This image, which specifically resolves the alienation introduced by the "voice" of "reproach" he heard from his past life (13.376–77), represents a careful shifting of terms between heaven and earth, an adjustment of the language of incarnation to suggest the foundation for a transcendental viewpoint. His initial connection to the lark comes directly out of the temporality of narrative and discourse—he has "protracted" his song, which makes it like the continuously present discourse of the lark. Like the lark, he is in the "unwearied" heavens; the transcendental song is possible, not because larks do not tire, but because they fly in a space that, like the moonlit landscape atop Mount Snowdon, does not permit of weariness. Once this position has been established, the lark/poet can "attemper" his voice to "the sorrows of the earth," reentering the earthly realm of the narrative but retaining the transcendental perspective. To "temper" a note on a musical instrument is to vary its pitch from the acoustically correct value so that it will sound appropriate in relation to other notes in a number of keys; in a move comparable to the hermeneutical circle by which the system of law adjusts to particular events, the "grammar" of the Pythagorean system is thus subverted by the contingencies of practical application to specific musical keys. Wordsworth's choice of this word is thus very appropriate; the lark/poet's ability to reenter the narrative language of earthly sorrow entails a tempering of or divergence from the grammar of music in the "unwearied heavens." Furthermore, the bird's song, like that which Keats will attribute to his nightingale, has no content of its own and thus can be fitted to both a transcendental and a human text. This supple image thus permits the incarnation of language to be viewed from the point of view of the source of the incarnation, in an autobiographical "I" that approaches post-textual status.

The poet who thus rises above the text "as if on wings" is very different from the discursive voice who says "I am lost" in book 11, or who describes "Imagination! lifting up itself / Before the eye and progress of my song" in book 6. The lark/poet is not the "I" who has been struggling through *The Prelude*'s tropological maze, not the self who *is writing* the poem, but the very different self who is defined as *having written* the poem. That post-textual self must assert itself as the source of the incarnated language, and as the reader of a completed text. It must be able to stand confidently between this text and *The Recluse* (*in* neither) and say

> Having now
> Told what best merits mention, further pains
> Our present labour seems not to require,
> And I have other tasks.
> (13.367–70)

The fragmentary nature of the text is partially acknowledged: the poet says he has told only the best parts of the story, and is not necessarily finished; he chooses to halt this painful labor to move on to other things. Still, the rhetoric of his exit from the autobiography demands that the text be totalized as other to the post-textual voice, which is related to his text as the lark is to the "world" below, to which he both does and does not belong.

The retrospective "post-textual" voice is of course an artifice within the text; its ability to look back over the "world" of the poet's life is not necessarily a formally satisfactory conclusion to the poem. As Irving Massey points out, "architectonic structures can create the illusion of having reached a stable conclusion, simply because they produce the necessity for a retrospective overview" (*Find You the Virtue* 2). The real post-textual voice is the inaccessible origin of the poet's consciousness, the unthematized subjectivity of Levinas's "saying." The rhetoric of the end of *The Prelude* involves a *staging* of the impossible withdrawal of the incarnate language into the silence of its source. The self that hovers around the borders of the text and is never quite articulated, but only pointed to by deictic figures such as that of the post-textual "I,"[24] is partly an "original" self: the adult consciousness that is the source of the incarnate poetic language, which consciousness seeks its own source in the pre-temporal origins of childhood described in the "Immortality" ode. However, it is also produced by the autobiography as the self that, having written *The Prelude,* is now theoretically able to complete a larger work. The representative of this original self within the text (the poet's voice at the end of *The Prelude*) is also a production of the text; it is a figure necessitated by the need to bring closure to *The Prelude.* This final version of the "I," figured by the lark, is thus poised between a self that is "above" and ontologically prior to the text, and one that is produced by the text.

Exactly when a final tropological divergence should occur, when the grammar of the text should dissolve into the "devouring sea" of the life from which it abstracts itself, we see instead a final recourse to the realm of figure. Wordsworth combines the textual and post-textual aspects of the final "I" by presenting himself, in dialogue with Coleridge, as an exemplum, a figure for the potentiality of mind in accord with nature, a moral figure that connects the text to the world. The exemplary dialogue is essential to the incarnational language of Wordsworth's strategy for poetic recuperation. For example, the death scene in the first "spot of time," which proved so terrifying as a lonely childhood experience, is later irradiated with "the spirit of pleasure" (11.322) by being placed into a memorializing dialogue when Wordsworth returns in 1787 "with those two dear ones" (11.316), sister and future wife. At the temporally significant nexus of the family from which he originates (Dorothy) and the family he will begin (Mary), the poet experiences an incarnation of meaning characterized not only by the interaction between presents (the revisiting with Mary and Dorothy and the present of the writing "I") and pasts (the past of the boyhood visit and the distant past of the execution and murder), but also by the experience of present dialogue that points toward past and future.

That the self is constituted in a process of dialogue is a commonplace of both the poetics and the theology of incarnation.[25] We know, most emphatically from "Tintern Abbey," that the poet could easily move from a dialogue with an invented past to a dialogue with Dorothy. At the end of *The Prelude*, the poet abandons narrative in favor of a dialogue in which his interlocutors are specifically named (Dorothy, Coleridge, and Calvert) and perceived within a dialectic of giving and receiving. The most important gift is that of *The Prelude* to Coleridge; Wordsworth refers to the poem as "this gift / Which I for thee design" (13.411–12). Earlier, in the passage between the two "spots of time," he does not desire to *represent* "substance"; rather he wishes to "*give* /... as far as words can *give* / A substance and a life" to what he feels (11.338–40; italics added), making it clear that poetic incarnation follows the logic of the gift. The gift of poetic incarnation, like the Father's gift of his Son, is an "emanation" involving an overflowing and increase of meaning that is not conserved in an economic exchange, and which is thus unearned and extra. As Gadamer says, "Essential to an emanation is that what emanates is an overflow. What it flows from does not thereby become less.... For if the original One is not diminished by the outflow of the many from it, this means that being increases" (*TM* 140). Augustine talks of both the divine and the linguistic incarnation in a similarly noneconomic way: "Both that word of ours becomes an articulate sound, and that other Word becomes flesh, by assuming it, not by consuming itself so as to be changed into it" (*On the Holy Trinity* 209).

Lewis Hyde has shown that the logic of the gift is asymmetrical and anti-economic; like the "gift" of the Incarnation and its repetition in the

Eucharist, what is "consumed" by the recipient is not thereby depleted (as it would be in an economic exchange) but rather increased. Hyde describes "what seems at first to be a paradox of gift exchange: when the gift is used, it is not used up. Quite the opposite, in fact: the gift that is not used will be lost, while the one that is passed along remains abundant" (*The Gift* 21).[26] This theory provides a partial answer to the dilemma faced by Hegel discussed in Chapter 1: the problem of the persistence of the objective materiality of language, the words that cannot be "read away" into pure love but must remain in their historical contingency. Hegel was leaning toward something like a Derridean theory of the supplement, or the idea that the persistent materiality and historicity of the signifier, always involved in endless chains of other signifiers, can never successfully disappear before a signified. In the logic of incarnational emanation and gift, however, as in Gadamer's judicial model of the generation of meaning, we can turn that persistence of the material around so that it demonstrates the abundance rather than the deficiency of meaning. Here the supplement does not so much defer access to presence (though it does that) as it positively constitutes an incarnational rather than a representational meaning. Incarnational meaning is less interested in representation of presence than it is in the translation of spirit into event, and as we saw in Chapter 2 this is for Wordsworth the process of translating thought into words as living, mortal things.

The "chastisement" in the second "spot of time" (11.369), whose excessiveness has puzzled many critics,[27] can be seen in these terms as a kind of negative gift. The poet describes his state of mind after his father's death:

> The event,
> With all the sorrow which it brought, appeared
> A chastisement; and when I called to mind
> That day so lately past, when from the crag
> I looked in such anxiety of hope,
> With trite reflections of morality,
> Yet in the deepest passion, I bowed low
> To God who thus corrected my desires.
> (11.367–74)

In purely human terms, the anxiety is innocent. Within the rhetoric of incarnation, however, the death of the father can be seen in a broader sacrificial sense: it is not felt as a response to particular human actions, but a reorientation of man's postlapsarian condition, a condition of unfulfilled desire, anxiety, and inadequate "trite reflections of morality" (11.372). It must be thought of in terms of the excess of the logic of the gift, not the exact reciprocity of an economic exchange in which an individual punishment matches an individual act. In positive terms, this superfluity permits an increase in being: the childhood events conditioned by the death of the poet's father become to the poet

>   spectacles and sounds to which
> I often would repair, and thence would drink
> As at a fountain.
>   (11.382–84)

They are a repeated source of meaning which, like a fountain, can continue to pour out of itself seemingly without depletion, thanks to the language of incarnation. In Levinas's terms, the very ability to become an incarnate subject capable of experiencing infinity is founded on the experience of being accused, or in Wordsworth's language "chastised" by an incomprehensible other, presented here as the "God who thus corrected [his] desires," who interrupts the subject's effort to assume the stance of an autonomous, totalizing entity. On the rhetorical level, the language of incarnation is a divergence from grammatical totalization; a grammar, like an economy, is subverted by the superfluity of meaning present in the gift of the language event. Seen negatively, this can be read as an achievement of homogeneity through the introduction of a radically heterogeneous element, like the dependence (in Pascal as read by Paul de Man) of the mathematical universe on the non-number zero, which stands for "nothing" but must be inscribed in the series of numbers as "something" ("Pascal's Allegory" 10). In the logic of incarnation, however, the nullity of death is reinscribed as the production of bountiful heterogeneity, as the poet feeds on memory's repetitions.

The double notions of gift and dialogue allow the poem to end with a combination of self-affirming closure and self-effacing openness. To engage in the fundamental interpretive experience of a dialogue is, according to Gadamer, to assert one's opinions and prejudices, but in a play of give-and-take that leads to a truth "which is neither mine nor yours and hence so far transcends the interlocutors' subjective opinions that even the person leading the conversation knows that he does not know" (*TM* 368). By presenting *The Prelude* to Coleridge as a "gift," Wordsworth affirms his written self, but does so by placing the autobiographical gift in the space of dialogue that transcends either partner. The language of the gift of incarnation is thus also the "giving" language of affective dialogue, which will justify the autobiographical enterprise: "to thee," the poet says to Coleridge, "the work shall justify itself" (13.410).

Gift giving is a form of dialogue that recognizes a fundamental difference as it hopes for a unity; hence we often give gifts at times of farewell or atonement. Thus the gift of *The Prelude* to Coleridge is an expression of hope "that thou art near, and wilt be soon / Restored to us in renovated health" (13.423–24). By packaging his life story as a "gift," the poet doubly removes it from his post-textual self: first, a gift is specifically something that is separated from the giver, and here it is sent off into the space of a dialogue that transcends the individual self. Second, at some point after a gift is given, the giver usually departs, having left a memorial to himself in the gift.[28] The gift of the narrative to Coleridge helps to palliate the absence that, according to Marin, accompanies narrative's elision of the discursive "I." The narrative, because it is of past events, leaves the present, discursive "I" on the outside, but as a gift that narrative can be packaged up and presented, in this case, to Coleridge, in the full enunciation of dialogical discourse.[29] Having left the packaged *Bild* of his life in the space of the dialogue with Coleridge, the poet is able to exit *The Prelude* and retreat into the silence of the post-textual self who (or so goes the plan) will be manifested in philosophical rather than autobiographical poetic texts in the future.

Dialogue retains a fluidity in which truth emerges from interaction instead of appearing as the telos of a line of argument; thus this ending dialogue with Coleridge is able to present a figure of closure that does not, however, have the teleological structure, with its attendant dangers of grammatical totalization, that characterized earlier, less successful figures. Thus truth resides, not in the telos of a concept or law, but in the exemplary life of an intersubjectively constituted person.[30] The dialogue between Wordsworth and the absent, ill Coleridge will mediate in the "redemption" of mankind (13.441) by serving as an *example* of affective dialogue: "What we have loved / Others will love, and we may teach them how" (13.444–45). The self-transcending effect of the exemplary dialogue with Coleridge has, even more than the imagery of Snowdon, oriented the speaking poet toward the transcendental side of incarnation. Instead of giving "substance" to thought, the incarnate substance of the textualized poet here looks toward its divine origin in a dialogue outside of the text. From this height, the dialogue between Wordsworth and Coleridge can be both an exemplary "figure," which will provide a "grammar" within which a redemptive plan can be read proleptically, and in the same gesture a source of repeated "auto-production," which, as we have seen, takes place in the tropological divergence from figural grammar.

It is no wonder that Coleridge, Wordsworth's most immediately important reader, in "To William Wordsworth," finds himself "in prayer" (112) after hearing his partner in dialogic redemption read *The Prelude*. Wordsworth had put forth a plan by which their creative/receptive dialogue would be recreated, not simply as an imitation, but, to borrow Lacoue-Labarthe and Nancy's formulation of this idea in the Schlegels, reincarnated as "a repetition of the very movement of the production or constitution of the subject. A mimesis, in sum, of auto-production" (*The Literary Absolute* 68). By repeating the process that Wordsworth has narrated and experienced in *The Prelude*, "the mind of man" can retrace the process of incarnation in order to become, according to the poem's last line, "of substance and of fabric more divine" (13.446–52). This mimetic apotheosis is an appropriate ending for the poem, because this is also the point at which the incarnate language of the autobiography dissolves into the silence of its source in the extratextual self.

This final act of figuration differs from previous figural structures in the *Prelude* in that it shifts the emphasis from epistemology to ethics. Wordsworth and Coleridge do not simply form a figural pair that, like earlier structures, represents the poet's life; instead, they function as an exemplum that will lead to future ethical acts of love: "What we have loved / Others will love, and we may teach them how" (13.444–45). Charles Altieri, in an effort to define an "expressivist ethics" that parallels my argument in its desire to discuss ethics in art and to escape the limitations of binary theoretical structures, draws on Nelson Goodman and Kant to argue that examples, as opposed to arbitrarily illustrative signs, perform an ethical communication that does not depend on rational categories: "Because examples possess and do not simply refer to properties, they can themselves provide forms that judgment can use without relying on abstract understanding" (*Canons and Consequences* 246). In addition to providing such forms, Altieri contends, examples, unlike abstract representations, testify to their own truth by demonstrating how "the truth is rendered or performed" (247), and also "allow us a range of projective sympathies so that we come to appreciate what is involved in given choices" (247). In this sense the *Bildung* that becomes an exemplary figure at the end of *The Prelude* is not at all abstract. By emerging from a developing life and a communicative interaction with Coleridge into an exemplary act of love, this final figure has the performative, ethical dimension that Altieri attributes to examples, and which is a fundamental part of Wordsworth's incarnational rhetoric. The example of love, not an abstract figure of love, will allow readers to share the experience and even the objects of Wordsworth's and Coleridge's love: "What we have loved / Others will love." As "joint labourers in the work...of...redemption" who will "speak / A lasting inspiration" (13.439–43), the human examples of love themselves will continue to perform the language of inspiration and redemption, testifying to the truth of the example by the continued performance of the example's content, and providing, not a fixed concept, but what Altieri calls "a range of projective sympathies" in this human incarnation of love.

This ethical aspect of incarnational language goes back to Augustine; as I pointed out in the first chapter, he saw both human and divine words as effecting (implicitly ethical) action: "As it is said of that Word, 'All things were made by Him,' where God is declared to have made the universe by his only-begotten Son, so there are no works of man that are not first spoken in his heart" (*On the Holy Trinity* 210). The shift in *The Prelude* from a grammatical, figural, semiotic view of language to a performative, tropological, incarnational view is a shift from epistemology to ethics comparable to the shift I discussed in "She Dwelt Among the Untrodden Ways" in the previous chapter. In that poem, the decay of the possibility of epistemological, representational knowledge produced an ethical relation like Cavell's acknowledgment of the loss of the other, or Levinas's assumption of responsibility for the death of the other. In *The Prelude*, the incarnational rhetoric that emerges from the decay of figural structures finds its final expression in a figural exemplum that is a call to ethical life as much or more than it is a representational structure.

Like a sacrament, this figure is both representational/epistemological and ethical: the Eucharist, for example, is supposed both to represent Jesus' past action and to exert an ethical force on the communicant, and Wordsworth's final figure is supposed to provide both representational closure for the poem and an ethical effect on the reader. If successful, this combination of roles shows the Wordsworthian incarnational word-as-living-thing at its best. As a set of incarnate things, the final words of *The Prelude* stand in the place of the poet's life, performing that representational function, but they also have the material force of performative event-things, exerting an ethical force on the reader. Hegel's dilemma between necessary objective materiality and equally necessary self-effacement before Christian love seems to have been resolved: the objective materiality that is so problematic on the representational level is translated into a force for ethical action that, while moving the whole question away from representational issues, is compatible with the principle of "pure" love to which, in representation, the "impurity" of objective materiality is opposed.

Thus, even though *The Prelude* ends with a totalizing gesture—wrapping up the autobiography as an exemplary figure—exposing the self *as* a sign, rather than representing the self as conceptualized within a system of signs, is exactly how the self participates in "saying," according to Levinas:

> Saying is thus to make signs of this very signifyingness of the exposure; it is to expose the exposure instead of remaining in it as an act of exposing. It is to exhaust oneself in exposing oneself, to make signs by making oneself a sign, without resting in one's every figure as a sign. (*OTB* 143)

The emergence of the incarnational self out of the decay of figural systems is Wordsworth's refusal to rest "in one's every figure as a sign"; by offering his experience as an exemplary sign at the end of *The Prelude*, he belies the act of representational figuration even as he enacts it. To speak to the reader as Wordsworth does to Coleridge is to

> interrupt the ultimate discourse in which all the discourses are stated, in saying it to the one that listens to it, and who is situated outside the said that the discourse says, outside all it includes.... This reference to an interlocutor permanently breaks through the text that the discourse claims to weave in thematizing and enveloping all things. In totalizing being, discourse qua discourse thus belies the very claim to totalize. (*OTB* 170)

Even as *Bildung* is reduced to a final *Bild*, Wordsworth's offering of his autobiographical subjectivity is "all gratulant" if it is "rightly understood" as "the signifyingness of sensibility, the one-for-the-other itself," which is "the preoriginal signifyingness that gives sense, because it gives" (*OTB* 78) in an ethical act of teaching. Though incarnational thought is precisely what interrupts representational figures in tropological divergence, the final representation of the self in an epistemological figure occurs in an incarnational, ethical act. Even though the completion of Wordsworth's autobiography is a totalizing gesture, his incorporation of Coleridge as reader into the end of the poem gestures toward the very nontotalized fate of the poem once it leaves the author's control (a control Wordsworth would not relinquish before his death, of course) and enters the world of interpreters. Levinas makes the point that books, even though they are the very medium by which "saying" is betrayed into the "said," reenter the conversation of "saying" once they enter the world:

> In the writing the saying does indeed become a pure said, a simultaneousness of the saying and of its conditions. A book is interrupted discourse catching up with its own breaks. But books have their fate; they belong to a world they do not include, but recognize by being written and printed, and by being prefaced and getting themselves preceded with forewords. They are interrupted and call for other books and in the end are interpreted in a saying distinct from the said. (*OTB* 170–71)

In this way *The Prelude*, even as it is wrapped up as a gift complete in itself—a "said"—is by its entry into the dialogue of gift giving immediately unwrapped, so to speak, by the interpreter to whom the gift of this book is given, whether that recipient is Coleridge or the poem's later readers, and thus becomes a "saying" in the noneconomy of gift exchange. As a gift to Coleridge, the poem is associated with Wordsworth's desire for Coleridge to be "restored to us in renovated health" (13.424); the desire to give is associated with a responsibility for the other that extends to the very basic level of his life and health, and that recognizes the fragility of both.

In comparing the conflict between representational and incarnational thought to the conflict between epistemology and ethics, I grant the obvious fact that Wordsworth, unlike Kant, could not ground ethics in a rational epistemology. Still, neither relationship is *simply* a conflict. The rhetoric of incarnation depends on the decay of non-incarnational figural systems, solving the representational problems faced by those figures even as those figures are destroyed, just as the original Incarnation would have no meaning outside of the presence and decay of the Law, which it both abrogates and fulfills, and just as, in Levinas's terms, "saying" reveals itself in the interruption of the "said." Similarly, the ethical relation toward which the Lucy poems and *The Prelude* tend is intimately connected to the failing epistemological systems out of which the ethical relation emerges. In *The Prelude*, this difficult terrain seems to be traversed successfully; in *The Excursion*, as we shall see, the attempt to address these issues in a more self-conscious combination of poetry and philosophy points up their problematic aspects in a poem that is fascinating because it fails on a such grand scale.

4
The Excursion:
Incarnation and Philosophical Poetry

One of the main objects of the Recluse is, to reduce the calculating understanding to its proper level among the human faculties.
—Wordsworth to Catherine Clarkson, January 1815

INCARNATION AND THEORY

There is a tension between a poetics of incarnation like that developed in *The Prelude* and a theory of moral philosophy like that presented in *The Excursion*. If poetry is "the incarnation of thought," it does not analyze the world, totalizing it into a detachable representational theory, but rather adds a new incarnation to the world, which, in this fundamentally anti-economic move, prevents the economy of theory from gaining a foothold. *The Recluse,* though it proposed "to reduce the calculating understanding to its proper level among the human faculties," also proposed (in the preface to *The Excursion*) to embody a philosophical system that any reader could "extract... for himself" (*PrW* 3:6). In its pure form such a philosophical system would exist as a representation of the moral universe, not an active incarnated force added to it.

Neither *The Excursion* nor its philosophical forebears exhibit such purity, though the intention to represent a system rather than to trace one's personal origins pulls the poet in the direction of such a recognizably unreachable goal. As Alan Bewell has demonstrated, Wordsworth wrote before the human sciences were divided into specialized disciplines, within a tradition of encyclopedic systems of moral philosophy such as Adam Ferguson's *Institutes of Moral Philosophy* (1796) and

David Hume's *Treatise of Human Nature* (1739), a work which was originally planned to be more comprehensive than it turned out to be. On the one hand, these systems "present a loose architecture of concerns, comprehensive, heterogeneous, often redundant, and yet also fluid, to the point of eclecticism" (*Wordsworth and the Enlightenment* 14), but on the other hand, they manifest a drive toward systematization that led to Kant's and Hegel's "culminating expressions of the totalizing vision of late eighteenth-century moral philosophy" (16). As Harry M. Solomon points out in regard to Pope's *Essay on Man* (an important antecedent to Wordsworth's attempt at philosophical poetry), despite the praise heaped on Pope's combination of the poetic and the philosophical, both his contemporaries and later critics commit the error of reducing his figurative language to analogical argument:

> Pope's success in uniting the poetic and the philosophical uses of language was initially much praised; but perhaps because there was no critical idiom adequate to characterize his accomplishment, this praise was sometimes conducted in terms which distort the ontological status of his figurative language and which ultimately led to misinterpretation and to the discrediting of the "argument" of the poem. ("Reading Philosophical Poetry" 124)

Solomon proposes a theory of "regulative metaphor" (based on Kant's notion of regulative ideas), which, like the incarnational thought I am discussing, attempts to move beyond the binary categories of both Enlightenment and contemporary thought by showing how, in Pope's case, figurative language is able to combine the conflicting tasks of argument, inspiration, and ethical admonition.

Wordsworth engaged a tradition of philosophical poetry represented most immediately by Pope, who, despite the complexity demonstrated by Solomon, had no problem writing poetry within the economy of totalizing theory. Wordsworth, however, wrote in the era of the Coleridgean synthesis, which was in part a desire to create an English version of the philosophico-poetic writing of, for example, the Schlegel circle, whose writing on and in fragments demonstrated that philosophy did *not* mean theoretical, economic totalization. Thus for Wordsworth the requisite interpenetration of philosophy and poetry, and similarly of theory and incarnation, was far more complex than for Pope. Bewell argues convincingly that Wordsworth's mature poetry both used and displaced Enlightenment philosophical systems, particularly systems of anthropological inquiry. In terms compatible with my view of an incarnational rhetoric arising from and displacing a representational epistemology, Bewell sees the project of *The Recluse* as the displacement of philosophical inquiry with images and eloquence: "The idea of addressing moral topics with 'eloquence' and through 'images' emerged in the space left vacant by his expulsion of moral philosophical inquiry" (*Wordsworth and the Enlightenment* 11).[1] Furthermore, Bewell argues, Wordsworthian anthropology is imbued with autobiography—observations of human culture and origins are both reflected in and accomplished by means of self-observation—and therefore "the division between anthropology and autobiography, between *The Recluse* and *The Prelude*, should . . . be seen as a false one, because the 'experimental' language Wordsworth developed in reaction to moral philosophy also provided him with the vocabulary, speculative framework, the categories, and the narrational structure by which he organized his life and made sense of it" (46). I agree in the sense that Wordsworth's experimental language—what I am calling his incarnational rhetoric—critiques the language of systematic Enlightenment philosophy in both works. As I will show below, autobiography plays an important role in *The Excursion* also; however, because of the "theoretical" framework of *The Excursion*, its relationship between systematic, representational philosophy and incarnational expression is very different from that found in *The Prelude*. In *The Prelude* Wordsworth was able to use the notion of incarnation—in its full, noneconomic, contradictory nature—as an actively implemented rhetoric rather than as a fully articulated theory, but in *The Excursion* he attempted to present that rhetoric as an implicitly economic, representable theory.[2] *The Excursion* provides us with both an account of what I have been calling the rhetoric of incarnation and a demonstration of the problems that arise when incarnation—a concept inherently opposed to the notion of an isolable, implicitly representational "theory"—becomes precisely a theory to be expounded by an eloquent spokesman such as the Wanderer.

At this point I have collected a number of roughly equivalent variants of the opposition between "incarnational" and "representational" thought. Before going any further, I would like to summarize these oppositions; for the purposes of this chapter, I will use the general designations of "theory" and "incarnation" to name the two sides. The relationship between the two sides is far from simple, and the equivalences are only approximate. Under the idea of "theory" I include:

1. A binary system of representational signs, expressed for Wordsworth in the negative idea of language as clothing for thought, and in the

eighteenth-century tradition of language as a set of arbitrary tools, means toward the representation of an object or concept. This is the limited, instrumental use of language to which Gadamer opposes hermeneutics by saying, "signs... are a means to an end. They are put to use as one desires and then laid aside" (*Philosophical Hermeneutics* 87).[3]

2. A mode of knowing, based ultimately on the natural sciences as they developed in the seventeenth century, that sees epistemology as separate from ethics in the claim that we can "know" something in a way that is not dependent on a particular moral orientation.[4]

3. The related separation of a theoretical system from the narrated life-process of the individual articulating the system: the idea that the disengaged Lockean subject—what Taylor calls the "punctual self"—can produce a theory of knowledge that can stand on its own not, as in Plato, because it is a Truth that is ontologically prior to the modern subject/object split, but by virtue of its correspondence with objective universal laws that are empirically or rationally discoverable and able to be manipulated by detached subjects. This is what Coleridge envisioned Wordsworth as presenting when he said of the plan for *The Recluse* that "Wordsworth should assume the station of a man in repose, whose mind was made up, and so prepared to deliver upon authority a system of philosophy" (*Table Talk,* 21 July 1832, in *Collected Works* 14[part 1]:307). The man should be detached, in repose, and his mind should be "made up," and thus not dependent on a developing process of *Bildung,* as was his mind in *The Prelude.* This is part of what Levinas calls "totality" and "the said": the notion that both the world and human subjectivity can be understood as isolable conceptual themes separate from the concrete ethical interactions of real humans.

I hope the previous chapter has made clear in a practical sense what I mean by the "incarnational" side of things, but it may be useful for the present discussion to extract these general characteristics of "incarnational" thought as they are opposed to "theoretical" thought:

1. A mode of meaning in which language is not locked into a binary signifying relationship with thought, but is instead an "incarnation" of thought in Gadamer's sense that through language thought enters the world as historical event.

2. A "critical" mode of meaning in the sense that Jesus' historical incarnation is a demythologizing act, critiquing both earlier mythologies and the very possibility of a mythological relationship to the world. (I am using "mythological" in something like Hans Blumenberg's sense of myth as a construction built to compensate for our inability to adapt to the world.) Implicit in this view of Christianity is Girard's (as well as

many modern theologians') reading that Christianity reveals and confronts, rather than conceals and mythologizes, the violence inherent in our being in the world. If incarnation is thus a "critical" stance, it is natural that the incarnational rhetoric should, as we saw in the last chapter, rise out of a critique of the "theoretical" rhetoric of binary representation. This is also Levinas's view that the trace of the incarnate subject appears in the interruption of totality and the "said" by the infinity of the absolutely other in a "saying."

3. A stance that cannot separate epistemology from ethics—in fact, a stance that cannot think in terms of that opposition. To put it in Charles Taylor's terms, the self that articulates thought is not an autonomous agent that can detach itself from its systems of knowledge and thereby deny its moral dimension; that "self" is itself constituted by its moral orientation to the world, and thus its thought is always "affective," to use a favorite Wordsworthian term, and "knowing" is an irreducibly moral act.[5] An alternate description of this stance is provided by Stanley Cavell's notion, discussed earlier, of "acknowledgment" as that which supersedes "knowing." Just as Cavell sees acknowledgment as a recognition of the other in his/her disappearance and death, in a way that neither embraces nor denies epistemological skepticism, but that resituates the skeptical impulse in its ethical life-context, the incarnational impulse becomes a reinterpretation of rationality (as it rises out of the ashes of binary figures) that situates itself in an ethical relation to death and disappearance. For Levinas, this is the irreducibility of the incarnate subject's responsibility for the other: that ethical relationship precedes any possibility of a theorized autonomous subject, even the autonomous subject characterized as dialectical self-consciousness, and even though the incarnate subject appears only as a precisely unintelligible trace interrupting the totalized conceptual structures that "betray" incarnational subjectivity.

I present this very non-incarnational, "theoretical" characterization of the two poles for its heuristic value, rather than as a description of isolable elements within Wordsworth. The situation is complicated in *The Excursion* by the fact that we are presented with a "theory" of an "incarnational" way of thinking, and much of what I have to say in this chapter stems from Wordsworth's struggle with that paradoxical situation. Furthermore, this isolation of the two poles is something that in certain instances is very clear for the poet—as when he distinguishes "incarnation" from "dress" as an analogy for thought in the third "Essay Upon Epitaphs"—but it is a separation that is far from clear within the labyrinthine rhetoric of the poetry.

In Wordsworth's early poems, those who expound rational, representational theories are often targeted for critique. The rational "adult" interlocutors of "We Are Seven," "Anecdote for Fathers," and other poems always turn out to be bettered by the nonrational intuition of children.[6] It is too easy, however, to say that this turn in *The Excursion* toward the positive presentation of an adult theorist is an example of Wordsworth retreating from the imaginative intuitions of the early works to the dogmatism of the later ones. In a sense this *is* what happened, as critics have noticed since the poem first appeared, and the later revisions of both *The Prelude* and *The Excursion* certainly are more dogmatic and orthodox. Still, the situation of *The Excursion* is yet more complicated, beginning with the obvious fact that the first book dates from 1797. That it was conceived from the beginning as a "philosophical poem" (a term involving a complex and partly oppositional relationship among epistemology, rhetoric, and ethics) is the key to its success as well as its failure as an incarnational exposition.

The Prelude's solution to the tension between binary representation and incarnational thought, as I read the final books, is to use the rhetoric of incarnation to transform the very problems of a binary system of representation into a sustaining rhetoric that builds on the critical "turn" of incarnation. That is easily and appropriately done in a poem whose autobiographical nature makes it a fading of one system into another, ending with the fading of the very idea of system into the post-textual self. Precisely this process of successive figural destruction constitutes the process of *Bildung* presented in *The Prelude*. In *The Excursion*, however—Wordsworth's only extended attempt to engage in the exposition of "ideas" instead of the incorporation of ideas into the stream of written life—the problems are different, because the representation of ideas in binary figures is a necessity throughout the poem, and cannot simply take a tropological turn into incarnational rhetoric. In fact, from the "theoretical" perspective of *The Excursion*, the supersession of figures is an indication, not of the process by which an authentic life is developed, but of the secondary importance of philosophy. The Wanderer says of the denizen of Truth's "pleasure grounds" (4.588),

> If tired with systems, each in its degree
> Substantial, and all crumbling in their turn,
> Let him build systems of his own and smile
> At the fond work, demolished with a touch.
> (4.603–6)

Out of the context of autobiographical *Bildung*, the supersession of figural structures is mere solipsistic play, and not a series of events "all gratulant, if rightly understood" (*The Prelude* 13.385).

What this means is that, in *The Excursion*, the incarnational rhetoric of *The Prelude* is in a different kind of tension with the binary structure of a theoretical heritage with which Wordsworth was far from comfortable. This tension between the "representational" or "theoretical" on the one hand and the "incarnational" on the other gives the poem—to invoke a metaphor in the spirit of Wordsworth's own analogy between clothing and language as counter-spirit—a surface fabric that is tightly stretched over a body of violence, death, and sacrifice, so that by the end we will see exposed the violence that Hegel sensed in the problem of the Incarnation.

THE WANDERER AS INCARNATIONAL THEORIST

The conflict between incarnation and theory can be seen from the outset in the role of Wordsworth's chief theoretical spokesman in the poem, the Wanderer. The critique of subjectivity carried out by so much modern theory tends to make us overlook the fact that every theory demands a theorist. Even a brief glance at the celebrity status of modern literary theorists, especially those committed to a semiological starting point for their work, and the power exerted by their names and personalities, bears out Gadamer's point that the erection of a theory based on a system of signs (even if the theory undoes that structure) is a dominating move; the elision of subjectivity from the theory itself (or the reduction of subjectivity to a Nietzschean perspectivism) forces the problem of the subject to reappear on the level of theorist himself, as the powerful manipulator of those signs from whose network he in some sense has pretended to escape (even if that "escape" comes in seeing his subjective presence as inevitable and arbitrary). As Gadamer points out, particularly a theory of semiotic representation—the kind of theory Wordsworth called "counter-spirit"—dominates the object of investigation by placing it in a position of controllable otherness. This is true regardless of the status of the subject within the theory itself; it applies both to Enlightenment systems of representation, in which the subject was unabashedly in control, and more recent systems, in which the subject is supposedly decentered, absent, or historicized. Ever since Plato's *Craty-*

lus, says Gadamer, "the concept of the image (eikon) has been replaced by that of the sign (semeion or semainon)," leading to "the self-conquest of language by a system of artificial, unambiguously defined symbols," the "ideal of the eighteenth- and twentieth-century Enlightenments (*TM* 414). This ultimately scientific knowledge is knowledge for domination:

> The world of objects that science knows, and from which it derives its own objectivity, is one of the relativities embraced by language's relation to the world. In it the concept of "being-in-itself" acquires the character of a *determination of the will.* What exists in itself is independent of one's own willing and imagining. But in being known in its being-in-itself, it is put at one's disposal in the sense that one can reckon with it—i.e., use it for one's own purposes. (*TM* 450)

In the Enlightenment, when the modern notion of the self was being established instead of threatened, the subjectivity entailed by a disengaged reason—part of what I am calling "theory"—is even more evident. Charles Taylor points out that the rational objectification of the world that began with Descartes and found its fulfillment in Kant—the idea that the mind can disengage itself from the world and use reason instrumentally, as opposed to the older Platonic notion of reason as a substantive part of the world to be contemplated—also involves a radical subjectivization:

> The philosophy of disengagement and objectification has helped to create a picture of the human being, at its most extreme in certain forms of materialism, from which the last vestiges of subjectivity seem to have been expelled. It is a picture of the human being from a completely third-person perspective. The paradox is that this severe outlook is connected with, indeed, based on, according a central place to the first-person stance. Radical objectivity is only intelligible and accessible through radical subjectivity. (*Sources of the Self* 175–76)[7]

This detachment stems from a desire for control: "Instead of being swept along to error by the ordinary bent of our experience, we stand back from it, withdraw from it, reconstrue it objectively, and then learn to draw defensible conclusions from it.... We fix experience in order to deprive it of its power, a source of bewitchment and error" (163). The detached theorist is also Martha Nussbaum's male, Platonic, hunter-like agent who strives after self-sufficient reason, which she opposes to the androgynous, Aristotelian, plant-like agent who is receptive to luck and external contingency. In *The Fragility of Goodness* she describes the tension between "the aspiration to rational self-sufficiency... the aspiration to make the goodness of a good human life safe from luck through the controlling power of reason," and the force of "luck," or "a raw sense of the passivity of human beings and their humanity in the world of nature... the special beauty of the contingent and the mutable, that love for the riskiness and openness of empirical humanity" (3).[8]

One of the forms of philosophical writing that lies behind *The Excursion* is the philosophical dialogue, popularized by Shaftesbury, Dryden, Hume, and others in the eighteenth century. In "Conversation and Political Controversy" Timothy Dykstal argues convincingly that such skeptical writers, no longer able to ground their thought in absolute religious or rational authority, appealed to an ideal of disinterestedness that in fact masked political interest: "But these philosophers may also profess disinterestedness to obscure the political interests that they actually do have, much like (if in a more sophisticated manner) the disputatious dialogue writers that they often define their efforts against" (312). *The Excursion*'s relationship to this tradition is of course a complex combination of influence and reaction, and is beyond the scope of this study. It does seem important to note, however, that the tension Dykstal discusses between political interest and philosophical disinterestedness in the eighteenth-century dialogue reappears in a modified form in the Wanderer's paradoxical role as Wordsworth's incarnational theorist, caught between the interested engagement of incarnational subjectivity and the detachment of the theorist's "punctual self." According to Dykstal, the "retreat from consensus" in the eighteenth-century dialogue, much like the skepticism of postmodernists such as Rorty and Lyotard, had the effect of removing art and literature to the inner circle of cultural elite: "By dodging the need for consensus, they helped turn criticism into an activity for the like-minded few, rather than the 'interpreter' (Habermas's term) for the many that their own Enlightenment program seemed to promise" (315). Without necessarily accepting Dykstal's Habermasian position, I also argue that the problems of disguised interest and detachment from the ethical appear in both Enlightenment and postmodern "theory," and are brought into sharp relief by the Wanderer's position as a "theorist" whose job it is to critique just such deficiencies of theory.

The Wanderer's problem is that he is, on the one hand, a detached, controlling, post-Cartesian theorist, presenting a system of knowledge that should be mastered and presented as a complete epistemological system. On the other hand, that theory promotes an *incarnational* existence, a life that exists as a criticism of precisely the theoretical, representational, semiotic, detached stance of even the incarnational theorist, a life that does not master contingency in the manner of Nussbaum's "hunter" but embraces it in the rhetoric of incarnation. This emerges as a paradoxical combination of self-assertion and self-effacement; he states this succinctly as the ethical problem of how to combine virtuous selflessness with the self-assertion necessary to separate oneself from the world:

> how shall man unite
> With self-forgetting tenderness of heart
> An earth-despising dignity of soul?
> (*The Excursion* 5.576–78)

The Wanderer clearly presents himself as a dominating theorist: the Poet's contributions to the conversation are nearly always ancillary, and the Wanderer, despite his superficially carefree life, will accept no variations in the trip's itinerary, authoritatively generalizing on the evils of interruption:

> he, who intermits
> The appointed task and duties of the day,
> Untunes full oft the pleasures of the day.
> (2.147–49)

His complex statement at the end of book 4 is a subtle exploration of the incarnational relationship between epistemology and ethics that certainly carries much of the authority of the autobiographical voice. However, the problem of the theorist's authority manifests itself partly as precisely a *problem* of autobiography, since what is at stake in the dominating tendency of a theoretical voice is in fact the authority of the autobiographical voice: the extent to which the expounded theory becomes "my" theory, dominated by the personality and autobiography of the theorist. Of course, autobiographical authority works differently in "autobiographical" and "theoretical" works. In his autobiographical poem, Wordsworth's problem was how to incarnate a *Bildung* in the somewhat resistant text of a poem, giving appropriate authority to the variety of "selves" that needed to be incarnated. In *The Excursion,* the problem is how to present non-autobiographical (in the sense that they should be universally applicable, even if rooted in self-formation) ideas through a voice that will have the authority to be persuasive without adopting the dominating stance of the theorist manipulating a system, particularly in light of the fact that the rhetoric of incarnation is supposed to be an antidote to the dominance of putatively objective theory.

As part of his "incarnational" argument in book 4, the Wanderer argues vehemently against the abstractions of empirical representation: science should not be "chained to its object in brute slavery" (4.1256), but, subservient to the moral, should "watch / The processes of things, and serve the cause / Of order and distinctness" (4.1257–59). Instead of "viewing all objects unremittingly / In disconnection dead and spiritless" (4.961–62), we should *listen* to the universe with the "ear of Faith," hearing "authentic tidings of invisible things" as the child, committing an empirical "error" listens to a shell:

> I have seen
> A curious child, who dwelt upon a tract
> Of inland ground, applying to his ear
> The convolutions of a smooth-lipped shell;
> To which, in silence hushed, his very soul
> Listened intensely; and his countenance soon
> Brightened with joy, for from within were heard
> Murmurings, whereby the monitor expressed
> Mysterious union with its native sea.
> Even such a shell the universe itself
> Is to the ear of Faith; and there are times,
> I doubt not, when to you it doth impart
> Authentic tidings of invisible things.
> (4.1132–44)

Similarly, in a passage originally inspired by one of Dorothy's journal entries, the imaginative relation to nature suggested by the solitary raven is an access to that which beyond sight, achieved via the dying echo of the heard cry:

> The whispering air
> Sends inspiration from the shadowy heights,
> And blind recesses of the caverned rocks;
> . . . .
> Within the circuit of this fabric huge,
> One voice—the solitary raven, flying
> Athwart the concave of the dark blue dome,
> Unseen, perchance above all power of sight—

> An iron knell! with echoes from afar
> Faint—and still fainter—as the cry, with which
> The wanderer accompanies her flight
> Through the calm region, fades upon the ear,
> Diminishing by distance till it seemed
> To expire; yet from the abyss is caught again,
> And yet again recovered.
>
> (4.1170–87)

I pointed out in the first chapter how Wordsworth's incarnational thought reversed Augustine's priority of sight to hearing, and these passages in *The Excursion* show how hearing serves in the incarnation—rather than the representation—of meaning. Hearing is hermeneutically prior to sight, not, as Mary Jacobus has argued,[9] because it occasions an idealized representational "presence" of the kind Derrida critiques in Husserl, but rather because it gives access to a trans-subjective dialogue, which, as we saw in *The Prelude,* is an important part of Wordsworth's incarnational rhetoric. Hans-Georg Gadamer's discussion of hearing, part of his discussion of "belonging" (*Zugehörigkeit*) bears this out: the sense that "in genuine dialogue, something emerges that is contained in neither of the partners by himself":

> If we are trying to define the idea of belonging (*Zugehörigkeit*) as accurately as possible, we must take account of the particular dialectic implied in *hearing* (*hören*). It is not just that he who hears is also addressed, but also that he who is addressed must hear whether he wants to or not. When you look at something, you can also look away from it by looking in another direction, but you cannot "hear away." (*TM* 462)

Thus hearing "is an avenue to the whole" (462) because it involves a context—formulated in dialogue with God and nature—that is larger than and prior to subjectivity. Vision, by contrast, disparaged in "Tintern Abbey" as controlling an immature

> feeling and a love,
> That had no need of a remoter charm,
> By thought supplied, nor any interest
> Unborrowed from the eye,
>
> (80–83)

is reductive because it reduces the other to the same; it depends on a totalizing relationship established by light. As Levinas says,

> Vision is not a transcendence. It ascribes a signification by the *relation* it makes possible. It opens nothing that, beyond the same, would be absolutely other, that is, in itself.... Vision is essentially an adequation of exteriority with interiority: in it exteriority is reabsorbed in the contemplative soul and, as an *adequate idea*, revealed to be apriori, the result of a *Sinngebung*. (*TI* 191, 295)

The images of the child with his shell and the raven bear out this contrast. The child *hears* the sea, and meaning is incarnated much as it was for the Boy of Winander. Bypassing an epistemological theory that would call his experience an illusion, he is taken out of whatever subjectivity he has, and placed in the context of the invisible (but heard) sea, which (even in a literal geographical sense since Britain is what the Pastor calls in book 9 a "sea-girt isle" [9.683]) surrounds him. The communication with the "smooth-lipped" shell also approaches the status of a kiss, bearing out the incarnational notion that the interpretive relation to the world is like a relation to a human other.

The invisible echo of the raven comes from a place of blindness and shadows, and thus cannot be visualized. It is "caught" and "recovered" in a dialogue between the abyss and the ear, placing the hearer in a position of "belonging" to an existence that extends, through the radical difference that comprises an incarnational relationship, from the fathomless abyss to the physicality of the human ear. The unrepresentable bird is incarnated as a death-laden event: the sound "fades upon the ear" and "seemed / To expire." The "recovery" of the bird occurs, not through its presence, but, in keeping with the mortality of incarnated meaning, through the repeated echo of its very disappearance: the repetition of its apparent expiration becomes the incarnation of what is "above" our perception.

This priority of voice is not any kind of direct access to either a presence or an abyss. In fact, as Gadamer points out in a discussion of Christian hearing versus Greek ocularity, voice has nothing to do with self-presence: "The word is what one person speaks and another understands. How does presence play a role in this? Who listens at all to his or her own voice?" ("Letter to Dallmayr," in Michelfelder and Palmer, eds., *Dialogue and Deconstruction*, 95). The heard sea is mediated by the shell, and the raven's cry is mediated by the echoes. The important thing is not that hearing is a more direct representation of anything, but that the auditory experience is affective, incarnational, and trans-subjective, whereas the visual experience is representational, theoretical, and radically subjective in the sense demanded by radical objectivity. We choose what to look at; vision exerts the tyranny of the subjective eye upon the separate objective world. Hearing, on the other hand, chooses us, so we are taken up into a trans-subjective dialogue. Vision, like the divisions of the sundial, (which will be discussed below as an important image of moral law in *The Excursion*) tends to divide into parts, but hearing mediates between us and a whole. Vision is highly representational, but hearing is the realm of living, incarnational communication.[10]

These two passages contain all the richness of the incarnated, mortal living things that grounded the generation of meaning in *The Prelude*; however, all this incarnational advice is intended as a program of recuperation for the Solitary; thus, the Wanderer must package this, not as an exemplary gift entering a dialogue (the final figure of *The Prelude*), but in terms of forms and laws that apply equally to all, despite his disclaimer that there are "manifold and various" means of "restoration" (4.1112–13). This need for a detachable "theory" is implicit in the Wanderer's almost Kantian discussion of "forms":

> Duty exists;—immutably survive,
> For our support, the measures and the forms
> Which an abstract intelligence supplies;
> Whose kingdom is, where time and space are not.
> (4.73–76)

Later, the Wanderer explains how the incarnational relation to "the Forms / Of nature" (4.1208–9)—imaged in the relation to the raven and the shell—will provide a kind of detachable theory for a very epistemological, representational access to the recuperative spiritual beyond:

> And further; by contemplating these Forms
> In the relations which they bear to man,
> He shall discern, how, through the various means
> Which silently they yield, are multiplied
> The spiritual presences of absent things.
> (4.1230–34)

The Wanderer is thus torn between his need to provide a pseudo-Kantian formula of representational categories prior to personal and historical contingencies, and his demand for a content for that formula that is grounded in nonrepresentable, anti-epistemological, incarnational interpretive acts such as the hearing of the sea and the raven.

Wordsworth's careful situation of the Wanderer in relation to the autobiographical voice reflects his sensitivity to this paradox of authority in which the Wanderer must theorize about that which goes against the very notion of theory. In 1843, Wordsworth told Isabella Fenwick that "the character I have represented in [the Wanderer's] person is chiefly an idea of what I fancied my own character might have become in his circumstances. Nevertheless, much of what he says and does had an external existence that fell under my own youthful and subsequent observation" (*Poetical Works* 5.373). Here we see Wordsworth struggling with the tension between the autobiographical and the extra-autobiographical implications of the poem's chief theoretical spokesman. The Wanderer has some of the essential authority of Wordsworth, but "his circumstances" make him a very different kind of voice, one who, among other things, does not speak from the standpoint of a poetic ego carrying the added authority (and attendant problems) of authorship. As an *alternate* autobiographical possibility, he both carries and avoids the authority of the autobiographical voice. The objective status of his claims—the idea that they are not tied to a particular voice—is emphasized in the insistence that "what he says and does had an external existence." What is important here, it seems, is not that other people who did and said these things existed, but that the actions and ideas themselves had an existence independent of any person.

This interplay or ambiguity between the Wanderer as autobiographical voice and as the impersonal vehicle of ideas is precisely the problem of the Wordsworthian theorist: on one hand, his voice must have objective authority as the carrier of universal ideas, and thus that voice cannot simply emerge from the autobiographical self—either the ideas will not stand on their own outside of the context of the autobiographical voice, or if they are given an independent otherness, the semiotic will to domination described by Gadamer will come into play, and the theorist will become a dominating manipulator of signs, which is the kind of communication Wordsworth wants to avoid. On the other hand, the theoretical voice needs to be recognized as Wordsworth's, both because the ideas have an unavoidable relationship to a particular self oriented to the world in a particular way and because the theories present in *The Excursion*, though they are intended to be universal, are also indissolubly linked to exactly the kind of self-formation traced in *The Prelude*. The Wanderer must be a "punctual self," instrumentally manipulating independently sustained sign systems, while at the same time embodying an incarnational *Bildung* that denies exactly that kind of subject-object separation in favor of incarnational dialogue.[11]

The problem of the Wanderer as a theorist also reflects in a complex way the word's problematic status as both "sign" and "thing." This is especially complex because through this lens the problem of agency and domination is almost exactly the reverse of the theorist's problem as described above. As a theorist, presenting a representational, epistemological structure of ideas, the Wanderer must be not only an aggressive proponent of self-sufficient reason (Nussbaum's male, Platonic force), but also a passive "sign," effacing himself before the universal ideas he is presenting. He must assert himself on the *incarnational* side, not as a dominating theorist but as a living "thing," a concrete incarnation that can both speak and exemplify the ideas. Ethically, he must exhibit both "self-forgetting tenderness of heart" and "earth-despising dignity of soul"; he must allow his subjectivity to dissolve before universal moral existence, but he must also act as an exemplary moral agent. The rhetorical dimension of this is that the Wanderer must be both the transparent voice of the ideas, disappearing before them, and at the same time a powerful persuasive presence, pragmatically and by his personal example convincing the Solitary to change his ways. Just as Hegel struggled with the need for both determinate objectivity and spiritual purity in the Eucharist, Wordsworth's Wanderer is torn between self-effacement before pure theory and living existence as speaker and exemplum, while at the same time he is torn between the potential domination exerted by the theorist and the demythologizing, dialogical embracing of the materiality and contingency of language that we have seen as characteristic of incarnational rhetoric. He is thus unable to achieve easily the sacramental combination of representational efficacy and ethical force that we found in the exemplary figure of the Wordsworth-Coleridge pair at the end of *The Prelude.*

His role can be placed in a broader context if we look at how this problem is handled by two other important speakers: the poet's voice in the Prospectus, and the Pastor's voice, which takes over from the Wanderer much of the explanatory work in the last half of the poem. The Prospectus to *The Excursion* is a complex self-quotation—it is announced as taken from "the conclusion of the first book of *The Recluse*"— in which Wordsworth's own voice becomes a complex echo of Milton's. This voice, thus clearly distinguished from the Poet who is a rather ineffectual character in *The Excursion,* has the objectivity of a detached quotation, and is thus for the most part removed from the exigencies of the living, developing autobiographical voice of *The Prelude.* It gives clear priority to the "Vision" to be beheld over the man contemplating the vision, but reserves the right to treat of the man also, suggesting the poet's concern for both the "sign" and the "living thing":

> And if with this
> I mix more lowly matter; with the thing
> Contemplated, describe the Mind and Man
> Contemplating; and who, and what he was—
> The transitory Being that beheld
> This Vision; when and where, and how he lived;—
> Be not this labour useless.
>   (94–99)

Here the Miltonic humility before the necessary Muse is invoked in order to ground the relationship between the signified "Vision" and the incarnate man. This is of course a traditional solution to the problem of the poetic ego's relation to its poetic vision: "my" poem has its sources elsewhere, in a higher realm of authority, and thus the living presence of the poetic self is balanced with its effacement before the higher authority. Such a Miltonic solution is of course ultimately not possible for characters such as the Wanderer who must face head-on the problems of autobiographical utterance. For them, because the source for poetic authority (seen theologically or linguistically) is not simply transcendent, but resides on both the transcendental and the incarnate sides of the incarnational relation—or rather in the nonbinary passage from one to the other—the tension between "sign" and "living thing" cannot be resolved into such a balance.

The Pastor, who, like the poet of the Prospectus, stands outside and above the Wanderer's rhetorical problems in a number of ways, sheds a complementary light on the Prospectus-poet's role and provides another context within which the relationship between conceptual and personal authority is played out. The Pastor claims to able to dispense with any need for personal poetic authority because his ideas have an unshakable objective authority:

> —Life, death, eternity! momentous themes
> Are they—and might demand a seraph's tongue,
> Were they not equal to their own support;
> And therefore no incompetence of mine
> Could do them wrong.
>   (8.10–14)

His almost complete self-effacement before the transcendental side of the incarnation is suggested—with attendant rhetorical problems—as we meet him, when he appears as a timeless monument that interrupts the Poet's attempts at the difficult interpretation of the monuments in the Pastor's graveyard:

> 'These dim lines,
> What would they tell?' said I—but, from the task
> Of puzzling out that faded narrative,
> With whisper soft my venerable Friend
> Called me; and, looking down the darksome aisle,
> I saw the tenant of the lonely vale
> Standing apart; with curvèd arm reclined
> On the baptismal font; his pallid face
> Upturned, as if his mind were rapt, or lost
> In some abstraction;—gracefully he stood,
> The semblance bearing of a sculptured form
> That leans upon a monumental urn
> In peace, from morn to night, from year to year.
>   (5.205–17)

The Pastor provides the interpretive key to the "faded narratives" in the churchyard, often bypassing written texts altogether and going straight for spoken memory, pronouncing "Authentic epitaphs" (5.651), as requested by the Wanderer, on the dead who alone can be represented as complete forms, no longer in process: "with these / The future cannot contradict the past" (5.663–64), and "the transit" has been made "that shows / The very Soul, revealed as she departs" (5.666–67). With such an interpreter around, oral record is preferred to written:

> These Dalesmen trust
> The lingering gleam of their departed lives
> To oral record, and the silent heart;
> Depositories faithful and more kind
> Than fondest epitaph.
>   (6.610–14)

There is a price to be paid, however, for this role of pure signification assumed by the Pastor, this ability to bypass the materiality of the written sign in an effacement before pure meaning. In his introduction, he is standing apart, reclining on the baptismal font—literally supported by the receptacle that welcomes the living into the institution of the Church. By the end of the passage, however, after his "rapt" state of self-loss is observed, he looks as if he has been absorbed into a funerary monument, "the semblance bearing of a sculptured form / That leans upon a monumental urn." His ideal self-effacement into the process of interpretation—his nearly pure existence as a sign—means that insofar as he is a thing, his permanence is that of death: he must "die" into the universality he is able to signify. As in the passage on the silhouetted horse rejected from book 13 of *The Prelude*, and as suggested by the buried objects in book 5 of *The Prelude*, to become a sign is in one sense an escape from "living thingness," but it is an escape whose only route is the death upon which living thingness is grounded.[12]

The Pastor, of course, is not bothered by this. His detachment from the autobiographical problems implicit in the Wanderer's role, because it entails self-effacement before God, apparently does not bring up the problem of the detached theorist's subjective domination. He has, after all, purposefully withdrawn from a position of both political and academic power:

> The calm delights
> Of unambitious piety he chose,
> And learning's solid dignity; though born
> Of knightly race, nor wanting powerful friends.
> Hither, in prime of manhood, he withdrew
> From academic bowers.
> (5.110–15)

According to *Ecclesiastical Sonnets* 3.18, the "pastoral character" should consist in an extreme humility, which the authority of Christ can transform into extreme power:

> Though meek and patient as a sheathed sword;
> . . . .
> . . . can earth afford
> Such genuine state, pre-eminence so free,
> As when, arrayed in Christ's authority,
> He from the pulpit lifts his awful hand?
> (3.18.5–11)

Thus a pastor should be able to go straight from humility to divine power, bypassing the problems of human subjectivity.

The Pastor's detachment enables him to make the poem's most absolute statements about the accessibility of wisdom. His recognition of human limits and his desire for a transcendent perspective are well reflected in the balance of the almost Popean phrase, "we / Are that which we would contemplate from far" (5.490–91), and he admits that, given our general inability to follow Duty's law, moral truth is largely a matter of perspective:

> We safely may affirm that human life
> Is either fair and tempting, a soft scene
> Grateful to sight, refreshing to the soul,
> Or a forbidding tract of cheerless view;
> Even as the same is looked at, or approached.
> (5.526–30)

His narratives of the dead buried in his churchyard are presentations of just such varying perspectives. It is only his own unique and somewhat impossible position, one of self-effacement before the transcendental end of the incarnational process, that places these various perspectives within a theological whole, and prevents his perspectivism from becoming Nietzschean. Were he any more of a "living thing"—were he even as interested a party as the Wanderer is in Margaret's story—his would tend to be another perspective, instead of a transcendent ground for a multiplicity of perspectives.

The foregoing suggests, too simply, that the Pastor merely stands above the incarnational process. In fact, the conclusion to book 8 reveals just how carefully the Pastor can orchestrate a therapeutic program for the Solitary that is specifically incarnational rather than representational. The Solitary feels better, not because of any concepts represented to him, but because of the give-and-take of conversation itself:

> While question rose
> And answer flowed, the fetters of reserve
> Dropping from every mind, the Solitary
> Resumed the manners of his happier days.
> (8.524–27)

His attempt to provide a representational context, to *represent* the Pastor's life beginning with the words, " 'A blessed lot is yours!' " (8.542), is interrupted by the *event* of the two boys rushing in. The boys present in their being and language a combination of diversity and unity that cannot ever be resolved: one is compared to "a bold brook that splits for better speed" (8.578) and the other to "the still lake" (8.582), and they are from different social classes. They present as the content of their narrative the catch of trout,

> And, verily, the silent creatures made
> A splendid sight, together thus exposed;
> Dead, but not sullied or deformed by death,
> That seemed to pity what he could not spare.
> (8.568–71)

Solace is provided by the event (not the representational content) of a dialogue that is interrupted by diverse, nontotalizable life, a life that carries with it a kernel of death. In a converse image of our first view of the Pastor, in which his monumental permanence concealed a relation to death, here we have fish that are obviously dead, but which achieve a kind of "unsullied" permanence as a memorial to the life of the young, fully incarnate anglers.

Interruption, which, as we have seen, is an important component of incarnational rhetoric, characterizes both this scene and its context. The boys' entrance interrupts the Solitary's sentence, and the party's movement into the Pastor's house—an event of human interaction, not of representational concepts—was an interruption of the discourse on children: in the middle of the argument, "the Vicar interposed / With invitation urgently renewed" (8.439–40). We are reminded of this context of interruption at the end of book 8, when the Wanderer's sight of the real children (as opposed to the abstract children in the interrupted discussion) leads his mind to return "Upon this impulse, to the theme— erewhile / abruptly broken off" (8.591–92). As in the disruption of figural structures in *The Prelude,* meaning arises within a context in which conceptual *structures* are interrupted by incarnational *events.*

The book ends with the Pastor's prayer, delivered from the full transcendence of his unique position

> as One
> Who from truth's central point serenely views
> The compass of his argument.
> (8.598–600)

However, we appropriately do not hear the "clear and steady tone" (8.601) of this transcendent prayer. It is literally beyond the bounds of the poetic text, suggesting that what we see of the Pastor's transcendent role provides a kind of Kantian boundary between the incarnate phenomenal and the transcendent noumenal, positing a necessary realm beyond our incarnate existence, but restricting our business to the earthly side of this boundary.[13] His self-effacement before the transcendental side of the incarnational process gives him an "objectivity" even above that of the detached theorist (he does not seem to have or need even a "punctual" self), but his very transcendence also demonstrates the strict limits to human authority.

We have seen that within *The Excursion* the Wanderer, the Pastor, and the church all participate in various ways in the process of incarnational thought. If we step back and look at the poet's relation to the text, the tension between the authority of the poet and the authority of the incarnational "theory" remains at issue, and helps to explain the Wanderer's role as the poem's chief theoretical spokesperson. The tension implicit in this role is clearly at stake when Wordsworth writes in the Preface to *The Excursion,*

> It is not the Author's intention formally to announce a system: it was more animating to him to proceed in a different course; and if he shall succeed in conveying to the mind clear thoughts, lively images, and strong feelings, the Reader will have no difficulty in extracting the system for himself. (*PrW* 3:6)

What Wordsworth *is* announcing in the above passage is suspended precisely between the autobiographical and the objective, as he intends to "convey" thoughts, images, and feelings that seem to be objectively transferable, though his reasons for that, if we pursue the implications of his images, are grounded in an autobiographical desire for self-animation. Wordsworth transfers to the reader the responsibility for creating the system that he is *not* announcing.[14] That transference also happens to the Poet in *The Excursion*; he becomes, as Frances Ferguson has noted, a "reader" of the Wanderer (who is himself a reader not a poet) rather than a poet to be read (*Language as Counter-Spirit* 204–5). This "readerly" exposition of the ideas on both levels is one way of circumventing the power of the theorist and thereby empowering the reader, and it has serious implications for how meaning is to work in the poem.

As Thomas Weiskel has pointed out, the difference between the "reader's sublime" and the "poet's sublime" is that the former presents an excess of word and an underdetermination of meaning, whereas the latter presents an excess of meaning and an underdetermination of the word (The Romantic Sublime 29–32). Without accepting Weiskel's semiotic premises wholeheartedly, we can find that insight useful here. To translate Weiskel's terms into my own, the "readerly" orientation operates from the perspective of the incarnated word to be interpreted—as event in history, as living thing—and its access to meaning is restricted by boundaries such as that thrown up by the Pastor. The poetic or "writerly" perspective operates from the divine/thought side of the incarnational relationship, the side of "meaning," the side in which meaning is excessive and the problem is not accessing it but rather incarnating it. At the end of *The Prelude*, we saw the poet problematically adopting that "divine" poet's perspective, a move justified only by the impending exit into the post-textual self, and in book 8 of *The Excursion* we saw the Pastor positing such a transcendental position but recognizing its inaccessibility. For a "theoretical" work such as *The Excursion*, such a "writerly" perspective would be unbearably dominating, precisely because it could not be a transient figure open to its own supersession, but would instead have to be a consistent theoretical voice exercising a very non-incarnational authority over its theoretical material.[15] The Pastor is the only one qualified to do this, but, unlike the poet soaring for a moment like a lark over his own text at the end of *The Prelude*, the Pastor's very transcendence becomes a reminder of the impossibility of transcendence.

Perhaps this is why the Wanderer, not the Pastor, must be *The Excursion*'s main theoretical spokesman. By positioning the Wanderer firmly on the earthly, readerly side of the incarnational relationship, Wordsworth makes it less likely that his spokesman will be seen as a dominating, writerly theorist, as he increases the potential compatibility between the Wanderer's incarnational and theoretical roles. The Wanderer's authority within the poem itself is as divided as Wordsworth's relation to him. The Poet's deference to the Wanderer's views grants him a monological authority, but the presence of the Solitary as a questioning voice grants the sense of dialogical development of ideas that was so important in the incarnational rhetoric at the end of *The Prelude*.[16] In accordance with the Socratic model that Wordsworth is following there is a combination of authoritative assertion and dialogue in this man who is "like a Being made / Of many Beings" (1.430–31). Socrates and the Wanderer always win, but the "winning" ideas emerge from the back-and-forth play of conversation, not from a linear series of propositions.

The Wanderer's ambiguous position is related to his role as an exponent of "excursive" power. In a key passage from book 4, the Wanderer calls for science to be properly understood as

> a support
> Not treacherous, to the mind's *excursive* power.
> —So build we up the Being that we are.
>   (4.1262–64)

The world outside the mind has a corresponding excursive power:

> Whate'er exists hath properties that spread
> Beyond itself, communicating good,
> A simple blessing, or with evil mixed.
>   (9.10–12)

This poem is an "excursion" both by title and by idea. An excursion, in the tourist sense, involves "a journey, expedition, or ramble from one's home, or from any place with the intention of returning to it" (*OED*), but the emphasis is on the act of moving outward from a point of origin, and crossing the boundaries of that point: "progression beyond fixed limits," in Samuel Johnson's succinct definition (quoted in *OED*). *The Prelude* also opens with an excursive gesture: "Now I am free, enfranchised and at large, / May fix my habitation where I will" (1.9–10). The movement there, however, is ultimately a move toward rather than away from a center; there will be a fix[ed] habitation, and it appears a few lines later:

> I made a choice
> Of one sweet vale whither my steps should turn,
> And saw, methought, the very house and fields
> Present before my eyes.
>   (1.81–84)[17]

Though in the famous "Imagination" passage in book 6 the imaginative "home" is specifically excursive—"Our destiny, our nature, and our home, / Is with infinitude, and only there" (6.538–39)—*The Prelude* maintains a "homing" teleology in which all excursions lead back to the post-textual dialogue with Coleridge, as we saw in the previous chapter. *The Excursion* establishes a contrary outward orientation not just because it "was designed to refer more to passing events, and to an existing state of things" (*Poetical Works* 5.2), but also because, in stepping out of autobiography, Wordsworth makes the risky move of framing ideas that do not begin and end in the kind of self-consciousness built up in *The Prelude*. The "*excursive* power" helps in "build[ing] . . . up the Being that we are," but it is an outward, public *Bildung* that is at stake, not one that ends in self-consciousness.

Though removed from the autobiographical context of *The Prelude*, this excursive power is clearly incarnational. Almost as if to anticipate a Derridean critique, the Poet makes it clear that the excursive power of the Wanderer's own speech is not dissemination, but an emanation and a gift from a *gebildet* life that gains its life in the poet's own life:

> The Words he uttered shall not pass away
> Dispersed, like music that the wind takes up
> By snatches, and lets fall, to be forgotten;
> No—they sank into me, the bounteous gift
> Of one whom time and nature had made wise.
> (4.1284–88)

Proceeding according to the logic of the gift rather than the logic of economic exchange, the Wanderer's words are an emanation without loss that achieves incarnate reality in the Poet, not a dispersal and fragmentation of meaning. Again we see the efficacy of the Poet's role as reader; he is able to interpret as a believer. Wordsworth is able to justify the Wanderer's language by appealing to the Calvinist doctrine of the mutual guarantee between language and faith:

> The word has not much certainty with us, unless confirmed by the testimony of the Spirit, for the Lord hath established a kind of mutual connection between the certainty of reverence for the word, when by the light of the Spirit, we are enabled therein to behold the Divine countenance; and, on the other hand, without the least fear of mistake, we gladly receive the Spirit, when we recognize him in his image, that is, in the word. (John Calvin, *Institutes of the Christian Religion*, 1.ix, quoted in John Dillenberger and Claude Welch, *Protestant Christianity*, 46)

As the Poet sees it, the Wanderer's language achieves incarnation when his words interact with the "spirit" infused in the Poet, according to this "mutual connection." Neither word nor spirit can be isolated as poles of a binary system; rather, the infusion of Spirit provides a hermeneutic link, which grants the word an incarnate life as it is "read" by the poet.[18] Thus the Wanderer both presents a doctrine of excursiveness and embodies an excursive quality that enables his language to be read incarnationally.

The Wanderer's own role as an outsider is significant both for his role as the manifestation of an excursive incarnational rhetoric and for his problematic status as the poem's incarnational theorist. His excursive homelessness is cited as an affective advantage, because it paradoxically gives him both autonomy and sympathy:

> in himself
> Happy, and quiet in his cheerfulness,
> He had no painful pressure from within
> That made him turn aside from wretchedness
> With coward fears. He could *afford* to suffer
> With those whom he saw suffer.
> (1.366–71)

As in his rhetorical autobiographical status, his narrated life combines a strong selfhood and an excursive going-out in which, in an almost Keatsian way, the self disappears into the affective object. In this way he can combine "self-forgetting tenderness of heart" with "earth-despising dignity of soul." The problematic relation between signs and things is expressed on both levels. As I noted above, the autobiographical persona needs both to efface itself before the ideas to be presented, in line with a sign's goal, and persist as a "living thing" both to guarantee the ideas and, for Wordsworth, to incarnate them in a living process of *Bildung*. Similarly, in his narrative incarnation the Wanderer is both an autonomous living thing and an excursive being that disappears into others, and his ability to be one depends on his ability to be the other. For example, his very status as an itinerant without a domesticity of his own gives him a sympathetic entrance into the domesticity of others:

> we took our seats
> By many a cottage-hearth, where he received
> The welcome of an Inmate from afar.
> (2.58–60)

He gains a special place as an "Inmate" precisely as he is "from afar."

His homelessness in space is matched by his temporal status as an anachronism. Having failed as a teacher, he takes up the work of a pedlar, of which the poet says, "their hard service, deemed debasing now, / Gained merited respect in simpler times" (1.327–28). The Wanderer himself takes up this theme at the end of book 7 when he compares himself to the similarly anachronistic Knight:

> I too shall be doomed
> To outlive the kindly use and fair esteem
> Of the poor calling which my youth embraced
> With no unworthy prospect.
> (7.1047–50)

As important as this is for the theme of social change developed in book 8, it also reinforces the Wanderer's status as a voice that is outside of, and in a sense usurped by, the progression of events. We sense here Wordsworth's recognition of the tragic potential of the theoretical voice. As Charles Taylor points out, the disengaged theoretical position that develops out of Deism entails the suppression of history: in theological terms, God's role as the providential founder of a logically interlocking system is incompatible with his direct intervention in history; hence Deism's heightening of the Protestant suspicion of miracles.[19] Wordsworth, with the strong sense of history entailed by his incarnational rhetoric, approaches this from the opposite direction. The gap between the objective theorist and historical life is potentially tragic, not because history is marginalized, but because the theorist is marginalized to the extent that he is usurped by history. History, not theory, is the stronger force, and that is why the situation is one of current events usurping the Wanderer, rather than one of those events being usurped by his objective position.[20]

The very tragedy of this usurpation, is, however, part of the Wanderer's incarnational status, not surprising if we see the incarnational as arising from the decay or interruption of the theoretical. As Levinas points out, the incarnational subject is always anachronistic, because out of step with a totalizable present, and thereby open to the ascendancy of the other:

> In the form of an ego, anachronously *delayed* behind its present moment, and unable to recuperate this delay—that is, in the form of an ego unable to conceive what is "touching it," the ascendancy of the other is exercised on the same to the point of interrupting it, leaving it speechless. (*OTB* 101)

Although the Wanderer is never left "speechless," his anachronistic status and consequent usurpation by history is an indication that his theoretical objectivity is constantly threatened by the irreducible fact of his incarnate subjectivity, constituted precisely by such usurpation. In part because he has outlived his calling and has thus been usurped by history, he has the unique narrative status that the poem's rhetoric seems to need. This historical self-effacement—the sense in which his anachronistic status prevents him from having his own historical identity—matches his homelessness as a quality that enables him to fade sympathetically into the lives of others, or, in Levinas's terms, take a selfless responsibility for others. Thus, in both time and space this displaced sense of self, though it makes him an "outsider," gives him a special kind of critical but sympathetic "inside" role. This combination of self-persistence and self-effacement gives the Wanderer an immanent but critical status very much in line with the Incarnation itself—Jesus entered the world but was also critically positioned against it—and the analogous situation of the word's dual status as self-effacing sign and living thing. Like the similarly anachronistic minstrel, "protected from the sword of war / By virtue of that sacred instrument / His harp" (2.13–15), the Wanderer's dual status both protects him and allows him to speak.

This ability of the Wanderer to straddle the incarnational fence between silent spirit and incarnated word, both effacing himself and presenting himself, is something no poet, tied to the "sad incompetence of human speech" can have. The barrier and bridge of text, which prevents the poet from either full self-effacement or full self-expression as it constitutes his connection both to the spirit inside and the world outside, is a mediating force that the Wanderer seems to be able to do without. He does read—primarily urtexts such as the Bible and Milton—but his reading is based on a nonlinguistic communion:

> No thanks he breathed, he proffered no request;
> Rapt into still communion that transcends
> The imperfect offices of prayer and praise,
> His mind was a thanksgiving to the power
> That made him; it was blessedness and love!
> (1.214–18)

Though in this state "thought was not" (213), this "still communion" is no immature, ocular, unthinking union with nature described in this passage from "Tintern Abbey":

> The sounding cataract
> Haunted me like a passion: the tall rock,
> The mountain, and the deep and gloomy wood,
> Their colours and their forms, were then to me
> An appetite: a feeling and a love,

> That had no need of a remoter charm,
> By thought supplied, or any interest
> Unborrowed from the eye.
>   (77–84)

The autobiographical writing in such poems as "Tintern Abbey" and *The Prelude* shows the poet moving from this stage through an engagement with mediating forces such as texts to a more mature affective relationship, whereas the Wanderer goes directly to the stage of supralinguistic communion. Perhaps this is what allows him to make his tale a transparent presentation of Margaret's plight:

> He had rehearsed
> Her homely tale with such familiar power,
> With such an active countenance, an eye
> So busy, that the things of which he spake
> Seemed present.
>   (1.614–18)

The direct physical power of "countenance" and "eye" take precedence over language, but this is much more than "appetite," and rather than being a prelinguistic stage, it *enables* the very language in which he speaks.

Earlier I claimed that the Pastor can do without texts, and now I make a similar claim for the Wanderer. In order to understand "text" as a mediating force that a working poet needs and that the Wanderer does not, we must look at textuality in Gadamer's terms rather than Derrida's. From a Derridean point of view, to say that the Wanderer does without text makes no sense, and it would take only the most superficial deconstructive analysis to show that the Wanderer's language is firmly embedded in the textuality from which it appears to escape. My point makes sense only if we consider "text" in Gadamer's more limited definition. For Gadamer, text, whether spoken or written, "is not to be viewed as an end product the production of which is the object of an analysis whose intent is to explain the mechanism that allows language as such to function at all," but is rather "a mere intermediate product [*Zwischenprodukt*], a phase in the event of understanding that, as such, certainly includes a definite abstraction, namely, the isolation and reification involved in this very phase" ("Text and Interpretation," in Michelfelder and Palmer, eds., *Dialogue and Deconstruction*, 31). The appeal to this reified text is something that occurs primarily when interpretation becomes problematic:

One can almost say that if one needs to reach back to the wording of the text, that is, to the text as such, then this must always be motivated by something unusual having arisen in the situation of understanding. (33)

For a poetic autobiography, of course, that "something unusual" is there from the start; hence *The Prelude*'s struggle with various forms of autobiographical textuality.[21] *The Excursion* experiments with a speaker whose circumstances and peculiar relation to poetry give him what Gadamer would call a more authentic hermeneutic situation—for him, texts, including Milton and the Bible, are intermediary steps in a supratextual process of understanding.

The Poet in *The Excursion* is, as we have seen, more of a reader than a poet. One interesting result of this role is that he is able to translate the Wanderer's communion into what is precisely a *reversal* of the incarnational process. Relieved of the responsibility for incarnating thought (that's the Wanderer's job), the Poet can remember exclaiming,

> Oh! what a joy it were, in vigorous health,
> To have a body (this our vital frame
> With shrinking sensibility endued,
> And all the nice regards of flesh and blood)
> And to the elements surrender it
> As if it were a spirit!
> (4.508–13)

This same movement from flesh to spirit is of course a commonplace in Wordsworth, from the lines, "we are laid asleep / In body, and become a living soul" ("Tintern Abbey" 46–47), to this passage from the 1826 "Composed When a Probability Existed of Our Being Obliged to Quit Rydal Mount as a Residence":

> So, in moods
> Of thought pervaded by supernal grace,
> Is the firm base of ordinary sense
> Supplanted, and the residues of flesh
> Are linked with spirit; shallow life is lost
> In being; to the idealizing soul,
> Time wears the colors of Eternity,
> And Nature deepens into Nature's God.
> (63–70)[22]

The "idealizing soul," however, is not the working poet who bears the burden of the translation from spirit to event, thought to language, and the Wanderer—despite his own supralinguistic communion with the sources of his existence—takes the above-quoted "strain of transport" (541) from the Poet and reduces it to youthful desires that fade into a "noble restlessness" (548), appropriately translating the feeling into the more earthbound strains of his own excursive character. As the Wanderer notes in a different but related context, the real problem is not leaving the earthly but rather making the incarnational link: engaging in a dialogue with the eternal from the perspective of the earthly:

> 'Tis, by comparison, an easy task
> Earth to despise; but, to converse with heaven—
> This is not easy:—to relinquish all
> We have, or hope, of happiness and joy,
> And stand in freedom loosened from this world,
> I deem not arduous; but must needs confess
> That 'tis a thing impossible to frame
> Conceptions equal to the soul's desires.
> (4.130–37)

We see from the foregoing that the Wanderer has two potentially conflicting sides, one that allows him to escape the snares of textual mediation by basing his language on an unmediated communion with his origins, and one that presents an "excursive" character tying him to the earthly, readerly side of the divine/human relation. Thus his freedom from textual mediation is carefully balanced by a refusal to idealize. This double status of the Wanderer complicates the above distinction between the Gadamerian and the Derridean view of textuality, a complication implicit in Gadamer's discussion of the distinctiveness of poetic texts. For Gadamer, the authority of a poetic text differs in kind from that of other texts. It is not simply a midpoint on the route toward meaning. It is self-originating and does not, like other texts, point back to an originary speaking "behind" it:

> The literary text is text in the most special sense, text in the highest degree, precisely because it does not point back to some primordial or originary act of linguistic utterance but rather in its own right prescribes all repetitions and acts of speaking. ("Text and Interpretation," in Michelfelder and Palmer, eds., *Dialogue and Deconstruction*, 42)

That is, the poetic text does not efface itself before some utterance that it is conveying, but lives and as an originary thing itself prescribes the conditions for its own interpretation. Again, this self-origination is part of what Wordsworth and Coleridge mean when they talk about words being living things. The speaker of a poetic text must efface himself before the text, as the Wanderer seems to be able to do with Margaret's story; Gadamer says "the ideal speaker will not make him- or herself but only the text present" ("Text and Interpretation" 47).

The problem is that *The Excursion* itself—as well as many of the texts within it—is both kinds of text: on one hand, it is an intermediate text, which, like a sign, is supposed to efface itself before the system the reader should be able to extract from it. On the other hand, it is a poetic text, which, like a living thing, lives its own life, into which the reader must enter in order for the originary text to speak. The Wanderer manifests this duality in his status as both a self-effacing champion of unmediated communion and an authoritative, anti-idealizing earthly presence. This duality intersects (somewhat obliquely) with his dual role as detached theorist and a manifestation of incarnational excursiveness. In the former role he exerts a "punctual" subjectivity, but also presents a system, like that of the intermediate text, of supposedly universally transparent, and thus self-effacing signs. In the latter role the theorist's detachment is gone, but the living thingness of the Wanderer as incarnate man is foregrounded, and he resembles the self-originating poetic text.

This is one more version of the problem Hegel saw in the Eucharist: how can Jesus and the Host both disappear into the Spirit from which they emanate and maintain a necessary objective existence? How can *The Excursion* or the Wanderer's language both disappear into a signified theory and maintain an existence as a living thing? The simple answer, of course, is that neither can really do either; much of the interest of *The Excursion* lies in what is revealed in the conflict between these two different relationships of language to experience.

"ROMISH PHANTASY" AND THE ANGLICAN MIDDLE WAY

Language is not the only incarnational institution called on to perform a complex dual role in *The Excursion*. The institution of the church has a similar role, an examination of which will reveal what happens when Wordsworth's incarnational thought is read back into the religious context from whence it came, a context itself informed by an incarnational mediation between the theological and the institutional.

We saw above that the Pastor functioned as an enforcer of the boundary between the transcendental and the earthly. His sense of the need for such boundaries in the face of a feared infinity informs his explanation of the church: lest "Man's affections" be "betrayed and lost / And swallowed up' mid deserts infinite," "our wise / Forefathers... embodied and established these high truths / In solemn institutions," establishing a "channel" to concentrate and preserve those affections in a kind of ecclesiastical irrigation ditch so that they will not perish in the infinite desert (5.996–1007). Institutional limits are vitally necessary because for us mortals the infinite is not transcendence but death. This separation between finite and infinite is counterbalanced by the united force of love, which allows "life" to be both a divine and a human concept: "Life, I repeat, is energy of love / Divine or human" (5.1012–13).[23] A closer look at exactly how the institution of the church functions in *The Excursion* will show how this institution set up to protect us from the infinite while allowing us to partake in the energy of divine and human love participates in the poetic rhetoric of incarnation. As we saw in the first chapter, the idea of a spiritual institution, situated between pure subjective "love" and institutional, objective "religion," which Hegel considered paradoxical, brings up the problems central to incarnation's attempt to mediate between spirit and event, and thus between thought and language.

The relationship between the church as an inessential human institution, fundamentally different from our relation to God, and as the expression of God himself is of course tied up in the relationship between radical Protestantism and Catholicism, between which Anglicanism has always steered a careful middle course. Wordsworth's devotion to orthodox Anglicanism has been seen by many critics to increase as his poetic powers decreased. I am not about to argue the reverse, but I would like to claim that Anglicanism, which, after all, had been an important part of Wordsworth's intellectual and spiritual background all along, is not in itself to be blamed for any decrease in his poetic power. In fact, Anglicanism's middle course, as well as its self-definition in terms of history as well as in terms of theology, makes it an appropriate background to Wordsworth's incarnational rhetoric, which, as we have seen, depends on a historically mediated, nonrepresentational dialogue between what "theory" would see as incompatible positions. It can be argued that Anglicanism's middle ground between Catholicism and Evangelicalism can uniquely support rhetorical and even theological heterodoxy. As Dillenberger and Welch point out concerning the *Book of Common Prayer,* even such a fundamental point as the Real Presence in the Eucharist is stated ambivalently:

> The *Book of Common Prayer*... reflects the tendency to combine much of the ancient tradition of the church with some of the Reformation insights. Sometimes, the two aspects lie side by side, as in the following sentence from the communion service: "The body of our Lord Jesus Christ, which was given for thee, preserve thy body and soul unto everlasting life. Take and eat this in remembrance that Christ died for thee, and feed on him in thy heart by faith, with thanksgiving." Nothing less than the genuine presence of Christ in the elements is combined with the Zwinglian concept of remembrance. (*Protestant Christianity* 71–72)

In book 4, the Solitary accuses the Wanderer of abandoning his iconoclastic Calvinist heritage and heading for "Romish phantasy" (4.908) with his praise of the concretely incarnated and multiple Greek deities. It is true that this attempt to see God both as a transcendence and a concrete historical manifestation has a distinctively Catholic air.[24] Interpreted in the best light, this combination demonstrates the flexibility of incarnational rhetoric: the attempt to maintain the link between spirit and event, thought and language, as an interactive historical process, rather than as a simple unity or difference. As the Catholic ethicist Charles Curran states the relationship:

> There is no doubt that the "and" has traditionally characterized Catholic self-understanding—Scripture and tradition, faith and reason, divine and human, grace and nature, Jesus and the Church, Mary and the Saints. In my perspective it is precisely the Catholic "and" which is very satisfying.... At its best, the acceptance of Scripture and tradition recognizes that the word and work of God must be heard and done in the light of the historical and cultural circumstances of the given time and place. The word and work of God must become incarnate in present reality. (*Faithful Dissent* 76)

To these pairs of terms we would of course add "thought" and "language," between which Wordsworth sees just such an incarnational link by which Spirit can be connected to—though not subsumed under or identified with—historical contingency. Wordsworth's own qualified praise of the Virgin Mary in the *Ecclesiastical Sonnets* is stated precisely in terms of the incarnational link between "celestial" and "terrene":

> Yet some, I ween,
> Not unforgiven the suppliant knee might bend,
> As to a visible Power, in which did blend
> All that was mixed and reconciled in Thee
> Of mother's love with maiden purity,
> Of high with low, celestial with terrene.
> *(Ecclesiastical Sonnets* 2.25.10–14)

Nevertheless, "Romish phantasy" is also, from the perspective of the Wanderer and the Solitary, both of whom were raised in the Calvinist tradition, a misuse of representation in its assumption that the link between divine and human is simply and systematically expressible in permanent symbols, which can become dangerously misleading idols, worshipped for their own sake. Wordsworth's negotiation of a compromise between these two extremes is a very practical theological example of the problem of things and signs. The radical Protestant extreme, represented by the Wanderer's upbringing (which, of course has been tempered by contact with the natural world) deemphasizes the materiality of words and symbols so that a relationship of pure signification can exist between man and God. The Solitary thus contrasts the Wanderer's tendency toward "Romish phantasy" with

> those godly men
> Who swept from Scotland, in a flame of zeal,
> Shrine, altar, image, and the massy piles
> That harboured them.
> (4.897–900)

Perhaps it is this background which assists the Wanderer in his unmediated contact with nature, his ability to be "rapt into still communion that transcends" (1.215), even though that contact with nature in fact leads him away from an immaterial relation to transcendence toward one that emphasizes the importance of the objective world. At the other extreme is the Catholic emphasis on the church as an incarnation of God's spirit on earth—the Mystical Body of Christ incarnated in an institution. This extreme values the "living thing" end of the sign/thing continuum to such an extent that, for Wordsworth the Anglican, the transcendental link is lost in the acquisition of temporal power by Rome, in "monastic voluptuousness," and the other abuses detailed in the *Ecclesiastical Sonnets*. From this perspective, the soul must be

> freed from the bonds of Sense,
> And to her God restored by evidence
> of things not seen.
> (*Ecclesiastical Sonnets* 2.30.2–4)

The Anglican compromise between the extremes of Catholicism and radical Protestantism—"In doctrine and communion they have sought / Firmly between the two extremes to steer" (*Ecclesiastical Sonnets* 2.40.10–11)—is compatible with Wordsworth's incarnational rhetoric because it takes into account both the transcendental origin and the earthly incarnation in such a flexible way. By not resolving the question in favor of one extreme or the other, Wordsworth opens up a wide space between words as signs that efface themselves before a transcendent God and as "living things" that partake of mortal life. Furthermore, Wordsworth's Anglicanism defines itself within a history that is both continuous and discontinuous: the historical break with Rome is balanced by a felt continuity with the early Church. Wordsworth's tempered praise for monastic life and even the Virgin Mary in the *Ecclesiastical Sonnets* as he tells his version of Anglican history bears this out. This is exactly the kind of history implicit in the notion of the Incarnation itself, with Jesus as both the fulfillment and the abrogation of Jewish law, and, as we saw in *The Prelude*, the history of the self is an incarnational continuity built out of figures that are critiqued and superseded. The Anglican concentration on historical event rather than systematic theology—borne out in both the Pastor's narratives and the focus on ecclesiastical history in Wordsworth's sonnet sequence—makes it a natural faith within which to side with incarnation rather than theory.

Wordsworth's most explicit allegorization of the relationship between signs and image-things in their Catholic and Protestant contexts is *The White Doe of Rylestone*. Though Wordsworth's pride in this poem stemmed from the apotheosis effected by the doe, the banner is the poem's controlling image. The blameless, Protestant Emily makes, against her will, a banner depicting the Cross, which Norton, her father, will carry into battle at the head of the Catholic uprising. Norton wrongly places his faith in the efficacy of that image, treating it as a thing that will effect victory. He misunderstands its representational function as a sign signifying the cross and his own political intentions, and he ignores its intentional source in the daughter who opposes his campaign. Francis, the son who also opposes the father's cause, carries the banner away from the battle at his father's dying request. He is recognized because he carries the banner, and is killed. Though he doesn't share his father's faith in the efficacy of the banner as an image or thing, the banner *is* tragically efficacious as a representational sign. Since to Francis's pursuers it represents the father's ambitions, it causes the son to be recognized and killed.

The story is ultimately a warning against the Catholic misappropriation of images and an argument for a post-Reformation alliance with self-effacing signs, paralleling the Protestant substitution of representational text for venerated image-thing. Wordsworth himself pointed out in an 1816 letter that in this poem "objects (the Banner, for instance) derive their influence not from properties inherent in them, not from what they are actually in themselves, but from such as are bestowed upon them by the minds of those who are conversant with or affected by those objects" (*Letters* 3.2.276). This is certainly in line with the Protestant denial of the independent efficacy of images. Still, the situation is a little more complicated than that. At the moment of Francis's death, when the banner's representational function has had its tragic effect, we suddenly move out of the realm of representation into the realm of living things. One of his assailants seizes the banner from him,

> But not before the warm life-blood
> Had tinged more deeply, as it flowed,
> The wounds the broidered Banner showed,
> Thy fatal work, O Maiden, innocent as good!
> (*White Doe* 132n)

According to these lines, revised several times between 1815 and 1845 (this is the final version), the banner is no longer a sign of the Catholic uprising, but a real-life mingling of the blood of Francis with the blood of Christ that is depicted on the banner. The 1836 version makes the identification even more graphic, as Francis's blood tinges "the embroidered show / Of His whose side was pierced upon the Rood!" (132n). It is as if the very tragedy of *representation* resulting from the banner's *mistaken* status as a thing that could act rather than simply represent (Norton's faith that the banner would guarantee victory) produces a new kind of nonrepresentational thingness. This new thingness is specifically incarnational, depending on the mortal mingling of blood between the Incarnation and the incarnate man. It also partakes of the Hegelian problem of the tension between the self-effacing signifying capacity of the object, suggested by the banner as a sign of Christ rather than a thing on its own, and its necessary living thingness, suggested by the mingling of blood. It is also another complication of the formula opposing incarnation and counter-spirit in the "Essays Upon Epitaphs": representational language, like the coat of Nessus, though it begins as a mere piece of clothing, results in a violent interaction. And though the essay distinguishes it from incarnational language, the language of counter-spirit reveals a powerful materiality in the apparently transparent sign—mere clothing becomes a thing that can kill—that is linked to the materiality of language as incarnation. (This idea will be explored further in the discussion of violence in *The Excursion.*) Thus, though this poem exposes what the Solitary in *The Excursion* calls the "Romish phantasy" of faith in things, it also points out how the tragedy of the history leading from Catholic "thing" to Protestant "sign" is expressed, not through the system of representation toward which that history putatively leads, but through a reinsertion of incarnational thingness (though a negative version of this thingness) that arises out of the *event* of that historical process of one kind of meaning superseding another.

In *The Excursion,* churches function differently depending on whether they are viewed abstractly as institutions or concretely as memorials to specific human acts of worship. Seen from a distance, the most important church in *The Excursion* is described with images of protectiveness that provide a social and political analogue to the Pastor's statement about the church as a moral and theological protection. The church not only protects man from the "deserts infinite," in which his affections would otherwise be swallowed, but also protects itself from the theological extremes detailed above, all the while protecting the integrity of England. Thus the first view of the Pastor's vale presents "a grey church-tower, / Whose battlements were screened by tufted trees" (5.80–81), a church both fortified and hidden. The opening of book 6 calls for a prayer for the English church and State,

> That, mutually protected and sustained
> They may endure as long as the sea surrounds
> This favoured Land, or sunshine warms her soil.
> (6.14–16)

The church needs better clergy for its defense against attacks:

> as on earth it is the doom of truth
> To be perpetually attacked by foes
> Open or covert, be that priesthood still,
> For her defence, replenished with a band
> Of strenuous champions, in scholastic arts
> Thoroughly disciplined.
> (6.53–58)

Looking at these descriptions together, we see that the church is fortified and protected as a locus of truth and political power as well as spirituality. On this explicit level, Wordsworth sidesteps the church's incarnational role as an objective manifestation—incarnation—of the spiritual. He is of course orthodoxly Anglican in thus avoiding a direct link between God and the Church in the Catholic manner; the Church is much more of a social and political than a spiritual institution, and thus its objectivity is securely contained within the "earthly" side of the incarnational relation.

Churches, however, become deeply involved in the whole of the rhetoric of incarnation when they are described in their personal and human contexts, and not simply viewed from the distance—whether the geographical distance from which the Pastor's church is seen or the distance of abstraction from which the institution of the church as viewed at the beginning of book 6—as institutions that protect and are worth protecting. The detailed description of the Pastor's church (based on St. Oswald's in Grasmere) blends the natural, the ecclesiastical, the moral, and the historical in a way that reflects the incarnation's translation of spiritual essence into historical event.

> Not raised in nice proportions was the pile,
> But large and massy; for duration built;
> With pillars crowded, and the roof upheld
> By naked rafters intricately crossed,
> Like leafless underboughs, in some thick wood,
> All withered by the depth of shade above.
> Admonitory texts inscribed the walls,
> Each, in its ornamental scroll, enclosed;
> Each also crowned with wingèd heads—a pair
> Of rudely-painted Cherubim. The floor
> Of nave and aisle, in unpretending guise,
> Was occupied by oaken benches ranged
> In seemly rows; the chancel only showed
> Some vain distinctions, marks of earthly state
> By immemorial privilege allowed;
> Though with the Encincture's special sanctity
> But ill according. An heraldic shield,
> Varying its tincture with the changeful light,
> Imbued the altar window; fixed aloft
> A faded hatchment hung, and one by time
> Yet undiscoloured. A capacious pew

> Of sculptured oak stood here, with drapery lined;
> And marble monuments were here displayed
> Thronging the walls; and on the floor beneath
> Sepulchral stones appeared, with emblems graven
> And foot-worn epitaphs, and some with small
> And shining effigies of brass inlaid.
>
> (5.144–70)

This description is in part an argument for ecclesiastical humility before the historicity of human worship: the few "vain distinctions" are "with the Encincture's special sanctity / But ill according." This "special sanctity" is not an earthly representation of divine perfection, "raised in nice proportions," but is "large and massy; for duration built," an enduring and changeful historical record of very mortal efforts at worship. Instead of a binary system by which God is represented, we are given a discontinuous history of events that nonetheless speak to us of a definitively incarnational "sanctity." The fact that the chancery's marks of vanity, surrounded by the "encincture" of the rest of the church, are *part* of the church indicates the church's incarnational ability to incorporate otherness into itself even as that otherness is critiqued. The cherubim are "rudely painted" traces of poor human endeavor rather than representations of the divine. Even the relative permanence of familial heritage and death are marked by contingency and temporality: the identifying colors on the heraldic shield do not present a unified sign for the family, but vary "with the changeful light" and a faded hatchment is contrasted with a more recent, unfaded heraldic death-monument.

The outer limits of this space fade not into the transcendent, but into the withering darkness: the "naked rafters" look like "leafless underboughs, in some thick wood, / All withered by the depth of shade above." This passage echoes the very description of a pagan landscape that led to the Solitary's accusation of "Romish fantasy"; near the end of that description the Wanderer depicted

> Withered boughs grotesque,
> Stripped of their leaves and twigs by hoary age,
> From depth of shaggy covert peeping forth
> In the low vale, or on steep mountainside.
>
> (4.879–82)

The withered boughs in both scenes—withered by age in the pagan scene, by "depth of shade" in the church—suggest the affinity between pagan and Christian rites in that the intimations of immortality are in both cases seen only from the mortal obverse of that immortality; the incarnational experience is bounded by death and darkness, even as its transcendental origins are acknowledged. The edge of that experience is of course also a blending of the human into the natural; just as the human monuments in "Hart-Leap Well" gradually fade into nature, the manmade rafters fade into grotesque natural undergrowth. The first church we see in *The Excursion* is the "bleached remains / Of a small chapel" (2.813–14) in which the dying man is found, suggesting even more extremely how the institution of the church fades into natural processes, one of which is human mortality.

Wordsworth's own explicit theological position is notoriously ambiguous, combining a politically conservative but theologically uncertain Anglicanism (at least by 1813) that resented Catholic interference in Parliament,[25] combined with a sympathy for (and, through John Keble, an influence on) the Oxford Movement's return to ritual,[26] and early acquaintance with Nonconformist preachers. Still, we do know that for Wordsworth both religion and poetry demand the incarnational translation of spirit into thing: Wordsworth describes the "affinity ... between religion—whose element is infinitude, and whose ultimate trust is the supreme of things, submitting herself to circumscription, and reconciled to substitutions; and poetry—ethereal and transcendent, yet incapable to sustain her existence without sensuous incarnation" (*PrW* 3:65). As I noted above, the difference implied within this affinity—that poetry's transcendence depends on its sensuous incarnation, to which religion deigns to "submit"—explains why poetry is more problematic than religion for Wordsworth, but perhaps this difference also helps to explain the ambiguity of the role of ecclesiastical institutions in the poetry. In addition to the theological tension generated by the problematic status of the institution of the church, we must consider that Wordsworth is speaking from the position of the poet, for whom the "sensuous incarnation" is even more important than in religion. Thus the church in *The Excursion* is seen through the double vision of a theology submitting itself to the circumscription of our world, and a poetics for which, despite its theological connections, such worldly "circumscription" is fundamental.

MORALITY AND REPRESENTATION

One of the fundamental ways in which systems of signification and incarnated life are related in *The Excursion* revolves around the importance of moral law, and with this in mind we will return to the question of the relationship between ethics and epistemology. In general, the "ethical" for Wordsworth is on the side of the incarnational and opposed to the representational; that is how I read the turn from epistemology to ethics in the Lucy poems. In Chapter 2, I spoke to how the living, mortal materiality of language entails a translation of epistemological knowledge into ethical relationship: the turn from "knowing" Lucy to recognizing "the difference to me." *The Excursion*'s explicit concern with moral philosophy and particularly moral law, as well as its entanglement in the rhetorical problems just discussed, provides us with another context in which we can see the relationship between epistemology and ethics. The concept of law, like the need for "theory" and the institution of the Church, is an overt presence in *The Excursion*, which complicates Wordsworth's incarnational thought in ways unimaginable in *The Prelude*.

In the background to my use of the term "ethical" are several theories that help situate ethics in relation to the concept of law. One is Charles Taylor's notion of an ethical orientation as an essential ground for self-knowledge: "To know who you are is to be oriented in moral space, a space in which questions arise about what is good or bad, what is worth doing and what not, what has meaning and importance to you and what is trivial and secondary" (*Sources of the Self* 28). That this moral space is a space of *questioning* has important ethical and hermeneutical implications. For Gadamer, the question is fundamental to an open-ended, historically sensitive hermeneutics, because all "answers" or statements must be put back into the context of the particular, historically contingent, prejudicial questions they answer:

> The significance of questioning consists in revealing the questionability of what is questioned. It has to be brought into this state of indeterminacy, so that there is an equilibrium between pro and contra. The sense of every question is realized in passing through this state of indeterminacy, in which it becomes an open question.... Posing a question implies openness but also limitation. It implies the explicit establishing of presuppositions, in terms of which can be seen what still remains open. (*TM* 363)

This notion of indeterminacy is in accord with the historically flexible notion of law as an interaction between legislative rules and judicial interpretations that I discussed above in relation to the development of the incarnational rhetoric of *The Prelude*. The idea of the foundational nature of the question is radicalized in ethics by Charles Scott, who uses Heidegger (Gadamer's mentor) to call for an ethics of questioning: "In the question of ethics, the emphasis falls on a continuing process of thinking that diagnoses, criticizes, clarifies by means of questions, destructures the components of meaning and power that silently shape our lives together, and also questions the values and concepts that have rule-governing and axiomatic power in our culture" (*The Question of Ethics* 7). Wordsworth's incarnational ethics are much less wholeheartedly deconstructive; still, the notion of the ethical as operating within the space of the question and the epistemological as operating within the space of reified "answers" that have forgotten their origin in questions is related to the notion of the incarnational as a demythologizing, critical stance that has its essence in the "questioning" of the representational. Another important version of the idea that ethics is the arena of the nontotalizable is Levinas's contrast, developed in *Totality and Infinity*, between "infinity"—the ethical realm of alterity, experienced in the face of the Other with whom we converse—and "totality": that which can be philosophically possessed, totalized into a closed system to be viewed from the outside. Cavell's distinction between knowledge and acknowledgment also remains useful here: the notion that skepticism is not an epistemological problem but rather a fundamentally ethical relationship to the world in its otherness, and that we need to see our knowledge of the world in the context of an *ac*knowledgment of an other person.

The opposition between an open-ended arena of ethical questioning and a closed space of epistemological answers is something like the double sense of ethical thought that Martha Nussbaum identifies in *The Fragility of Goodness:* the tension between self-sufficient reason and "luck." In seeing Greek ethical thought in both terms, Nussbaum is attempting to counter the influence of Kant, for whom "there is one domain of value, the domain of moral value, that is altogether immune to the assaults of luck" (4). This is particularly important for my purposes, because the tension Nussbaum discusses between Platonic-Kantian rational self-sufficiency and Aristotelian acknowledgment of contingency parallels in many ways *The Excursion*'s tension between "theory" and "incarnation," and will help to illuminate the relation between ethics and law. In an area even closer to the problems of the ethical dimensions of aesthetic experience, Charles Altieri argues that the concrete intentionality embodied in the experience of works of art can ground an "expressivist ethics" that is not dependent on universal categories:

> Where expressivist aesthetics sets itself against mimetic theories, expressivist ethics depends on contrasts to any rationalist model of values—be it deontological or consequentialist. Value is not

derived from a universal schema or principle but relies on how persons configure individual identities. (*Canons and Consequences* 241)

Wordsworth's incarnational thought attempts to reaffirm the role of the contingent in ethics by building up a moral life through the process of *Bildung* I discussed in the previous chapter, by seeing meaning—moral significance as well as epistemological signification—as tied to incarnational word as living event or contingent "thing" in history, rather than as representational sign within a figural system. This was Wordsworth's own reaction to the Kantian reification of rational self-sufficiency (though his direct targets were Hartley and Godwin); the final books of *The Prelude*, for example, show a contingency-conscious moral life being built out of the ruins of systematic attempts at rational or figural self-sufficiency. As Altieri formulates this process, an "expressivist ethics" "will have to put some concept of *Bildung* in the place of appeals to truth or to beauty" (241).

Despite the great differences among these thinkers, they all share with *The Excursion* the sense of a tension and interdependence between totalizing epistemological systems and ethical relationships that, because of their immersion in life's contingency, cannot be so totalized, but are in fact more fundamental than such systems. They are responding to a crisis in twentieth-century thought that has resulted from the progressive separation, since the Enlightenment, of ethics from epistemology. As David Hiley succinctly puts it, "Our problem in the twentieth century is that we have inherited the Enlightenment conception of the connection between the growth of knowledge and the improvement of ourselves and society, as well as the Enlightenment conceptions of reason, autonomy, and hope for ourselves and the future, yet we have rejected the metaphysical structure and teleological conception of history that made the Enlightenment view plausible" (*Philosophy in Question* 63). Wordsworth's fragmentary "Essay on Morals" complains, very much in the spirit of this area of thought, that moral philosophy is not very good at dealing with the nontotalizable contingency of human existence:

> You will at least have a glimpse of my meaning when I observe that our attention ought principally to be fixed upon that part of our conduct & actions which is the result of our habits. In a [?strict] sense all our actions are the result of our habits.... Now, I know of no book or system of moral philosophy written with sufficient power to melt into our affections, to incorporate itself

with the blood and vital juices of our minds, & thence to have any influence worth our notice in forming those habits of which I am speaking. (*PrW* 1:103)

This inadequacy of rational system to the force of custom can be translated into a simple Burkean conservatism, but it can also be read as a skeptical insistence on the priority of nontotalizable contingent life to epistemological systems, in the spirit of incarnational thought's emphasis on history and event.[27] By contrast with this sought-for ethics that will accommodate the living, contingent "blood and vital juices of our minds" (a reference to the concrete physicality of ethical subjectivity that sounds almost like Levinas), a Kantian moral law depends not only on universal applicability, but also on freedom from all empirical contingency:

> The ground of obligation here must not be sought in the nature of man or in the circumstances in which he is placed but apriori solely in the concepts of pure reason, and . . . every precept which rests on principles of mere experience, even a precept which is in certain respects universal, so far as it leans in the least on empirical grounds . . . may be called a practical rule but never a moral law. (Immanuel Kant, *Foundations of the Metaphysics of Morals*, 5)

Despite this contrast between "Wordsworthian" and "Kantian" ethics, both an incarnational, nontotalizable ethics and a Kantian (and Christian) sense of a universal moral law operate at a fundamental level of Wordsworth's argument. Though Wordsworth's 1798 essay on morals is more vehemently antisystematic than the later *Excursion*, the tension between the two views of ethics is still very much a part of the later work.

In its broadest terms, the problem of ethics in *The Excursion* is the problem of the role of epistemology in moral theology, or how one thinks of the human, ethical implications of theology—from faith to works—within or near the epistemological problems of "knowing" God through a system of representation, how, in the Wanderer's words,

> sense is made
> subservient to moral purposes,
> Auxiliar to divine,
> (4.1247–49)

whereas those *moral* purposes—expressed as the "law of conscience"—are also the earthly *representation* of God, "God's most intimate presence in the soul, / And His most perfect image in the world" (4.224–27). This combination of an ethical and an epistemological relation to God is of course a problem that goes back to Paul, Augustine, and the continuously uneasy relationship between Greek rationality and Hebrew faith that has characterized Christianity. The tension between faith and reason becomes much more intense with the Enlightenment's redefinition of reason as binary, representational epistemology, and its consequent separation from an explicit sense of ethics.

In linguistic terms, this tension is partly the incompatibility that Lyotard finds in Kant and Levinas between prescription and denotation. Kant's categorical imperative attempted (somewhat unsuccessfully, according to Lyotard) to reduce the prescriptive to a denotative norm. The paradox Lyotard finds in Levinas is that in order to feel the ethical force of an order or law, one must be the passive, nonconceptualizing addressee of a command, but one *understands* an order or a law by becoming an addressor using a denotative metalanguage, transforming the command into a representational statement of a norm. Lyotard expresses the resulting paradoxical position of the commentator on the work of Levinas who must attempt to "understand" Levinas in a denotative metalanguage: "If he understands it, he must not understand it, and if he does not understand it, then he understands it" ("Levinas' Logic" 304). The problem is that "the simplest prescription, instructively empty but pragmatically affirmative, at one stroke situates the one to whom it is addressed outside the universe of knowledge" (308), because the totalizing conceptualization of denotative knowledge is incompatible with the full acceptance of the other's alterity demanded by a prescription. The Wanderer, in negotiating between the denotative theoretical aspect of moral law (law as representing God) and the incarnational, prescriptive aspect (law as God's command) is faced with this paradox, which is not simply a linguistic problem but an even more complex element, both in Wordsworth's thought and in his inherited theological tradition, than Lyotard's paradox suggests.

The ethical life in general, usually expressed in this poem in terms of "conscience" and "duty," has two somewhat contradictory roles, whose incommensurability is a good index of the strange relationship between epistemology and ethics in *The Excursion*. First and most obvious, the ethical is seen as an alternative to the representational—a different and better standard of truth. Second, however, the ethical is seen as united from the start with epistemological representation: the ethical is not an alternative to representation so much as it is the *ground* of representation. (Already we see that the problem is more complicated than Lyotard's concern about the irreducibility of one category to the other.) The Wanderer suggests both relationships in the following passage, a commentary on the Pastor's venture into a carefully grounded perspectivism:

> 'We see, then, as we feel,' the Wanderer thus
> With a complacent animation spake,
> 'And in your judgment, Sir! the mind's repose
> On evidence is not to be ensured
> By act of naked reason. Moral truth
> Is no mechanic structure, built by rule;
> And which, once built, retains a steadfast shape
> And undisturbed proportions; but a thing
> Subject, you deem, to vital accidents;
> And, like the water-lily, lives and thrives,
> Whose root is fixed in stable earth, whose head
> Floats on the tossing waves.'
> (5.558–69)

On the one hand, this is a sharp distinction between the objective permanence of the "mechanic structure[s]" produced by "naked reason" and the more valuable but unrepresentable moral truth, which, like the water lily, is a "thing" (as words are living things) that can be firmly though invisibly grounded while tossing in the living waves and "vital accidents" of individual difference and historical contingency. This distinction suggests, of course, the incarnational combination of divine grounding and human contingency, and the impenetrable materiality of a *thing* in the world, which, like Hegel's leftovers, cannot be completely taken up into a system. A significant, if tenuous, connection to the Christian incarnation may be provided by the fact that this ethical, incarnational side of the picture, presented in the religious context of this conversation with the Pastor, is illustrated by the water lily, an aquatic cousin, at least in name, of a standard symbol of resurrection.

On the other hand, "we see . . . as we feel": ethical feeling is the *ground*, not the antithesis of representational, visual thought. This foundational aspect of the ethical is made even clearer when the Wanderer asks,

> But how acquire
> The inward principle that gives effect
> To outward argument . . . ?
> (5.571–73)

The fact that the nonrepresentable (the lily's fixed root is of course under water and unseen) is thus represented allegorically is exactly the paradox engaged by the strange connection between the representational and the incarnational: they are opposed, but if representation is also grounded in the ethical, then binary, epistemological representation is our only route back to the ethical and incarnational, at least for a "theorist" like the Wanderer who, as we have seen, must present the incarnational rhetoric in a non-incarnational mode. This kind of paradoxical necessity is explained by Levinas as the combination of necessity and betrayal in the relationship between the incarnational, ethical "saying" and the conceptualized "said." The said is the betrayal of the saying, but it is also the only way in which the saying is thematized "as" this or that:

> The saying that states a said is in the sensibile the first 'activity' that sets up this as that.... [T]he said is not added on to a preexisting knowing, but is the most profound activity of knowing, its very symbolism.... That knowing be conceptual and symbolic is then not a makeshift of a thought which would be incapable of opening intuitively upon the things themselves. (*OTB* 62)

At the same time as we acknowledge the fundamentality of this process—the process by which, for the Wanderer, the representational is grounded in the incarnational—we must also acknowledge the conflict and betrayal in the fact that the totalized conceptualization of "theory" denies the infinite ethical dimension present in incarnational saying. Thus philosophy practiced by thinkers such as the Wanderer has the dual role of originating in an inevitable betrayal and then phenomenologically reducing or exposing that betrayal:

> Thematization is then inevitable, so that signification itself show [sic] itself, but does so in the sophism with which philosophy begins, in the betrayal which philosophy is called upon to reduce. This reduction always has to be attempted, because of the trace of sincerity which the words themselves bear and which they owe to saying as witness, even when the said dissimulates the saying in the correlation set up between the saying and the said. Saying always seeks to unsay that dissimulation, and this is its very veracity. (*OTB* 151–52)

It might be argued that for the Wanderer the "outward argument" grounded by the ethical sense is in fact quite different from the rationality to which the ethical sense is opposed. This position could be justified by teasing out the various strands of rationality that operate on both sides of this duality. For example, one could argue that the Wanderer, while opposing ethical principles to a post-Cartesian, semi-Godwinian mechanism (the "mechanic structure" built on "naked reason"), allows those same ethical principles to ground a "seeing" or "outward argument" that is oriented more toward the contingencies of sense-experience. Empirical grounds for refuting "naked reason" are invoked in the lines,

> ... the mind's repose
> On evidence is not to be ensured
> By act of naked reason.

That is to say, the foregoing examples of knowledge varying by experience provide empirical evidence against a purely rationalistic view. That, however, is a reduction of Wordsworth's insight to his inherited philosophical categories, and if we thus try to turn him into an Enlightenment philosopher, he will turn out to be as inconsistent and uninteresting as many readers of *The Excursion* have complained he is. For my purposes, the differences between the two kinds of epistemological thought are less interesting than their similarities: both are epistemological, representational, detached, fixed, and ocular, as opposed to the ethical side, which has incarnation's antirepresentational combination of fundamentality and contingency. Wordsworth argues in his fragmentary "Essay on Morals" that rational moralists such as William Paley and William Godwin suffer from

> an undue value set upon that faculty which we call reason. The whole secret of this juggler's trick lies (not in fitting words to things (which would be a noble employment) but) in fitting things to words—I have said that these bad and naked reasonings are impotent over our habits, they cannot form them; from the same cause they are equally powerless in regulating our judgments concerning the value of men and things. (*PrW* 1:103)

The chief difference for Wordsworth is not between rationalistic and empirical systems—he lumps Godwin's rationalism and Paley's "evidence" together—but between systems of language and the world of "things."[28] The primacy of the "thing" for Wordsworth is not the empiricist's employment of the thing as the ground for a system, but rather the existential primacy of the thing as that which cannot be systematized, that which prevents any epistemological system from grounding our understanding of the *event* of the thing, even if such systems are the only means by which brute facticity can be "said." Wordsworth's very inability or unwillingness to make fine distinctions between philosophical systems allows him to express the more fundamental—philosophically and poetically—distinction and relationship between epistemological systems in general and his own incarnational practice. The tension between incarnation and representation, ethics and epistemology, is a stronger force in Wordsworth than are distinctions among various epistemological doctrines.

Wordsworth's intention to ground thought—even scientific thought—in the affective sphere,[29] and to found a rhetoric based on the event of incarnation rather than a binary system of representation has a natural corollary in the idea that an adequate morality will compensate for an inadequate system of representation; in this sense the ethical and the representational are clearly opposed.[30] He seems implicitly to accept Kant's restriction of our access to the noumenal, and to agree that this restriction makes room for faith, but Wordsworth would not, of course, accept the argument for a rational ground for ethical judgment—the ethical and the rational are, in this first strand of thought, more radically opposed. In *The Excursion,* this notion of the ethical as an alternative to the rationally representational comes through with particular strength in that it is one of the few areas in which the Solitary and the Wanderer show some agreement. The Wanderer prefers soulful superstititon to soulless truth:

> Life's autumn past, I stand on winter's verge;
> And daily lose what I desire to keep;
> Yet rather would I instantly decline
> To the traditionary sympathies
> Of a most rustic ignorance, and take
> A fearful apprehension from the owl
> Or death-watch: and as readily rejoice,
> If two auspicious magpies crossed my way;—
> To this would rather bend than see and hear
> The repetitions wearisome of sense,
> Where soul is dead, and feeling hath no place;
> Where knowledge, ill-begun in cold remark
> On outward things, with formal inference ends;
> Or if the mind turned inward, she recoils
> At once—or, not recoiling, is perplexed—

> Lost in a gloom of uninspired research;
> Meanwhile, the heart within the heart, the seat
> Where peace and happy consciousness should dwell,
> On its own axis restlessly revolving,
> Seeks, yet can nowhere find, the light of truth.
> (4.611–30)

Even with the pressure of age's need to sustain the philosophic mind, a decline in the order of reason to a false epistemology is preferable to reasoning that begins with "cold remark / On outward things" and ends in "formal inference[s]," as long as that representationally false epistemology is rooted in human moral traditions. Epistemological "illusions," even if, as the Solitary will remark, they tend toward "papist" idolatry, can be "outward ministers / Of inward conscience" (4.836–37); theories of knowledge should serve the ethical, not the other way around. In telling the histories of various mythologies, the Wanderer gives credit to those whose "imaginative faculty was lord / Of observations natural" (4.707–8). Despite the Greeks' "gross fictions" (4.732), they possessed a spirit by which emanations and felt bonds exercised an authority over both philosophy and war:

> emanations were perceived; and acts
> Of immortality, in Nature's course,
> Exemplified by mysteries, that were felt
> As bonds, on grave philosopher imposed
> And armed warrior.
> (4.738–42)

Given the "excursive," outward orientation of the ethical/incarnational power, the relationship between inward and outward is particularly interesting in the Wanderer's recognition of the importance of "traditionary sympathies," because this passage shows just what happens when we try to ignore or subvert the inevitable priority of the ethical over the representational. In this situation "inward" turning does not lead to "the inward principle that gives effect / To outward argument"; instead it *isolates* the "heart within the heart," forcing it to rotate solipsistically "on its own axis" and preventing the excursive movement that would provide an authentic relationship between inside and outside. A little later, this solipsism is seen as the result of analytical thought itself. In dividing the world into parts, analysis reduces the world:

> And still dividing, and dividing still
> [We] break down all grandeur, still unsatisfied
> With the perverse attempt, while littleness
> May yet become more little.
>   (4.963–66)

Ultimately, this process reduces the universe to a mere mirror of our own solipsism,

> a mirror that reflects
> To proud Self-love her own intelligence;
> That one, poor, finite object, in the abyss
> Of infinite Being, twinkling restlessly!
>   (4.991–94)

Thus the problem with analytical thought ends as a problem of its misplaced and ultimately solipsistic faith in a system of representational signs: in attempting to encode the external universe by means of an analytical process, what we think is an increasingly accurate representation of the world becomes, through the reductive power of analysis, a mirror of the least admirable part of our ethical being: self-love. This connection between prideful solipsism and formal reason is familiar from the contemporary "Essay Supplementary to the Preface" of the 1815 edition of the *Poems,* in which Wordsworth criticizes readers who let their own ethical stance cloud their view of poetry:

> To these excesses, they, who from their professions ought to be the most guarded against them, are perhaps the most liable; I mean those sects whose religion, being from the calculating understanding, is cold and formal. For when Christianity, the religion of humility, is founded upon the proudest faculty of our nature, what can be expected but contradictions? (*PrW* 3:65)

Charles Taylor points out that the priority of the ethical over the epistemological is inevitable, because our notions of truth are inevitably grounded in our orientation (often unarticulated) toward an idea of the good. But as Enlightenment naturalism leads to classical utilitarianism, theories become "debarred by the ontology they accept from formulating and recognizing their own moral sources.... This means that the place of moral sources in this philosophy ... is strange" (*Sources of the Self* 338). Wordsworth's version of this insight seems to be that an epistemology which does not recognize moral sources, a refusal to make "sense ... / Subservient still to moral purposes" (4.1247–48), will end up mirroring the unarticulated ground of the impulse toward pure epistemology. That ground turns out to be "Self-love," manifested philosophically as solipsism. This is also another demonstration of Wordsworth's insight into the radical subjectivism that is a dangerous corollary to a radically objective or "theoretical" stance, and that runs counter to the "humility" of incarnational engagement, which he presents in his "Essay, Supplementary to the Preface" as characteristic of Christianity rightly viewed.

Though the Solitary does not share the Wanderer's faith that we can "live by Admiration, Hope, and Love" (4.763), his cynicism is the converse of the Wanderer's presentation of the ethical as an alternative to the representational, and thus between them we get a broad picture of this problem. His position stems from the negative side, of course; he is keenly sensitive to the inadequacy of binary representation and understands the force of

> The outward ritual and established forms
> With which communities of men invest
> These inward feelings.
> (5.312–14)

In discussing the discrepancy between rituals (such as baptism) and the life they express, he desires an escape from the illusoriness of such representational structures that posit a correspondence between inner and outer: "Far better not to move at all than move / By impulse sent from such illusive power" (5.321–22).

In general, the Solitary is cynical about both the ethical and the epistemological ramification's of the Kantian restriction of access to the noumenal. Why should the soul, he asks,

> quit the beaten track of life, and soar
> Far as she finds a yielding element
> In past or future; far as she can go
> Through time or space—if neither in the one,
> Nor in the other region, nor in aught
> That Fancy, dreaming o'er the map of things,
> Hath placed beyond these penetrable bounds,
> Words of assurance can be heard; if nowhere
> A habitation, for consummate good,

> Or for progressive virtue, by the search
> Can be attained,—a better sanctuary
> From doubt and sorrow, than the senseless grave?
> (3.213–24)

Even though we can posit a realm beyond the "penetrable bounds" of time and space ("that may by pure abstraction be conceived," according to a draft version of line 218), no ethical communication—"words of assurance"—with that realm is possible. The best sanctuary from epistemological "doubt" and ethical "sorrow" is the grave. Yet when the Poet wants to turn the Solitary's argument into one that styles philosophy a lesser poetry—"a dreamer of a kindred stock, / A dreamer yet more spiritless and dull" (3.339–40)—the Solitary counters with a pragmatic argument for the *moral* effect of philosophy:

> Slight, if you will, the *means*; but spare to slight
> The *end* of those, who did, by system, rank,
> As the prime object of a wise man's aim,
> Security from shock of accident,
> Release from fear; and cherished peaceful days
> For their own sakes, as mortal life's chief good,
> And only reasonable felicity.
> (3.360–66)

This pragmatic argument comes in part, of course, from the Voltaire he has been reading and to which the Wanderer will object as reductive. The Solitary would agree with Richard Rorty's assent to William James's preference for "what it is better for us to believe" over "the accurate representation of reality" (*Philosophy and the Mirror of Nature* 10) as the appropriate view of truth, whereas the Wanderer argues against representation on foundational rather than merely pragmatic grounds. However, the distinction that the Solitary makes between valuable moral ends and questionable philosophical means parallels in an important way the Wanderer's distinction between the ethical spirit of even erroneous philosophies and the reductiveness of analytic thought, even though the Solitary is arguing against those very same erroneous philosophies that the Wanderer is trying to protect. Despite their explicit disagreement, both admit the futility of the attempt to represent the world accurately, and both see, in different ways, the only value of thought as residing in its ethical effects.

The Wanderer's greater optimism resides not simply in his more positive evaluation of those ethical effects, but in his ability to negotiate an uneasy union of the representational and the ethical, which constitutes the second relationship between incarnated ethical life and systems of signification: the use of the moral law, not as an alternative to epistemological representation, but as the *ground* for systems of representation. As in the first view, the ethical is primary, but in this strand of thought the link between the ethical and the representational is more intimate. This view has clear sources in Kant's and Coleridge's arguments that morality should be the basis for a theological epistemology, rather than the other way around.[31] Wordsworth's version is presented most explicitly in the Wanderer's account of the relationship between God and duty. The theology is orthodox, but that orthodoxy presents a rhetorically heterodox combination of representational and ethical criteria:

> But, above all, the victory is most sure
> For him, who, seeking faith by virtue, strives
> To yield entire submission to the law
> Of conscience—conscience reverenced and obeyed,
> As God's most intimate presence in the soul,
> And His most perfect image in the world.
> (4.222–27)

Conscience is not only God's ethical presence in the world, but also God's represented "image in the world." This combination is in large part an Augustinian union of Jewish faith in God and Greek faith in Ideas: the *person* to whom we look for judgment becomes an *idea* that can function within a representational hierarchy. As Charles Taylor explains it, "Augustine gives us a Platonic understanding of the universe as an external realization of a rational order. Things should be understood ultimately as like signs, for they are external expressions of God's thoughts" (*Sources of the Self* 128). That is, the moral effect of God in the world can be translated into the rational signification of God in the world. This translation of effect into signification shows how Wordsworth's incarnational theory is not simply a reversal of the Enlightenment prioritizing of rational signification over ethical effect, but presents instead a more complex relationship between them. Above, we saw how the representational is subordinated to the ethical, but here we see that the representational and the ethical are joined at the source. For the Wanderer, the "law / Of conscience" is not only the "intimate presence" of God—the Protestant inner light—but is also the image of God in the world, functioning in *both* an ethical and a representational way, with the former grounding the latter.

The problems that arise when this "law / Of conscience" combines representational and ethical criteria are suggested by the image of the shepherd lad who has an internal ethical sundial that corresponds to the clock he carves into the turf:

> —The Shepherd-lad, that in the sunshine carves,
> On the green turf, a dial—to divide
> The silent hours; and who to that report
> Can portion out his pleasures, and adapt,
> Throughout a long and lonely summer's day
> His round of pastoral duties, is not left
> With less intelligence for *moral* things
> Of gravest import. Early he perceives,
> Within himself, a measure and a rule,
> Which to the sun of truth he can apply,
> That shines for him, and shines for all mankind.
> (4.800–810)

This is partly an answer to the Solitary's question of how error can be recognized by imagination if it cannot be recognized by reason:

> Is it well to trust
> Imagination's light when reason's fails,
> The unguarded taper where the guarded faints?
> (4.771–73)

It is exactly this assumption of the prior claim of reason's "guarded taper" that the Wanderer challenges by offering the tale of the shepherd lad, which places moral and rational sources into a complex relationship. The boy carves a dial into the turf in order to "divide / The silent hours" so that he can in turn "portion out his pleasure" and "adapt" his duties to that makeshift sundial's "report." This external sundial is then compared to the internal "moral" sundial, a standard of measurement to be applied to "the sun of truth," which shines on him in his solitude and on the rest of mankind.

The sun's light is historically a fundamental image for exactly the philosophical questions at stake here: it is an analogy for the Platonic idea of the Good as the source of knowledge and truth, easily connected to God as the source of light in the Gospel of John. As Taylor points out, Augustine joins these traditions, grounding a rational vision of cosmic order in the notion of a loving God:

> Augustine takes over the image of the sun, central to Plato's discussion of the Idea of the Good in the *Republic,* which both nourishes things in their being and gives the light to see them by; but now the ultimate principle of being and knowledge together is God. God is the source of light, and here is another junction point, linking up with the light in the first chapter of John's Gospel. (*Sources of the Self* 128)

For both Plato and John, the ethical is prior to the representational. It will not be until well after Descartes that an Enlightenment reversal of that relationship will be possible; however, once the tables are turned, the Christian source of the sun image as the origin of the light of love will help counter the representational vision of reality that descended from the Greek source of the sun image as the origin of illumination for accurate representation.[32] The sun is a complex metaphor of origin for Wordsworth, as we saw in book 10 of *The Prelude,* where the sun that rises as natural light sets as an artificial "gewgaw."

Here in *The Excursion* the image moves from the sun shining upon the earth, illuminating both the construction and the use of the man-made sundial, to the sun as the *object* of investigation ("the sun of truth"), to which the internal sundial will be applied as a standard. As is often the case in Wordsworth, the ambiguity of the analogy is precise. As the passage progresses, we are forced to turn from the ground on which the natural sun is shining to the sun—the source of the light for the first, external kind of measurement—which we then measure with our internal moral sundial. The gaze soon turns back to earth, as this internal sundial regulates the shepherd lad's daily life, but the image goes through a strange turn toward the sun on the way. On the surface, this metaphorical sundial seems to be an objectively constituted tool—an internal ethical clock—distributed to shepherd lads at an early age. The object to be "measured," however, "the sun of truth," is the same as the sundial's source of illumination, which means that the standard of measurement is in fact not independent of the object to be measured; the representational tool depends on the sun in order to function even as it "measures" the sun. The dual image of the sun as both functional illumination and truth to be ascertained via the process of measurement seems to confuse two different kinds of reason: the instrumental concept of reason derived from post-

Cartesian philosophy, by which reason becomes a tool manipulated by subjects, and the substantive, ethically grounded notion of reason in Plato, in which reason is not a tool, but a higher state, associated with the Good, to which we aspire (the aspect of Plato that was so easy for Augustine to combine with John).[33] There is an inherent conflict between the idea of a rational instrument for representation—the sundial—and the ethical "truth" suggested by the Platonic or Johannine "sun" as contemplated source of light.

Wordsworth, in presenting the former as a route to the latter, engages at the source the paradox entailed by joining Platonic-Christian moral sources and post-Enlightenment representational criteria. Put otherwise, the conflict between instrumental and substantive reason is a version of the tension between epistemological representation, which depends on an instrumental concept of reason (we represent the world by systematically applying representational tools to it) and representation based on moral sources (we represent the world as we do because of our moral orientation—"we see, then, as we feel"). To have a standard of measurement with which we can actually measure (and thus look at) the sun is the goal of the desired link between the ethical and the epistemological, but it requires us to combine the two incompatible types of reason: in order to have a moral standard that will really work as the foundation of representational standards, it needs to be something toward which we orient our whole selves even as it illuminates the process of representation. One must not simply look at a sundial on the ground—a secondary or tertiary level of truth—but must stare straight into the *source* of the Good (Plato) *or* God as light (John). This puts one in the paradoxical (and blinding) position of having to apply a standard of truth to the source of truth, the very source from which that standard comes.

To the extent that the criteria are two different standards, there is no problem: if we see the ethical (substantive) measure as simply prior to and different from the epistemological (instrumental) measure, then it makes sense that the internal, ethical measure be applied even to the source of epistemological truth, the "sun" of truth. Yet when we attempt to merge the two standards, so that God's ethical influence in the world is seen in epistemological, representational terms—when "conscience" becomes God's "most perfect image in the world"—the same sun-image must function both as the object to be measured by representational tools and the moral source by which that act of representation is grounded. In practical terms, our "conscience" is both the ethical grounding for our acts of representation and—as God's incarnated image in the world—a paradigm for representation itself. If Wordsworth were a true Platonist, this would not be paradoxical—a substantive notion of reason automatically grounds representation in orientation toward the Good; however, the concept of instrumental reason inherited from Descartes and developed by Locke and others into a system of arbitrary tool-like signs has attempted to jettison its moral sources, so there emerges a fundamental conflict between the pseudoscientific notion of the sun as an object to be measured by our internal sundials, and the sun as the moral source upon which representation must be grounded. In the first case it illuminates our tools so that we can see as we work; in the second case it is the source of those tools' ability to *do* their work.

The movement from external to internal sundial is also an attempt to escape from the solipsistic isolation that often results from external, instrumental reason (discussed above in relation to the Wanderer's preference for superstition to empty reason), to the communality entailed by a substantive notion of reason. The shepherd lad begins with the representational organizing of his "long and lonely summer's day," but when the analogy turns to the inner sundial that is both ethical and representational, he has access to a shared experience of "the sun of truth . . . / That shines for him, and shines for all mankind," a much wider experience of truth. The ethical sundial provides that larger context even though the "measure" and "rule" are "within himself." Again, we see Wordsworth negotiating the fine line between the tradition of subjectivity that he himself radicalized into what is now known as the Romantic self, and the equally forceful dangers of subjectivity: not only the dangerous *power* of the autonomous imagination, which Hartman demonstrated so clearly, but here particularly the solipsism to which "objective" thought can lead. The sundial image begins as the ultimately solipsistic application of a system of signs—the sundial organizes the boy's day—but when the context of the image is expanded to the realm of ethically grounded representation, that self is placed within a larger context, achieved by looking *inward.*[34]

The foundational nature of the Wanderer's moral imperative is best understood in terms of the notion of *law* as that which makes the problematic link between the ethical and the representational. Here again is the central passage on submission to the law of conscience, which is God's image in the world:

> But, above all, the victory is most sure
> For him, who, seeking faith by virtue, strives
> To yield entire submission to the law

> Of conscience—conscience reverenced and obeyed,
> As God's most intimate presence in the soul,
> And His most perfect image in the world.
> (4.222–27)

At issue here is the tension between the "law" as that to which one must submit—an ethical, performative, hortatory force with the power of poetry's living, material language—and the law as a system of representation by means of which we know God.[35] The earlier "Ode to Duty" poses a similar tension between Duty's hortatory function, personified as "stern Lawgiver," and the idea of Duty as God's image, "wear[ing]," and thus expressing his grace the way a smile represents a person's disposition:

> Stern Lawgiver! yet thou dost wear
> The Godhead's most benignant grace;
> Nor know we anything so fair
> As is the smile upon thy face.
> (49–52, in *Poems, in Two Volumes* 107)

The following statement by the Wanderer exhibits both views of law while demonstrating how incarnation precludes representation:

> The vast Frame
> Of social nature changes evermore
> Her organs and her members, with decay
> Restless, and restless generation, powers
> And functions dying and produced at need,—
> And by this law the mighty whole subsists:
> With an ascent and progress in the main;
> Yet oh! how disproportionate to the hopes
> And expectations of self-flattering minds!
> (7.999–1007)

There is an inevitable conflict between the spatialized "frame" of the "law" supporting the whole of social existence and the expectations of the concrete individual. One reason, however, for that disproportion is precisely the law's nonsystematic, incarnational flux of death and generation, which prevents us from representing it as a whole. This passage does not simply promote a Hegelian synthesis of contingent process and absolute wholeness, but rather the presence of both as a fundamental *aporia* in the concept of law itself, and as an indication of the inadequacy of those "self-flattering minds" who expect to totalize existence in representational systems.

That relation between the incarnational and the theoretical or representational view of law can be shifted to the question of the relation between systems of representation and moral sources. Because, as we have seen, *The Excursion* presents two different relationships between morality and representation (morality as an alternative to representation versus morality as the source of representation), and because of this poem's status as a problematically "theoretical" work, the question of law in *The Excursion* is more complex than in *The Prelude*, even though its theology is much more orthodox. Unlike *The Prelude*, *The Excursion* does not present the kind of autobiographical rhetoric that would enable an incarnational conception of law to emerge from the decay of a semiotic one. Furthermore, the Wanderer's role as a "theorist" *and* a Calvinist, at least in origin, makes the issue of law an explicit concern:

> The Scottish Church, both on himself and those
> With whom from childhood he grew up, had held
> The strong hand of her purity; and still
> Had watched him with an unrelenting eye.
> (1.397–400)

The Calvinist respect for Old Testament law seems to be an implicit part of the Wanderer's language.[36] The "strong hand" and "unrelenting eye" suggest both the restrictiveness and an ocularity (usually indicating representation rather than incarnation for Wordsworth) of a rigidly representational concept of law. Just as the Wanderer has a real stake in his role as purveyor of objective theory, he has an autobiographical investment in a concept of law more rigid than that of a middle-of-the-road Anglican. Thus the confrontation between the theoretical and the incarnational is in *The Excursion* a matter of constant tension, not to be resolved in *The Prelude*'s development of the latter out of the former.

The long-standing controversy over the role of law in Protestant Christianity intersects in an important but complex way with the role of law in *The Excursion*. The major theological question, of course, is the extent to which Christ fulfills or abrogates the Jewish law, and consequently what role the notion of law—as opposed to the infusion of the Christian spirit of love—should play in the life of a Christian. As William Lazareth explains it, the law was seen as having three uses:

> The first use of the law is to show persons their sin (*usus theologicus*); the second is to hold people in civil restraint (*usus civilus/politicus*); the third defines the validity of the law for the "regenerate" (so Melancthon and the *Formula of Concord*) or for "believers" (so Calvin). The third use is distinguished from the other two by the fact that it serves only to inform the regenerate or the believers, and hence the old dogmaticians called it the *usus didacticus.* ("Love and Law in Christian Life" 104)

Luther and Calvin agreed that law served a useful purpose for those who had not yet attained the status of righteousness as well as for civil order, but the controversy arose over the third use: the question of whether law served a purpose for those who already had access to the love of Christ, which had supplanted the Jewish law. According to Lazareth, Luther's response turned on a distinction between natural and Mosaic law: the Ten Commandments are to be obeyed, not because a concept of Mosaic law is in any way still operative, but because they summarize important principles of natural law: Insofar as

> the Christian remains sinful, he is bound only to that part of the Decalogue which coincides with the natural law (civil righteousness). Insofar as he is righteous, however, he is free from all law—Mosaic and natural alike—in the liberating power of God's grace (Christian righteousness). (108)

Calvin, on the other hand, sees the third, didactic use of the law as important for believers, both because "its instruction will bring Christians to a better understanding and confirmation of God's will" and because "its exhortation and mediation will excite Christians to obedience" (111).

Within the Luther-Calvin controversy, there is a tension between the function of law as a system of representation and its function as a command to action, the tension that Lyotard finds in Levinas. In general, both Luther and Calvin suggest that as the law loses its commanding role, it retains a representational one: if the law can no longer function to guide my life, it serves instead the representational purpose of showing me my sinfulness; it gives me knowledge through representation (upon which, of course, action might be based) more than direct instruction for action. For Luther, the law's purpose is purely representational, rather than hortatory (to the extent that it has a function at all) both in the sense that it represents natural law and in the sense that its aim is "to make original sin manifest and show man to what utter depths his nature has fallen and how corrupt it has become" (*The Smalcald Articles* 3.3, quoted in Lazareth, "Love and Law," 112). For Calvin, however, the law retains its hortatory function alongside the representational one.

The move from a hortatory to a representational concept of law can also be seen in a tradition much closer to Wordsworth, in the work of Richard Hooker, the early Anglican divine praised in Ecclesiastical Sonnet 2.39. Hooker defines law in general as follows:

> All things that are, have some operation not violent or casual. Neither doth any thing ever begin to exercise the same, without some fore-conceived end for which it worketh. And the end which it worketh for is not obtained, unless the work be also fit to obtain it by. For unto every end every operation will not serve. That which doth assign unto each thing the kind, that which doth moderate the force and power, that which doth appoint the form and measure of working, the same we term a *Law*. So that no certain end could ever be attained, unless the actions whereby it is attained were regular; that is to say, made suitable, fit and correspondent unto their end, by some canon, rule, or law. Which thing doth first take place in the works of God himself. (*Of the Laws of Ecclesiastical Polity* 109)

As A. S. McGrade and Brian Vickers, the editors of this edition, point out, Hooker "has omitted from the definition of law what for many thinkers is its most essential property: authoritative or coercive imposition by a superior.... The most immediate consequence of Hooker's non-coercive concept of law was that it allowed him to apply the idea to God" (19). By seeing law as a systematic correspondence between means and ends, and not as a command from God, Hooker paved the way for the notion of divine law as a system of representation rather than a set of commands. Furthermore, if this "correspondence" concept of law, unlike a "violent or causal" concept, can then be applied to God himself, we are not far from Wordsworth's claim that law can be a representation of God as well as a command originating from him; the correspondence between means and ends in God himself can be reflected in the similar correspondence within the laws of human conscience, which can thus become God's "most perfect image in the world." The Wanderer is in both camps, perhaps because the hortatory Calvinist strain is still strong: as we have seen, moral law is both prior to the representational (suggesting the primacy of law's hortatory function) and coeval with the representational (suggesting the primacy of law's representative function).

For Luther, the representative function of the law is negative: it represents to man his sinfulness. For Wordsworth, the law's representative function is positive: the law of duty is the image of God's goodness, not man's sinfulness. Part of this turn can be ascribed to the Enlightenment. If, as various forms of deist and postdeist thought suggest, the order of the universe being revealed by empirical science reflects a providential interlocking of purposes, then the laws of nature are a more appropriate representation of God than his interventions in history or his exhortations to obedience. The representative function of law can thus be seen as positive because it represents the order of the universe. Although Luther's distinction between divine and natural law is blurred in this new formulation, he had in fact prepared for this by calling Mosaic law a codification of natural law.

That Wordsworth in one sense crosses over from morally imperative law to scientifically representative law is suggested by the image of the sundial discussed above: the internal moral law becomes an instrument of scientific measurement. The post-seventeenth-century concept of natural law in fact moves the whole discussion from the moral toward the representational and epistemological, as Charles Taylor has demonstrated. The end result of this shift from divine command to the natural laws of human life will be the Victorian notion that the law of duty is not even a *representation* of God, a means by which we can know him, but a form of life that is a kind of *substitute* for prayer to a God who can be acknowledged but not known: As Arthur Clough has it,

> O not unowned, thou shalt unnamed forgive,
>   In worldly walks the prayerless heart prepare;
> And if in work its life it seem to live,
>   Shalt make that work be prayer.
>   ("Qui Laborat, Orat" 17–20)

Ludwig Feuerbach's anthropological notion of God takes this substitution of moral law for God to its logical extreme: "It is the consciousness of love by which man reconciles himself with God, or rather with his own nature as represented in the moral law" (*The Essence of Christianity* 50). Here the moral law has come fully to the human side of the incarnational relationship, representing man's nature, not God's. Broadly stated, the moral "law" moves from God's command to a system of moral law by which God is represented to that system of moral law detached from its divine referent.

Wordsworth, however, was neither a deist nor (even in *The Excursion*) a Victorian, and of course argued *against* the exclusion of moral grounds in a purely epistemological worldview (and thus against the reduction of law from command to human representational system), but also *for* law as a representation of, not a substitute for God. Thus the concept of law for him strongly reflects the *tension* between law as representation and law as exhortation, rather than one or the other extreme. Law is *both* an epistemological system—a tool of measurement by which we can know truth and a set of signs for God—and an act of will. The law of duty represents God, partly in its representation of a natural order (Wordsworth, certainly saw natural and divine order as compatible without opening himself to the charge of pantheism) but it is also God's command in that duty is the "Stern Daughter of the Voice of God," as the opening line of the "Ode to Duty" has it. For Wordsworth, caught as he is in *The Excursion* between the demands of theory and incarnation, law must function both ways, and law as semiotic codification cannot simply be restored to an original notion of law as divine will.

A miniature emblem of this tension is provided within the pastor's church:

> Admonitory texts inscribed the walls,
> Each, in its ornamental scroll, enclosed;
> Each also crowned with winged heads—a pair
> of rudely-painted Cherubim.
> (5.150–53)

These "texts" are fundamentally hortatory, as evidenced by the first word in their description, but they are also enclosed within "ornamental" scrolls that in their purely decorative mimetic role are *detached* from any sense of the "admonitory," and even from any meaningful sense of representation. The presence of cherubim translates this tension into the relation between the representational and the incarnational: those "ornamental" scrolls are on second glance not at all detached if we consider their incarnational function. They are superficially representations of divine beings, but because they are "rudely painted" they actually tell us more about their very human, historical, local context of real events than about how cherubim might look. Thus the real "moral" of these admonitory texts lies not in what they admonish, but in the incarnational humility that appears through their transparently crude efforts at representation.

This concreteness is of course fully in line with Wordsworth's tendency to think of the church in terms of village churches rather than in terms of abstract theology. More important for my purposes, however, these scrolls reflect the parallelism, very problematic for Wordsworth, between the movement from admonition to representation and the movement from image to text. Protestantism's replacement of icons with biblical text is in part a move from "things" to "signs": our relation to God is, in theory, no longer mediated by ecclesiastical objects, or the bodies of saints, but rather by God's own biblical language, which provides us with purer, more transparent signs of his presence. Wordsworth is of course operating within that tradition, but the incarnational emphasis on words as "living things" forces him to go against the grain of Protestant progress from image to sign, insofar as that progress is leading toward representation and away from the concrete, incarnational experience of words as things. Therefore the scrolls in the church must be both the representational signs of God's law and the concrete images of human events.

There is a side of *The Excursion* in which law remains an ultimately negative epistemology—negative both because it is an epistemology, and thus partakes of the problems of representation, and because it operates within the Protestant tradition of law as the representation of sin. I will discuss this later in the context of the violence revealed by the theoretical-incarnational tension in *The Excursion*. Still, insofar as the law is seen as a force of will, rather than a structure of representation, some resolution between its potential restrictiveness and the human need for freedom is possible, because in this sense law is expressible in the language of incarnation. In stanza 6 of the "Ode to Duty," deleted by Wordsworth after 1807, the poet argues that submission is really choice:

> Yet not the less would I throughout
> Still act according to the voice
> Of my own wish; and feel past doubt
> That my submissiveness was choice:
> Not seeking in the school of pride
> For 'precepts overdignified',
> Denial and restraint I prize
> No farther than they breed a second Will more wise.
>
> (41–48, in *Poems in Two Volumes* 106–7)

Similarly, in *The Excursion* the law of duty is invoked by the Wanderer, and submission and choice are linked:

> O blest seclusion! when the mind admits
> The law of duty; and can therefore move
> Through each vicissitude of loss and gain,
> Linked in entire complacence with her choice.
> (4.1035–38)

The deleted stanza from the "Ode to Duty" argues that God's stern, commanding will—that which *limits* human freedom, it would seem—can be turned into human choice precisely because the relationship between divine will and human will is incarnational rather than representational. The negative, restrictive effect of law can be translated into human freedom, though human freedom of course cannot logically "represent" divine law.

Schelling's distinction between *Wille* and *Willkür*, reflected in Wordsworth's notion of the "imaginative Will," allows human choice to be a manifestation of a higher absolute will, sometimes even without our knowing it. The Wanderer tells the Solitary that even such a discourse as his, which consciously desires oblivion and death, is illuminated and colored by that problematic "sun" we have seen before:

> Your discourse this day,
> That, like the fabled Lethe, wished to flow
> In creeping sadness, through oblivious shades
> Of death and night, has caught at every turn
> The colours of the sun. Access for you
> Is yet preserved to principles of truth,
> Which the imaginative Will upholds
> In seats of wisdom, not to be approached
> By the inferior faculty that moulds,
> With her minute and speculative pains,
> Opinion, ever-changing!
> (4.1122–32)

The "imaginative Will" is a concept no doubt derived from Schelling via Coleridge by which individual choice is subordinated to an all-encompassing Will. Elsewhere in Wordsworth (particularly in the "Imagination" passage of *The Prelude*, book 6) and in Coleridge (the definition of the primary imagination in book 13 of the *Biographia*

Literaria as "a repetition in the finite mind of the eternal act of creation in the infinite I AM"), the emphasis is on forging a link between finite choice and the infinite will—*Willkür* and *Wille* in Schelling's terminology. As Schelling puts it, the connection is intimate: the finite will is the only vehicle by which the absolute will can manifest itself: "But insofar as the absolute will appears, it can only do so, in order to appear *as* absolute, in the form of choice" (*System of Transcendental Idealism* 191).[37] Most important for my purposes, the incarnational stance allows for the transformation of spirit into event in a way that does not require adequate representation for the operation of the will: *Wille* can be expressed as *Willkür*, or spirit can become event, without forcing the issue of the inadequacy of the latter to the former, since they are in an incarnational more than a representational relationship, with all the difference and connection thus entailed. It is in this sense that the human will can be an "incarnation" of a higher imaginative will, the "second Will more wise" (48) of the "Ode to Duty," while at the same time the difference between particular human choice and the whole "imaginative Will" can be recognized, as the Wanderer does in his discussions with the Solitary in book 4 of *The Excursion*.

For Levinas, the ambivalent position in which the subject is placed by responding to a command that has not yet been heard—a version of Wordsworth's experience in book 6 of *The Prelude*, for example, of discovering after the fact that unwittingly crossing the Alps reveals individual choice to be in the service of an infinite but also subjective imaginative power—is the very diachrony of incarnational subjectivity:

> The possibility of finding, anachronously, the order in the obedience itself, and of receiving the order out of oneself, this reverting of heteronomy into autonomy, is the very way the Infinite passes itself. The metaphor of the inscription of the law in consciousness expresses this in a remarkable way, reconciling autonomy and heteronomy. It does so in an ambivalence, whose diachrony is the signification itself, an ambivalence which, in the present, is an ambiguity.... This ambivalence is the exception and subjectivity of the subject, its very psyche, a possibility of inspiration. It is the possibility of being the author of what had been breathed in unbeknownst to me, of having received, one knows not from where, that of which I am author. (*OTB* 148–49)

Like Levinas, Wordsworth draws on the Judeo-Christian imagery of a "breathing" between the infinite and the finite (most notably in the "correspondent breezes" passage, which opens *The Prelude*) as well as the inscription of divine law in human consciousness to formulate the constitution of the subject. For Wordsworth, the conflict between the hortatory and the representational aspects of moral law—the duality of the law of conscience as both that which commands us even before we know it and that which represents God—is able to "breed a second Will more wise" or constitute the subject as infinite even as it delimits the subject, through this kind of incarnational logic, which refuses to reduce the heteronomy of the ethical command to the autonomy of the representational statement even as it recognizes their ambivalent interdependency.

INCARNATION AND VIOLENCE

For Wordsworth, law is both a system of representation and a living, commanding voice, both an epistemological system of signs and an incarnational event. God's law is a system of signs that represent him in the human conscience, but it is also (and more fundamentally) his ethically commanding voice, demanding that he be, in Cavell's terms, *acknowledged* in historical action, not *known* in a system of signs. There is a great potential for violence in this view of law; Wordsworth's most graphic acknowledgment of this is the boy's terror-stricken flight from the site of a violent execution in the first "spot of time" in *The Prelude*. This violence, however, is not simply a conflict between system and event, between a set of rules and contingent events that do not conform to those rules. Such a conflict would be the violence described by de Man in his discussion of Rousseau (see Chapter 3), by which the grammar of law must exclude contingent events that nevertheless interrupt and at the same time ground that grammar. As we saw, Wordsworth can turn that violence into the hermeneutical circle of incarnational meaning. The violence in Wordsworth is much more fundamental, because it resides both in the relation of representational systems to the world and in the very world that is acknowledged by an incarnational hermeneutics.

In the famous contrast between incarnation and counter-spirit, violence is ascribed mainly to "counter-spirit." If words are not incarnational, but merely representational, they will "prove an ill gift; such a one as those poisoned vestments, read of in the stories of superstitious times, which had power to consume and to alienate from his right mind the victim who put them on" (*PrW* 2:84–85). If words are merely signs in dead representational systems, they will "kill" the living materiality that they are unable to systematize. This resembles the conflict between system and event described by de Man. That violence, however, is preceded by violence of an even more fundamental variety, because the very distinction between incarnation and counter-spirit is based on the violent potential in words. The above passage is prefaced by the statement, "Words are too awful an instrument for good and evil to be trifled with: they hold above all other external powers a dominion over thoughts" (*PrW* 2:84). That power is not just the conflict between system and event, but rather a power and potential for violence that precedes the idea of system. The relationship is complex, however, because it is also a violence that is both revealed and (violently) suppressed by linguistic and legal systems. This violence goes back to the violent death of Jesus that is an essential part of the original Incarnation, and to the precultural violence that Girard sees Judeo-Christian scripture as revealing.

The deep level at which violence enters the concept of law is suggested by Hegel's struggle with the notion of penal law in his early essay, "The Spirit of Christianity and Its Fate," which I discussed at length in Chapter 1. His analysis of penal law, though it leads into a discussion of reconciliation through love, is the point at which he comes closest to seeing violence at the root of the Judeo-Christian system. A simple law such as "thou shalt not kill" sets up a relationship of opposition between the mastering universality of the law, alien to life, and the subservient particularity of the individual "thou," an opposition which Hegel sees as the fundamental Jewish alienation described above. The opposition can be easily transcended by the Christian directive to "love thy neighbor," which annuls the opposition between person and law by replacing the oppositional law with an "is," a principle intimately connected with (instead of specifically alien to) existence itself. That annulment is easy because there is no contradiction between the two: to love one's neighbor fulfills the earlier law as it annuls it; the conflict is merely in the form, not the content: "Since law was opposed to love, not in its content, but in its form, it could be taken up into love, though in this process it lost its shape" ("The Spirit of Christianity," in *Early Theological Writings* 225). The alien universality of law is replaced by a very different, existential principle that is in life rather than alien to it, but that formal difference is masked by the fact that there is no contradiction in content between the fulfillment of a law and the command to love one's neighbor. This resembles the positive incarnational rhetoric of *The Prelude*: youthful figural systems, such as the equation of the French Revolution and natural liberty, are annulled, but the decay and supersession of those systems is precisely the existential, incarnational event of a creative autobiographical *Bildung*. The content—

"liberty"—remains; its form simply needs to be changed from a representational to an incarnational one.

But with penal law the case is more difficult, because for it to be annulled by love both its form (as law) and its content (punishment, which is opposed to love) would have to be annulled. This is impossible because here the relationship of opposition that obtains on the universal level *must* also obtain on the existential level. Hegel maintains that penal law always maintains a relation of opposition between the contingent, individual person and the universal law, because the law needs the reality of punishment in order to be more than merely an abstract concept. "The law merely says that [the trespasser] must lose the rights comprised in the law; but, because the law is directly only a thought, it is only the concept of the trespasser which loses the right; and in order that this loss may be actualized, i.e., in order that the trespasser may really lose what the concept has lost, the law must be linked with life and clothed with might" (225–26). To fulfill the law is always to set up a relationship of opposition between the universal and the particular. On the side of the law's administration, this is a conflict between the unbending universality of the law and the human life of the judge: "There may be a contradiction between [justice] as universal, as thought, and it as real, i.e., in a living being. . . . [A] judge can give up acting as a judge, i.e., can pardon. But this does not satisfy justice, for justice is unbending" (226). On the side of the trespasser, this conflict manifests itself as a bad conscience, which can never reconcile the reality of its action to the universality of the law it has violated: "The trespasser always sees himself as a trespasser; over his action as a reality he has no power, and this his reality is in contradiction with his consciousness of the law" (227). Similarly, though law in *The Excursion* is not simply penal, it must hold within it on all levels the conflict between the universality of a system of representation and the particularity of a forceful command; this conflict reflects the conflict between the philosophical poem's need for both representational theory and antitheoretical incarnational thought. The system of law, conceived as penal law, cannot simply be superseded in an incarnational process.

To explain how Christianity can overcome this opposition, Hegel introduces the concept of "fate" (*Schicksal*). Fate turns the relationship between victim and law from one of mastery by a force other to life into one of opposition between forces *in* life. Fate is then an enemy to be fought rather than (as in law) a master who will always be in control:

> In the hostile power of fate, universal is not severed from particular in the way in which the law, as a universal, is opposed to man

or his inclinations as the particular. Fate is just the enemy, and man stands over against it as a power fighting against it. Law, on the contrary, as universal, is Lord of the particular and has subdued this man to obedience. (229)

According to the principle of fate, murder is no longer the violation of a universal law, a law which will punish the murderer, but is rather the perversion of life into an enemy. This relationship of opposition occurs within the orbit of life, and thus does not depend on an opposition between the particularity of life and the universality of law. Hegel sees this as an advantage where reconciliation is desired: "Fate, so far as reconcilability is concerned, has this advantage of the penal law, that it occurs within the orbit of life, while a crime falling under law and punishment occurs on the contrary in the orbit of insurmountable oppositions [i.e., the universality of law] and absolutely real events [i.e., deeds that conflict with those universals]" (230). In fate one fears separation and longs for what is lost, but because these oppositions occur within the sphere of life, they are open to the possibility of reconciliation. Fate sees a trespassing deed as a part of a whole with which reconciliation is possible; penal law sees the deed as a fragment that forever fixes the person (now defined by his fragmentary deed as nothing but that deed, as a "criminal") in a relationship of opposition to the universal law.

Hegel's interest in this move from law to fate is to solve the problem of punishment in the Christian supersession or abrogation of Jewish law; however, we do not need to shift his terms very far to see the potential for violence revealed in this Christian process, a violence that can be linked to incarnation and Wordsworth's incarnational thought. The translation of a universal principle (law) to the force of a human other (fate) resembles the way in which Cavell's skeptic deals with the conflicting drives toward resolution of skepticism (the desire for universals) and skepticism itself (the desire to value contingency over universality) by translating the object of investigation—the world—into a living human other, thus moving the problem of knowledge from an epistemological question to a potentially violent relationship to another human.[38] Just as Cavell's animated world can be engaged by a murderous relationship (as when the mariner kills the albatross), Hegel's world of "fate" turns the punishing force into a human other to be fought. Thus, instead of the conflict between universal and particular, held apart through the differentiation of law, we have a Girardian rivalry between two similar characters, a rivalry whose end result may not be Christian reconciliation, but rather the reduction of differences to the chaos of the Same. Seen in the context of "fate," punishment presents Hegel's criminal with a mirror image of himself, with whom his relationship must be one of rivalry, it would seem: "Punishment as fate is the equal reaction of the trespasser's own deed, of a power which he himself has armed, of an enemy made an enemy by himself" (230). The otherness of the other is in this situation only apparent; in truth the other's deed is merely a reaction to one's own: "A fate appears to arise only through another's deed; but this is only the occasion of the fate. What really produces it is the manner of receiving and reacting against the other's deed" (233).

It is tempting to recast this move from the universality of law to the existential reality of an opposition in life into Levinas's emphasis on priority of concrete human relations to universal concepts, and Hegel does move in this direction in suggesting that "in the case of punishment as fate ... the law is later than life and is outranked by it. There, the law is only the lack of life, defective life appearing as a power" (230). Hegel's move does engage the irreducibility of the contact with the human other that is central to Levinas's ethics. Law is a defect of life, a later expression of the more primitive oppositional force of fate. This priority of nontotalizable, humanly lived, relational experience over ontological system looks forward to Levinas's disruption of systematic "totality" by the "transcendence" of absolute alterity manifested in face-to-face dialogue: "The void that breaks the totality can be maintained against an inevitably totalizing and synoptic thought only if thought finds itself *faced* with an other refractory to categories" (*TI* 40). Though Hegel very definitely totalizes the experience of fate into the unified Christian life of love, Levinas's more radical preservation of alterity, which, as we saw in the Lucy poems, entails a foundational sense of the ethical as responsibility for the *death* of the other, can just as easily be inferred from Hegel's substitution of life for law. Nevertheless, the early Hegel is still Hegel, and true to form he sees the goal of this move as a reconciliation impossible on the level of universal law, not, as in Levinas, the preservation in concrete life of an alterity lost in the totalization of universal laws and concepts. By seeing the move from law to life as a move toward unification, Hegel runs the risk, (implicit rather than explicit in his argument) that unification turns into what Girard analyzes as the violence of the Same, the violence that is averted by systems of differences. This Christian principle of "life" as prior to "law" parallels Wordsworth's incarnational insistence on the ethical as prior to the epistemological, but the very desire for unification in this life brings to the fore the violent potential in a life that is prior to law and thus "lawless" in a very real way. This is a violence present in Levinas's emphasis on the subjection of the subject to the command of the other, but palliated by Levinas's emphasis on the fundamentality of alterity, which allows him to avoid the Girardian problem of the erasure of differences—if I may be permitted a serious pun, Levinas's preontological anarchy has a friendlier face than Girard's.

In the first chapter, I suggested that Hegel intuited the violent potential in the principle of unity promoted by the Incarnation: there is a fine and perhaps invisible line separating the desired subjective unity of Christian love—a principle derivable from the "life" forces of punishment-as-fate—from the violent collapse of structures of differentiation into the chaos of the Same. As Girard points out in many circumstances, the principle of violence is often reversed into a principle of unity, for example when the blood of murder and contagion is turned into a purifying agent through the ritual of sacrifice.[39] Hegel seems to be straddling the fine line, on which such a reversal turns, between the Christian principle of fate as an opportunity for wholeness and reconciliation (because it lacks differentiation between universal and particular, allows for a reconcilable opposition between forces within life), *and* as a revelation of an originary violence (because it is prior to the preservative differentiation of law, and because the opposition between mirrored life-forces is the endless cycle of reciprocal violence that culture seeks to control).

In the remainder of this chapter, I want to show not simply that Wordsworth shared that intuition, but that the violence both exposed and controlled by incarnational thought is an important key to the relationship between the two kinds of thought I have been examining in *The Excursion*. My thesis might be summarized like this: as incarnational thought is forced to face up to its formulation within the differentiated structure of a "theory," it becomes increasingly clear that this differentiated structure both conceals and reveals the violence that results from the power of theoretical words ("awful instruments"), functioning within a differentiated system, in tension with incarnational concepts, which do not comfortably fit into such differentiation, and the incarnation's own violent origins. Again, though *The Prelude* contains plenty of violence (the drowned man of Esthwaite, the execution site, the French Revolution, etc.), the very implicitness of the incarnational rhetoric was able to channel that violence into an effective *Bildung*, and thereby enact an incarnational subjectivity. In *The Excursion*, the bare exposure of theoretical principles in tension with incarnational thought forces the violence to the surface.

As I pointed out in the previous chapter, incarnational thought is fundamentally anti-economic; it operates according to the logic of the gift, not reciprocal exchange. God must become man with no loss of Godhood, and this means adding something extra to the system. An economy does not add anything new to the world (that would literally be uneconomical), whereas incarnation does. Just as Jesus was God's unearned gift to man (Coleridge was particularly bothered by the absurdity of an *economy* of atonement[40]), the translation of thought to language does not follow the principle of conservation of energy. Language is not an economy of signs in which the objective matter of the words can be converted into the pure energy of meaning; instead, thought's transition to language effects a noneconomic increase in being. Words do stand as signs, but they also have their own materiality—a surplus from the point of view of meaning—both in the philosophical sense that they are and should be living things, and in the very literal sense of being physically proliferated through publication and circulation. The noneconomic nature of the Incarnation has been obscured or at least ameliorated by Christianity's attempt to align itself with a Greek rationality that sees perfection as equivalent to economically perfect proportion, which leads to ideas of Christianity as a pure economy. Thus we get the Pauline economy of sacrificial exchange suggested by the idea that Jesus died to restore the balance upset by sin, and Milton's promotion of the baroque concept of an aesthetic economy as the representation of divine order; the arrival of the savior is seen as the fulfillment of an implicitly not-yet-full prophetic economy. From Gadamer's point of view, the economic "fiction" is part of the pseudoscientific domination of the sign, a manifestation of an Enlightenment desire to see the object of investigation as completely other to the observer, describable in structural terms that convey a systematic completeness, with nothing "left over" that would force interpretation into an endless process.

This anti-economic status of incarnational thought has both a positive and negative dimension: on the positive side, it is the logic of the gift as described by Lewis Hyde and as executed in *The Prelude*; meaning occurs as a noneconomic, incarnational emanation or overflow that is an increase of being.[41] As Gadamer says of the relation between original and representation in an artistic presentation, "Every such presentation is an ontological event and occupies the same ontological level as what is represented. By being presented it experiences, as it were, an *increase in being*. The content of the picture is ontologically defined as an emanation of the original" (*TM* 140).

Nevertheless, there is also something dangerously impure about such a violation of economic rules, especially when seen from the point of view of the rationalist tradition to which Hegel and Wordsworth had such a complex relation. In Hegel this is the problem of the objective remainder, the incarnate, objectified word/Word not susceptible to complete subjectivization or consumption; it is the problem of the word that refuses to be "read away." Derrida gives the most radical interpretation of this leftover in his theory of the "supplement," the extra element that is always outside the desired economy of language, but on whose existence the economy depends.[42] Gadamer, building on the hermeneutic tradition that sees the inadequacy of the finite to the infinite as an invitation to interpretation, sees precisely that endless, anti-economic process of interpretation as a generation of meaning, an addition to the world analogous to the increase in Being resulting from the Incarnation. For Derrida, the economic metaphor is also inadequate, but for the opposite reason: the objective leftover, the violation of economic purity that results when the word persists in its materiality when it is supposed to be functioning as a sign, is not the increase in Being promised by the Incarnation, but the repetition of the persistent otherness in language that prevents desired meaning from emerging. Or, to invoke Girard's concrete anthropological context, the incarnational argument against economy reveals the violence that was to have been concealed by economic structures of differentiation that promise falsely the equality-in-difference of a system of balanced exchange. In analyzing Wordsworth's relation to economic systems, we must keep in mind that the anti-economic strain in incarnational rhetoric can lead both toward the fulfillment of our desire for meaning's generation and toward the revelation of why such a desire must be frustrated. The Incarnation foils our desire for economic order by offering a tantalizing promise of the infinite's self-presentation in the finite that starts a hermeneutic process of similar increase, and at the same time demonstrating the irreducible difference that characterizes such a process of supplementation. This is part of the confrontation between incarnation and theory: the idea of the Incarnation mitigates against the economic totalization of theory, whether in the hermeneutic direction of an increase in being, a movement toward "truth" that is not reducible to theoretical "method," or in the deconstructive direction of a language that is too contingent to be totalized in theory.

For Hegel, the move from a universal economy of law to the contingency of life enables Christian reconciliation; however, the proliferation of words as things, the existence of those objective leftovers that troubled Hegel, also participates in the logic of violence and sacrifice as discussed by Girard and Michel Serres. Girard points out that economic systems of differentiation, such as law, function to control the proliferation of violence; without such economic structures, we have either the controlled violence of sacrifice, or, at an even more fundamental level, the chaos of the Same.[43] Serres argues that any act of formalization, such as the establishment of economies of law and representation such as I have been discussing, is an act of dialogue that works to exclude the "third man," and the anti-economic "noise" that is the necessary background to any communication:

> *The first effort to make communication in a dialogue successful is isomorphic to the effort to render a form independent of its empirical realizations.* These realizations are the third man of the form, its interference and its noise.... To exclude the empirical is to exclude differentiation, the plurality of others that mask the same.... Thus, the empirical is strictly essential and accidental *noise.* (*Hermes* 69–70)

It is only on a purely spiritual level that the Incarnation can be seen as an economy; in fact, one of the attractions, to Hegel, of the idea that the objective element is completely consumed in the Eucharistic consumption of the body, is that, unlike language, it is economically "pure." The objective has passed into the subjective with nothing left over in the exchange.

The Pastor comes closest to being able to believe in such a pure economy of incarnation. He avoids the material objectivity of language by having a graveyard with very few epitaphs, and his main concern is for the spiritual purity of the transcendental side of the Incarnation. He is thus worried about the proliferation of language as noise, because a pure economy will allow for no noise. He even goes so far as to justify the exclusion of poetry, despite its divine origins, by reference to its necessary engagement with a noneconomical noise that approximates the chaos of warfare:

> Noise is there not enough in doleful war,
> But that the heaven-born poet must stand forth,
> And lend the echoes of his sacred shell,
> To multiply and aggravate the din?
> (7.363–66)

This sacred shell echoes the one in the dream of the Arab Quixote in book 5 of *The Prelude,* to be buried in the face of the approaching catastrophe, as well as the child's shell in book 4 of *The Excursion,* which represents, among other things, "central peace, subsisting at the heart / Of endless agitation" (4.1146–47). Those shells are represented against a background of "noise"—the foundational chaos of the deluge and "endless agitation"—which must be excluded by the incarnational dialogue with the universe (in the case of the child) and from which the shell/voice must be protected (in the burying of the shell in *The Prelude*). The Pastor is willing to silence the shell of the "heaven-born poet" so that it does not become contaminated by the noise it must, from a poet's point of view, engage and exclude.

The Pastor, of course, is quick to exclude the noise of language's materiality because he is concerned with incarnation from a perspective opposite to that of poetry; he is concerned with connecting the incarnate back to the spiritual, not with transforming spirit/thought into language/event. With less investment in language—that is, with less concern for separating the language of poetry from its background noise— he is happy to see words dematerialize as they are uttered, particularly in the case of a priest known both to him and to the Wanderer. After a century or so of verbal memorialization aided by the "simple stone" marking the man's grave,

> Then, shall the slowly-gathering twilight close
> In utter night; and of his course remain
> No cognizable vestiges, no more
> Than of this breath, which shapes itself in words
> To speak of him, and instantly dissolves.
>   (7.356–60)

The Pastor is dismissing noise more than he is suppressing or excluding it; his incarnational insight allows him to recognize its presence and danger, but his supratextual status relieves him of the responsibility to force language into confrontation with its background noise, to make the shell of poetry heard against the din of the chaos from which it springs. Unlike the Wanderer, he has no need of theories; he tells stories and takes care of people's spiritual needs, and thus can dismiss the noise instead of suppressing it by means of a theoretical, implicitly economic "accounting," which would place knowledge into an ordered system of reciprocal differences by which that knowledge can seem to represent the world.

The Wanderer's—and, in a more radical way, the Solitary's— theoretical bent, however, sets up a tension between the positive and negative aspects of the incarnational anti-economy and the economic differentiation of theory. As always, the Wanderer must play both sides of the game: he must argue against the reductive economies proposed by the Solitary, and thus argue for the positive materiality of incarnational thought, but at the same time his construction of a theory is a fundamentally economic act, intended to suppress the negative proliferation of linguistic materiality as violence or noise, and also implicitly in tension with the very incarnational materiality he wants to foster.

The Solitary clearly turns to a very restricted epistemological economy as a way of suppressing dangerous questions of origin. In book 3, while exploring the Solitary's vale, the travelers view strange rock formations whose origin is in a dim region between nature and culture. The Wanderer says,

> Among these rocks and stones, methinks, I see
> More than the heedless impress that belongs
> To lonely nature's casual work: they bear
> A semblance strange of power intelligent,
> And of design not wholly worn away.
> ... And I own,
> Some shadowy intimations haunt me here,
> That in these shows a chronicle survives
> Of purposes akin to those of Man,
> But wrought with mightier arm than now prevails.
>   (3.80–91)

The side of those "shadowy intimations" that suggests precultural violence is here only dimly suggested by the presence of what looks like "a stranded ship, with keel upturned" (3.54), and "a fragment, like an altar" (3.60), and by the fact that the orderly distinctions between nature and culture are blurred. The themes of death, fragmentation, and sacrifice implied in these images will be made more explicit in book 9. Here we have a sublime sense of a natural power of design that is linked to man, but that is more powerful. The Solitary sees this relation between man and nature as ironic:

> The shapes before our eyes
> And their arrangement, doubtless must be deemed
> The sport of Nature, aided by blind Chance
> Rudely to mock the works of toiling Man.
>   (3.124–27)

This ironic perspective—and this could be said of much of the Solitary's position—represents an insight that is both more and less than that of the Wanderer. The Solitary's insight is greater in that he recognizes the violence implicit in the conflict between natural and human purposes. His is not simply a Hobbesian view of the state of nature as full of conflict; the interaction with human culture is more subtle. Here nature is granted something of an animistic force, but one whose relation to human life is that of rude mockery—not a force to be acknowledged as a mortal other. Nature's work does resemble man's, but in a rivalry in which man is the loser. As Girard says of Greek tragedy, "Violence invariably effaces the difference between antagonists" (*Violence and the Sacred* 47); the resemblance between man and nature threatens to become, not the interactive, incarnational dialogue epitomized in the Mount Snowdon episode of *The Prelude,* but rather the symmetrical reciprocity that leads to violent nondifferentiation, the taboo mixture of categories that cultural systems strive to keep different.

The Solitary backs off from this position, however, and prefers the satisfaction of "the wandering Herbalist" (3.161) who "peeps round / For some rare floweret of the hills" (3.165–66), or the amateur geologist who "resolve[s] his doubts" about the nature of the rocks disguised by natural processes,

> And, with that ready answer satisfied,
> The substance classes by some barbarous name
> And hurries on.
> (3.182–85)

In other words, the system of differences, however trivial or transitory, imposed by these systems of classification, is preferable to the reciprocal violence that is exposed when the relation between nature and man is viewed directly. A representational economy is overlaid on the precultural violence, and the tragedy of the Solitary's situation is that he knows this is what he is doing. For him, the erection of systems of difference is a cynical, desperate gesture that in the end only reinforces his recognition of the illusory nature of such gestures.

The Solitary shows great sensitivity to the danger that economically based systems of difference will dissolve into the chaos of the Same. In an aside on the development of factories (his main point is that degradation was present long before industrialization), he notes that factories mingle cultural categories in a way that produces a kind of mutual infection. He talks of a time before "these structures rose, commingling old and young, / And unripe sex with sex, for mutual taint" (8.339–40). Wordsworth seems somewhat preoccupied with the idea of "taint" at this point in *The Excursion;* the Poet laments the loss of "honest dealing, and untainted speech" (8.241), and later the Solitary cynically refers to the oppressors who instruct the poor to die "with the least taint and injury to the air / The oppressor breathes" (9.150–51). As Girard points out, contagion is a common cultural image of the destruction of differences because it is a force that makes people the same—they all have the same sickness—in a "diseased" way, opposed to the "healthy" differentiation of normal society, and it leads to the ultimate nondifferentiation of death. Thus sacrificial victims are often seen as the source of diseases or plagues, since they represent the threat of nondifferentiation. Girard says of the epidemic associated with Oedipus, the paradigmatic victim, "The epidemic that interrupts all the vital functions of the city is surely not unrelated to violence and the loss of distinctions. The oracle itself explains matters: it is the presence of a *murderer* that has brought on the disaster" (*Violence and the Sacred* 76). The Solitary, both in his fear of "taint" and in his own desire for isolation, seems to feel this threat of contagion with particular force. In book 2, the Wanderer suggests a source for this feeling, when he sees the Solitary as having taken a "mortal taint" from the nondifferentiated support for the French Revolution, "that righteous cause" which

> bound
> For one hostility, in friendly league,
> Ethereal natures and the worst of slaves.
> (2.227–29)

The result, described in the language of contagion and disease, was that

> An overweening trust was raised; and fear
> Cast out, alike of person and of thing.
> Plague from this union spread, whose subtle bane
> The strongest did not easily escape;
> And He, what wonder! took a mortal taint.
> (2.241–45)

The Solitary experienced firsthand the threat of contagion and nondifferentiation. Whereas in *The Prelude* misplaced support for the French Revolution could be seen in a supersession of figures for liberty, here—

where that kind of autobiographical *Bildung* is not possible—the result is a chaotic, contagious erasure of difference.

Whereas the Solitary fears contagion because he recognizes the threat of violence in nondifferentiation, the Wanderer rejects the Solitary's position—and the closely related fundamentality of sacrifice—because it goes against the "law / Of life, and hope, and action" that he is promoting. On one level, this is perfectly consistent with the contrast, drawn in the third "Essay Upon Epitaphs," between language as incarnation and language as the coat of Nessus, a counter-spirit that takes sacrificial victims. In this sense, sacrificial violence is a characteristic danger of non-incarnational language in which words are separable clothing for thought. In Ovid's version,[44] this coat, stained with blood and poison because Nessus had been shot by the jealous Hercules, is given to Deianira by the centaur Nessus, purportedly to help make her love him, but actually as an act of revenge. Later, thinking that the coat will help Hercules love her, and jealous of Iole, the young captive Hercules has brought back from war, Deianira sends the coat to him. Hercules puts the coat on, lights a sacrificial fire, and the poison is activated, beginning a cycle of violence that ends in Hercules' death (though this is also the occasion of his deification). The coat—Wordsworth's analogy for improperly used language—which is intended by one party to protect, connect, and express (it is meant to reconcile Hercules and his wife), instead exerts a negative power stemming from the contagious mixture of categories (the blood and poison); violence resulting from rivalry's reduction of differences to the same (both the shooting of Nessus and the sending of the coat are acts of jealousy, as the pairs Hercules-Nessus and Deianira-Iole begin to resemble each other); and the ritual sacrifice (Hercules' sacrificial fire activates the poison). Thus it is no wonder that the Wanderer objects to these three dangers. He recognizes the danger of the "tainting" contagion and mixing of categories, as noted above in his analysis of the Solitary's condition. He clearly fears the erasure of differences: his final complaint about the Solitary is that he erases differences among humans in universalizing his own condition; his "wounded spirit" is

> habitually disposed
> To seek, in degradation of the Kind,
> Excuse and solace for her own defects.
> (9.786–89)

At two important points in *The Excursion*, the Wanderer makes his objections to sacrifice explicit. The position he takes in book 9 is the clearest. He objects to sacrifice because it treats humans as means or instruments, in a position consistent with incarnational thought's preference for the living thing and rejection of instrumental reason's emphasis on words (or in this case people) as mere tools:

> Our life is turned
> Out of her course, wherever man is made
> An offering, a sacrifice, a tool
> Or implement, a passive thing employed
> As a brute mean, without acknowledgment
> Of common right or interest in the end.
> (9.113–18)

Incarnational thought (at this point in concert with the Kantian imperative) treats the living thing as in some sense participating in its own end: Jesus is a human incarnation of God, not just a means toward God, and words translate spirit into living event; they are not simply tools that represent spirit. Man was created not for this instrumental role, but rather "to obey the law / Of life, and hope, and action" (9.128–29). The sacrifice objected to here is that in which sacrificial victims become part of economy of exchange—the theory of sacrifice to be developed in the late nineteenth and early twentieth centuries by theorists such as Henri Hubert and Marcel Mauss.[45]

The Wanderer's opposition to sacrifice is complicated, however, both by how law itself becomes a substitute for sacrificial violence, and by the violence inherent in the notion of incarnation. Just as the notion of moral law contains a tension between living moral force and semiotic representation, as we saw earlier, this simple contrast between the instrumentality of sacrifice and obedience to the moral law is complicated by the Wanderer's recognition elsewhere that sacrifice is a more fundamental notion than this. In the aforementioned discussion of factories in book 8, the Wanderer casts the workers as sacrificial victims:

> Men, maidens, youths,
> Mother and little children, boys and girls,
> Enter, and each the wonted task resumes

> Within this temple, where is offered up
> To Gain, the master idol of the realm,
> Perpetual sacrifice.
>
> (8.180–85)

The relation between this negative sacrifice and the Wanderer's Christian alternative is complex, because this industrial sacrifice is compared to the Catholic, pre-Reformation practice of keeping a constant vigil, by human presence or the burning of candles, to the presence of the Host:

> Even thus of old
> Our ancestors, within the still domain
> Of vast cathedral or conventual church,
> Their vigils kept; where tapers day and night
> On the dim altar burned continually,
> In token that the House was evermore
> Watching to God. Religious men were they;
> Nor would their reason, tutored to aspire
> Above this transitory world, allow
> That there should pass a moment of the year,
> When in their land the Almighty's service ceased.
>
> (8.185–95)

The modern rites are "profaner" (196), and the Wanderer cannot share the "proud complacency" (199) of those who "triumph" (196) in them; this suggests that the modern industrial sacrifice suffers in the comparison. The Wanderer's Calvinist background, however, would not allow him to approve of the literalization of the Eucharist implied in the Catholic rite, and in fact the ultimate point of the comparison is that there is a potential positive value to the modern sacrifice, which expresses

> An intellectual mastery exercised
> O'er the blind elements; a purpose given,
> A perseverance fed; almost a soul
> Imparted—to brute matter.
>
> (8.201–4)

In this sense, it is the *modern* sacrificial rite that grants a religious power to matter. The Wanderer's attitude toward sacrifice is clearly ambivalent. On the one hand, he rejects it as profane here, and as demeaningly instrumental in book 9. On the other hand, he relates it to a spiritually animating force.

For my purposes, the most important implication of this ambivalence is that it reflects the tension within the Wanderer's concept of moral law. He attempts, in lines 113–18 of book 9, quoted earlier, to contrast the profanity of sacrifice with the sacredness of Christian moral law. According to the Wanderer, order is maintained in the Christian law by a combination of humanly instituted difference and divinely ordered unity. Though he agrees with the Solitary on the negativity of human difference—"Alas! what differs more than man from man!" (9.206)—that difference comes "from himself" (9.207). He offers an alternative to that human difference by arguing for a divinely and naturally legislated equality:

> Throughout the world of sense,
> Even as an object is sublime or fair,
> That object is laid open to the view
> Without reserve or veil; and as a power
> Is salutary, or an influence sweet
> Are each and all enabled to perceive
> That power, that influence, by impartial law.
> (9.214–20)

This distinction, though grounded in the familiar Romantic notion of unifying the universal and the particular, and in the Kantian notion of a unitary concept of moral law available to reason, ignores the earlier insights by both the Solitary and the Wanderer that the erasure of differences is a greater problem than their existence. It is thus "too easy" to account for those differences within a preservative structure of natural and divine law, since the real function of law is not to unify differences, but to provide a ground for maintaining them. What the Wanderer is doing, then, in describing that ground, is articulating what in Girardian terms is a "blind" view of the function of law. The Wanderer is being highly "theoretical" rather than "incarnational" in positing a binary opposition between a legislated natural or divine unity and a human set of differences—an opposition that flies in the face not only of incarnational thought but also of the complex minglings of such categories of which both the Wanderer and the Solitary are implicitly aware.

A major force undercutting the distinction that the Wanderer is trying to impose—a force intimately related to the Incarnation—stems from the fact that Christian thought is based on the bloody sacrifice of the crucifixion. According to Girard, law fulfills the same function as sacrifice, and like sacrifice it conceals its mechanism of revenge:

> As soon as the judicial system gains supremacy, its machinery disappears from sight. Like sacrifice, it conceals—even as it also reveals—its resemblance to vengeance, differing only in that it is not self-perpetuating and its decisions discourage reprisals. (*Violence and the Sacred* 22)

The difference is that the judicial system "effectively limits [vengeance] to a single act of reprisal, enacted by a sovereign authority specializing in this particular function" (15). Religious law is a privileged example of this because law, like sacrifice, functions by means of a transcendentalizing authority that is rooted in religion:

> *Religion* in its broadest sense, then, must be another term for that obscurity that surrounds man's efforts to defend himself by curative or preventative means against his own violence. It is that enigmatic quality that pervades the judicial system when that system replaces sacrifice. This obscurity coincides with the transcendental effectiveness of a violence that is holy, legal, and legitimate successfully opposed to a violence that is unjust, illegal, and illegitimate. (*Violence and the Sacred* 23)

As I noted in Chapter 1, however, the Judeo-Christian Bible, as read by Girard, differs from the mythologies of Greece and other cultures in that it reveals the violence of cultural origins that myth usually works hard to conceal. For example, whereas the Oedipus story must be deconstructed to reveal that Oedipus is a scapegoat and a victim rather than guilty, the story of Jesus presents him openly as a victim of mob violence and a scapegoat.

The passage in which these issues are brought together most forcefully comes near the end of the final book when ancient rituals of human sacrifice are compared to modern Christian life. This comparison is in the words of the Pastor, and must be placed alongside the attitudes of the Wanderer and the Solitary in order to round out our view of these issues in *The Excursion*. I quote at length because of the importance of the rhetoric of this passage.

> "Once," and with mild demeanour, as he spake,
> On us the venerable Pastor turned
> His beaming eye that had been raised to Heaven,

"Once, while the name, Jehovah, was a sound
Within the circuit of this sea-girt isle
Unheard, the savage nations bowed the head
To Gods delighting in remorseless deeds;
Gods which themselves had fashioned, to promote
Ill purposes, and flatter foul desires.
Then, in the bosom of yon mountain-cove,
To those inventions of corrupted man
Mysterious rites were solemnized; and there—
Amid impending rocks and gloomy woods—
Of those terrific Idols some received
Such dismal service, that the loudest voice
Of the swoln cataracts (which now are heard
Soft murmuring) was too weak to overcome,
Though aided by wild winds, the groans and shrieks
Of human victims, offered up to appease
Or to propitiate. And, if living eyes
Had visionary faculties to see
The thing that hath been as the thing that is,
Aghast we might behold this crystal Mere
Bedimmed with smoke, in wreaths voluminous,
Flung from the body of devouring fires,
To Taranis erected on the heights
By priestly hands, for sacrifice performed
Exultingly, in view of open day
And full assemblage of a barbarous host;
Or to Andantes, female Power! who gave
(For so they fancied) glorious victory.
—A few rude monuments of mountain-stone
Survive; all else is swept away.—How bright
The appearances of things! From such, how changed
The existing worship; and with these compared,
The worshipers how innocent and blest!
So wide the difference, a willing mind
Might almost think, at this affecting hour,
That paradise, the lost abode of man,
Was raised again: and to a happy few,
In its original beauty, here restored.

"Whence but from Thee, the true and only God,
And from the faith derived through Him who bled
Upon the cross, this marvelous advance

>   Of good from evil; as if one extreme
>   Were left, the other gained."
>
>   (9.679–724)

The Pastor's role as one whose starting point is heaven rather than earth is emphasized at the outset of this crucial passage, as he turns "his beaming eye that had been raised to Heaven" to his earthbound companions. This perspective guides our interpretation of this passage—he is going to give us a theologically respectable account of the transition to Christianity, of the translation from violent sacrifice to the Christian law, which, in Girard's terms, veils the sacrificial mechanism, if thinly. Even within traditional Christian theology, however, the attitude toward sacrifice is ambivalent. As Frances Young points out, Christianity was founded partly in opposition to that part of the Jewish tradition which emphasized sacrifice, but Paul brought the objection to sacrifice back to sacrifice itself, in the notion that Christ's sacrifice had replaced the older notions of sacrifice:

> The Church modelled its worship on the Jewish synagogue rather than the Temple-cult; so there was no sacrifice. In this world-wide context, however, Paul had already begun to use sacrificial language to describe the worship and service of Christians.... Besides this, he had also used sacrifice as a means of understanding the death of Christ. In the Epistle to the Hebrews, this approach was taken further, so much so that it amounted to a rejection of Jewish sacrifices *on principle,* and the principle was an entirely new one. It was not just acceptance of the old criticisms of the practice. It was an assertion that *Christ's sacrifice had replaced them.* Sacrifice should no longer be offered by Christians, not because Christ's message was in conflict with the old Testament revelation of the past, but because he had so fulfilled it as to make it meaningless. (*Sacrifice and the Death of Christ* 49–50)

Not surprisingly, the Pastor shares the Wanderer's objections to sacrifice as presenting an illusion of instrumental efficacy. The false gods to whom humans will be sacrificed are created by the savages in part "to promote / Ill purposes," and the "female Power" is sacrificed to in the mistaken belief that she will effect "glorious victory." The Christian scene before the travelers gives, by contrast, the appearance of a recovery of "that paradise, the lost abode of man." The softly murmuring cataracts, which are now heard, were drowned out by the agony of the victims, even though those cataracts were "swoln" and wilder in those old, wild days, indicating that Christianity's triumph is also the triumph of a gentler nature.

The Excursion's view of pre-Christian sacrifice contrasts sharply with the similar image in book 12 of *The Prelude;* this contrast is a good demonstration of the difference between *The Prelude*'s incarnational praxis and *The Excursion*'s uneasy combination of incarnation and theory:

> I called upon the darkness, and it took—
> A midnight darkness seemed to come and take—
> All objects from my sight; and lo, again
> The desert visible by dismal flames!
> It is the sacrificial altar, fed
> With living men—how deep the groans!—the voice
> Of those in the gigantic wicker thrills
> Throughout the region far and near, pervades
> The monumental hillocks, and the pomp
> Is for both worlds, the living and the dead.
> (*The Prelude* 12.327–36)

The last five lines of this passage are borrowed from *Salisbury Plain* (121–26), in which the groans of the sacrificial victims are compared to those of the traveler, a victim of contemporary events. In *The Prelude*, the sacrificial scene is a restorative, invented memory (in the narrative of "Imagination, How Impaired and Restored" comprising books 11 and 12) that demonstrates the power of the poet's reviving imagination. He is able to call on the darkness and have this scene incarnated by the power of his own language, although that language is given less power in the 1850 version, when the scene appears to him "before the word / Was uttered" (13.327–28). The connection between the memory and the present scene is general—the reverie occurs "while through those vestiges of ancient times / [he] ranged" (12.317–18)—and darkness literally removes the objective world from the poet's sight, as if the power of imaginative recall can overcome any tension with the actual materiality of the world around the poet. As Bewell notes, "It should be obvious to any reader that the prehistoric past that Wordsworth saw so vividly and with such immediacy there on the lonely plains of Sarum was a fiction. Like the subsequent reverie, ... the scene that rose before his inner eye was ... derived from an imaginative response to his reading" (*Wordsworth and the Enlightenment* 45).

The scene in *The Excursion* is also fictional, but its fictionality has a very different status and genesis. Whereas *The Prelude*'s scene is a restorative "memory" incarnated by strong poetic language, *The Excursion*'s scene establishes the Christian incarnation in a complex binary relationship with pre-Christian human sacrifice. Unlike the generally situated scene on Salisbury Plain, it is precisely located "in the bosom of yon mountain-cove," put into a specific contemporary geographical context even as it plays a specific theological role in the contrast with Christianity. Neither the objective materiality of the contemporary world nor the contrast with Christianity can be ignored in the world of *The Excursion*, caught as that world is in the various tensions that we have been following between the presence and effacement of objectivity. *The Excursion*'s sacrificial scene returns to a relation to the contemporary objective world, as in *Salisbury Plain*, but here it is the universal world of contemporary Christianity, not the localized world of a victim of war. In *The Prelude*, despite the horror of the groans of living men being burned in a huge wicker man, this scene can express a "pomp . . . for both worlds, the living and the dead" that is almost like the proper epitaph's expression of the "joint offspring of the worth of the dead and the affections of the living" (*PrW* 2:58). In *The Excursion*, by contrast, the scene can only have value in an oppositional relationship with Christian sacrifice. In *The Prelude*, a scene of human sacrifice can be caught up as a product and affirmation of the poet's newfound incarnational language; in *The Excursion*, incarnation and representation pull in opposite directions: the incarnation itself (Christ's sacrifice on the cross) is part of the scene, but that original incarnation exists by virtue of a complex representational (as opposed to incarnational) relationship to the Incarnation itself.[46] This process is an example of what Jean-Luc Nancy discusses as the genesis of "Western" sacrifice (from Christ and Socrates through Hegel and Bataille) in a dialectical spiritualization of an invented notion of non-Western sacrifice. We view the "old" sacrifice as an economical process that has been replaced and sublated into the unique and universal sacrifice of subject, as Paul saw the sacrifice of Christ as a sublation of Hebrew sacrifice. This process demands both the rejection and the mimesis of sacrifice:

> Condemnation of this sacrificial "economism" runs through Plato and Christianity, Hegel and Bataille. Spiritualization has no doubt left us, from the outset, incapable of grasping the proper significance of the old sacrifice in its own context. . . . Everything finally occurs as if the spiritualization/dialectization of sacrifice could

not operate without a formidable disavowal of itself. It disavows itself beneath the figure of an "old" sacrifice, which it pretends to know and which in reality it fabricates for its own purposes. And it approves of itself in the form of an infinite process of negativity, which it covers with the "sacred" name of "sacrifice." This double operation brings to the center, simultaneously and in a painful ambiguity, the infinite efficacy of dialectical negativity *and* the bloody heart of sacrifice.... This same logic, which claims to be both rupture with and *mimetic repetition* of sacrifice, wants, by this same movement, to be both the sublation and the truth of sacrifice. ("The Unsacrificeable" 26–27)

In carrying out the process described by Nancy, the Pastor makes it clear that we are talking about extremes in comparing Christian and pre-Christian sacrifice, "as if one extreme / Were left, the other gained." That "as if" runs throughout both extremes: if the human sacrifice is the result of illusory expectations and the "inventions of corrupted man," the *appearance* of a restored paradise—"how bright / The appearances of things!"—is also an illusion, and an illusion dependent on the contrast provided by the invented vision of an economy of human sacrifice that has been sublated. It is clear that "living eyes" do *not* have "visionary faculties to see / The thing that hath been as the thing that is"; even the Wordsworthian autobiographer says in "Tintern Abbey" "I cannot paint what then I was." Thus if human sacrifice is built on illusion, so is the Pastor's inventive narrative of its atrocities. That illusion about the past can be invented partly because of cultural forgetfulness: aside from "a few rude monuments of mountain-stone," which, like the monuments in "Hart-Leap Well," are blending back into nature, all traces of the old world are "swept away." Thus what separates the past atrocities from the present peace is not illusion versus truth, but the fact of a differential opposition between two fictions and the West's dialectical sublation of sacrifice: it is only because the "difference" between these two fictions is "so wide" that the "willing mind / Might almost think"—but of course cannot, really—that we have a black-and-white contrast between a fallen and an unfallen world. Thus the Christian law of love is not only based on the violent death of Jesus, but is in its representational role caught in a dangerous binary relationship of reciprocal definition with that very pagan violence it is to replace.

This invention and illusion, both critiqued and practiced by the Pastor, suggests not only the process described by Nancy, but also Girard's definition of religion as "that obscurity that surrounds man's efforts to defend himself by curative or preventative means against his own violence," as well as Serres's definition of a theoretical system as a dialogue that defines itself in opposition to the "third man" of noise and violence. Here the differential structure of contrast between old and new rituals programmatically excludes the violence inherent in both, for not only are the past and present scenes equally illusory, and structurally interdependent in that the present is an illusory mirror image of the past, but they are also equally violent. The rituals informed by the "groans and shrieks / Of human victims" are replaced by "the faith derived through Him who bled / Upon the cross."

As Nancy points out, however, the violence of sacrifice is also ambiguously preserved in its very sublation, and as Girard points out (in a position somewhat at odds with Nancy's), Christianity recognizes violence on a more fundamental level than other systems do. In the pagan rites described by the Pastor, violence is not seen as fundamental, but as instrumental: sacrifice is a tool, a means, to gain an end of propitiation or success in battle (the invented "old" sacrifice described by Nancy). As we have seen, the purely instrumental use of reason or even of sacrifice is denigrated throughout *The Excursion.* It is in Christianity that the violence of the crucifixion is not simply instrumental, but is rather that fundamental fact from which faith is "derived." Thus behind the admittedly illusory vision of a present recovery of paradise, we have a faith derived from a violence that is excluded by the structure of the Pastor's fiction, but also recognized as even more fundamental than the violence of the old human sacrificial rites.

Herein lies the genius of Wordsworth's presentation of the Pastor in this final section of the poem. As I suggested in the beginning of my discussion of *The Excursion,* Wordsworth presents us with a poem whose main characters are more readers than they are poets, on the event/language rather than the thought/spirit side of the incarnational transformation. In presenting the Pastor, Wordsworth shows us the other side: a character very definitely from the thought/spirit side, who must lower his eyes even to see us. He must thus be read both from his point of view and from our more earthly one. We see his ethereal vision of the "wide difference" between the pagan and the Christian, and recognize it as theologically sound. At the same time, our event/language perspective causes us to see it as a structurally created illusion whose system of differences betrays the fundamental violence concealed by that system. We see Christianity, and by extension the incarnational foundation for thought, as both mythologizing and demythologizing: the Pastor's establishment of Christianity as an idealized myth built on an illusory system of differences and a sublation of old notions of sacrifice *is* the erection of a myth, but its admitted illusoriness and patently violent origins reminds us that the incarnation is a *de*mythologizing mechanism.

The role of violence in *The Excursion* and in the contrast between incarnational language and language as counter-spirit in the third "Essay Upon Epitaphs" give us another perspective on the paradoxical role of the objective element in language. In Chapter 1 I discussed Hegel's distinction—and confusion—between law and love in Christianity. The Christian message is one of love rather than law, but the demands of representation require the exteriority of law in order to effect the communication and expression of the interiority of love. We lament both the Host's necessary exteriority *and* its disappearance as it is eaten; the objective element is instrumental and ultimately dispensable—a means to an end—but also essential in that we mourn its loss. Words must be both "living" and "things": their incarnate life consists in a powerful, permanent thingness, but they also "die" as self-effacing signs. Conversely, and paradoxically, their existence in semiotic binary systems forces their inevitable thingness to run rampant, wreaking the violence of the coat of Nessus—they *cannot* simply efface themselves as signs— and the living nature of their incarnate thingness contains the seeds of death, because incarnation implies mortality: as book 5 of *The Prelude* has it, words are both "powers" for life and "frail shrines" for the dead.

This means that verbal "thingness" plays a role in both the incarnational and the representational views; their "awful power" as things is prior to either category. As in the image of the horse rejected from book 13 of *The Prelude,* words are "things" both as the dead objective remainders left over after a sign has done its representational work, and as the mortal "living things" by which authentic incarnation of thought occurs. The problem, of course, is that these two kinds of materiality are sometimes indistinguishable. This close interdependence of the incarnational and the representational is also evidenced by the rhetoric of the end of *The Prelude,* which I examined in Chapter 3: to argue that systems of representation lead to objective remains that cannot be effaced in semiotic representation is not so different from arguing, as I did in Chapter 3, that the incarnational rhetoric arises out of the subversion of a representational rhetoric. Here in *The Excursion,* the problem of a materiality that points both toward the negative side of representation and the positive side of incarnation returns as the problem of the very irrational, material, violent origins of the very Christian religion by which the "law of conscience" can represent God.

If we treat words as mere signs, we can claim that their objective portion is essentially fixed and dead, clothing whose sole purpose is to cover and express the body of thought. Yet this denial of words' "awful power" causes them to function in a precisely monstrous fashion: they become like animated corpses, which combine the categories of life and death illegitimately, and they exert a contagious violence (like that of the coat of Nessus) that no human system can control. The very attempt to treat words as "dead"—setting them up in binary opposition to the "life" they should express—causes this mixture to occur. In Taylor's terms, by not recognizing the moral sources behind a system, those sources function in unpredictable, and in this case violent ways. Incarnational thought counters this tendency, not by positing a transcendental unity, but by acknowledging the awful power of words as *living*, ethical things (before they are parts of an epistemological system) that are nonetheless essentially linked to the violent death of Jesus, which in effect unleashed the power of life. Thus thought and language are not opposed in the binary opposition of "live" thought and "dead" language, but are recognized as participating in the incarnational transformation of thought/spirit into language/mortal life: words are alive in the way that mortal beings are alive, which means that death—as a powerful, even violent force—is an acknowledged and fundamental part of that life.

Thus death and violence function in both the "incarnation" and the "counter-spirit" part of the formula, but in essentially different ways: in representational, binary thought (counter-spirit), it is the uncontrolled eruption of unacknowledged violence, whereas in incarnational thought it is the acknowledgment of and confrontation with the violent potential in language. As an idealizing theoretical theologian, the Pastor erects a system of figural representation by which Christianity and paganism are reciprocally defined, but this system veils the underlying violence only thinly. As an incarnational spokesman (though he sees incarnation from the other, transcendent side) the Pastor acknowledges, if somewhat backhandedly, the human, historical violence at the core of the Incarnation.

Notes

INTRODUCTION

1. The extent to which theology has come to be seen as an escape from, rather than as a species of, critical thought was brought home to me when a part of this study to be presented as a conference paper was rejected with the comment that I was "using the theological tradition to help Wordsworth and Romanticism fudge over real intellectual problems." I contend, of course, that "the theological tradition" and "real intellectual problems" are not mutually exclusive.

2. See *TM* 341–79.

3. John D. Caputo finds in Gadamer
    a deeply Hegelian streak which leads him to search for some hermeneutic version of the *Aufhebung*—some way to fuse the horizons so as to bear fruit in the present—rather than to undertake the radical Heideggerian step-back (*Schritt-züruck*) from all horizonality. He is too much interested in garnering the accumulated goods of the tradition, the "truth" (*verum, alethea*) which it has stored up, to ask the question of the *a-letheia* process itself, which Heidegger never ceased to pose and pose again, which never gave the "path of thought" any rest. (*Radical Hermeneutics* 96–97)

In defense of Gadamer against similar accusations, Gerald Bruns claims that "a careful reading of Gadamer produces an antitotalist conception of tradition that bears no resemblance to the sort of thing Eagleton and others claim to see in him. We miss the heteroglossia in Gadamer's notion of tradition. Gadamer's idea is that the encounter with tradition always brings our desire for totality up short" ("What Is Tradition?" 11).

4. Unless otherwise indicated, citations from *The Prelude* will be from the 1805 text in the Norton edition. Other Wordsworth poems are cited from the Clarendon edition of the *Poetical Works* unless otherwise indicated.

5. In a discussion whose concerns and texts are very different from mine, but whose conclusions parallel mine at a few points, Anthony Cascardi treats the Romantic attempt to recover nature in the wake of Kant in "From the Sublime to the Natural: Romantic Responses to Kant." Cascardi's broad categorization of Romantic texts, encompassing works from Shakespeare to Nietzsche, forces him to generalize about the Romantic attempt to recover the natural and conflate the noumenal and phenomenal in ways that I, from the specific vantage

point of Wordsworth's incarnational language, would question. Still, my interpretation of Wordsworth's incarnational thought shares Cascardi's emphasis on the Romantic desire to get beyond issues of representation and knowledge (115, 121), to see the "natural" as encompassing moral relationships (116), and to interpret the goal of nature's recovery (exemplified for Cascardi by marriage in *A Winter's Tale*) as a de-sublimating act that accepts life's contingency.

6. See Stephen Prickett, *Words and "The Word,"* 86–88.

7. Taylor's notion of expressivism responds to a range of problems and influences far broader than just the Kantian dilemma, and in fact he uses Kant's thought as a form of "modern internalization" that is an alternative rather than a challenge to expressivism, but I do not think my selective treatment of Taylor's argument distorts it in any way that would deny the validity of the point I am trying to make here.

8. Whereas philosophy had promised that our happiness

> would be achieved through our release from ignorance—from our escape from appearances to reality—Pyrrhonism was motivated by the realization that it was the promise of escape, not our ignorance, that was the real source of our unhappiness. With the subsequent development of skepticism, the purely epistemological aspects of Pyrrhonism increasingly overshadowed the moral ones and took on a life of their own. However, the original and fundamental point of skepticism was to call into question the possibility of knowledge and the reasonableness of belief in order to undermine their desirability. (Hiley, *Philosophy in Question* 10)

9. Hartman notes the tentativeness of Wordsworth's incarnational engagement with humanity, in contrast with Blake's unmediated relationship between imagination and the human: "He is not an anthropocentric artist and could never have said with Blake that 'Imagination is the Body of Man.' Nor will he ever attain that Christian or Blakean position. Christ is the 'one' related to human form, and the cross is an omphalos. But Wordsworth's imagination, on separating from nature and self-consciously seeking its own sphere of action, enters the world of men only precariously" (*Wordsworth's Poetry* 124).

10. For a brief and accessible account of the various senses of the "Word" of God, see Walter J. Ong's *Presence of the Word,* 182–91.

11. Studies that counter Abrams by emphasizing Wordsworth's participation in, rather than his secularization of England's religious traditions include Stephen Prickett, *Words and "The Word,"* and Richard Brantley, *Wordsworth's "Natural Methodism."*

12. See Stephen Gill's discussion of this point in *William Wordsworth: A Life,* 279–80.

13. I use "semiological" to refer to Saussurean and post-Saussurean sign theory, and "semiotic" to refer either to sign theory generally or to pre-Saussurean sign theory specifically.

14. See Dominick LaCapra's critique, in "The Temporality of Rhetoric," of the binary oppositions that limit both M. H. Abrams's *Natural Supernaturalism* and Paul de Man's "Rhetoric of Temporality" (in his *Blindness and Insight* 187–228).

15. Karen Mills-Courts, *Poetry as Epitaph:* "Hence, poets are compelled to seek exactly the right words, words which seem to 'belong' to truth, and which are unique and pure enough to master presence, to incarnate it and bring it into the world as meaning. Derrida has called this quest for the right word a 'nostalgia,' a 'longing for the master name' that never existed in the first place" (62–63).

16. One way to pursue the notion of language as event is through reader-response or reception theory, whose European versions are heavily influenced by Gadamer through Hans Robert Jauss. I do not take this approach, because I want to use Gadamer to focus on the production of meaning, rather than its reception; to emphasize meaning as constituted by its reception is to sidestep important questions about its production. Perhaps the most interesting recent development in reception theory's application to Romanticism is Tilottama Rajan's *Supplement of Reading,* in which she translates Derridean supplementation into a text's reconstitution by a reader:

> We cannot dismiss as a futile postponement of semiotic nihilism the sense that the problem of the text's difference from itself must be reconceived in terms of the reader. Writing is already thought of as an alienated medium that exists in the gap between signifier and signified. But reading in the romantic period is still to some extent conceived as an action, hence a medium in which the fracturing of the sign can be momentarily overcome, through a desire that creates understandings even if it does not uncover truths. (35)

I will try to put into question the semiological premises from which Rajan begins her move to reception theory; because she adopts a fairly standard deconstructive approach to the production of meaning, even her sophisticated move to the reader bypasses important questions about meaning's production. Still, I agree that the "event" of reading has an important role in what I am calling incarnational thought's attempt to respond to a crisis of representation.

17. Even the notion of an "unfallen" language does not necessarily refer to a simple, pretemporal unity. Irving Massey, in distinguishing between "prospective" meaning (temporal, unconscious, immediate, ethical) and "retrospective" meaning (spatial, conscious, distanced, nonethical) asserts the priority of the former by saying that "the unfallen language, the paradisal language of poetry is, then, paradoxically, purely temporal" (*Find You the Virtue* 12).

18. Prickett says of *The Prelude*, in arguing against a simple notion of progressive secularization, that "what is extraordinary about the poem is not its difference from Augustine's *Confessions* but its *similarity* [to that work].... Moreover, what strikes the reader about the *Prelude* is not so much its secularity, as a kind of disconcertingly inappropriate religiosity that suddenly obtrudes itself into the narrative for no very obvious reason" (*Words and "The Word"* 97).

19. Wordsworth here participates in the complex eighteenth- and nineteenth-century discussion of the relation between religious and poetic language, which Stephen Prickett traces in detail from John Dennis to John Henry Newman. See Prickett's *Words and "The Word,"* 37–68.

20. I am indebted to Joel Weinsheimer's discussion of this passage. See his *Philosophical Hermeneutics and Literary Theory* 120.

21. The problem is not only that we are tied to a general notion of meaning as residing in signs, but also that, through the somewhat accidental line of influence leading from Saussure to Lévi-Strauss to Derrida, much recent American criticism has restricted itself to a narrowly Saussurean definition of the sign, privileging Saussure's structuralism (as a system to be followed *or* overturned) over the competing theories of the sign offered by, to the east, the Prague structuralists, and, to the west, Peircean semiotics. A broader interpretation of the sign would usefully qualify many of the categorical statements that have been made in the past decade by the American followers of Derrida.

22. See also Richard Rorty's critique of representational thought, which he traces back to the image of the mind as a mirror of nature, in *Philosophy and the Mirror of Nature*.

23. See my "Viewing the 'Viewless Wings of Poesy.'"

24. See Paul de Man, "Political Allegory in Rousseau" and "The Rhetoric of Temporality" (in *Blindness and Insight* 187–228).

25. I am indebted to L. E. Marshall's discussion of the history of the Romantic concept of words as things in his " 'Words are *Things*': Byron and the Prophetic Efficacy of Language." See esp. 806–12.

26. See Hans Aarsleff, *From Locke to Saussure,* 24–31.

27. Jean-Jacques Rousseau, *The Second Discourse:* "Let us therefore begin by setting all the facts aside, for they do not affect the question" (103).

28. Laurence S. Lockridge points out in his *Ethics of Romanticism* that Romantic imagination readjusts the relationship between reason and morality:

> It is easy to see why the Romantics express no hostility to the term "moral sense." They enter their own brief against the rationalists, do not denigrate sense experience or analogies based on it, and conceive an interaction of the ethical and the aesthetic. For

them "moral sense," like "moral beauty," is no oxymoron. But the term "moral sense" is rendered largely obsolete by "imagination," which has, like the moral sense, a valuing power. (57)

29. See Cavell, *In Quest of the Ordinary,* esp. 4–9, 43–45, 55–56, and 171–78.

30. See Gerald L. Bruns, "Stanley Cavell's Shakespeare," 619. Levinas himself sees the history of skepticism as supporting the kind of temporality he promotes, in which the "saying" that precedes any thematization of representation is not reduced to the totalized synchrony of a "said":

> The periodic return of skepticism and of its refutation signify a temporality in which the instants refuse memory which recuperates and represents. Skepticism . . . is a refusal to synchronize the implicit affirmation contained in saying and the negation which this affirmation states in the said. . . . Skepticism . . . contests the thesis that between the saying and the said the relationship that connects in synchrony a condition with the conditioned is repeated. (*OTB* 167–68)

31. The careful reader may detect a contradiction in my use of both Gadamer and Levinas here, since, despite their common debt to Heidegger, Levinas's idea of "conversation" presupposes an *absence* of community, where Gadamer's idea presupposes the community of tradition and fusible horizons; Levinas explicitly objects to the "*we* prior to the I and the other" (*TI* 68) in Heidegger. Without denying the difference between Gadamer and Levinas, I see several points of contact that are useful for my argument. Both seek a relationship to the other that is prior to the totalized categories of subject and object, both treat language as conversation instead of representation, and in fact a nonconservative reading of Gadamer can view his sense of the tradition in which conversation occurs as similar to the temporality in which Levinas's relation to the "other" occurs. Gadamer claims that "hermeneutics must start from the position that a person seeking to understand something has a bond to the subject matter that comes into language through the traditionary text and has, or acquires, a connection with the tradition from which the text speaks," but he gives equal weight to the alterity in that relationship: "Hermeneutical consciousness is aware that its bond to this subject matter does not consist in some self-evident, unquestioned unanimity, as is the case with the unbroken stream of tradition. Hermeneutic work is based on a polarity of familiarity and strangeness" (*TM* 295). And to the extent that they are different, Levinas's radical notion of the subject absolutely separated from but in a relation of proximity to the other and Gadamer's notion of a conversation that fuses horizons reflect two sides of an ambivalence toward the subject and the community that is present in Romanticism itself.

32. See Robert Bernasconi and Simon Critchley, eds., *Re-Reading Levinas,* esp. xii–xiii. *Otherwise Than Being*'s intense recognition of the necessary reciprocity of "saying" and "said," as opposed to *Totality and Infinity*'s implicit assumption that "totality" can almost be escaped in favor of "infinity," makes the latter work more useful for my discussion (in Chapter 4) of the reciprocity of theoretical and incarnational thought in *The Excursion.* Still, our tendency to view Levinas through the lens of Derrida's writing has perhaps exaggerated the difference between the two works; it is largely by rather narrow deconstructive criteria that *Otherwise Than Being* can be said to supersede *Totality and Infinity.*

33. "Signifier" here of course means "s/he who signifies," not the material component of the Saussurean sign.

34. As Cavell puts it, the emphasis on consciousness in Romantic criticism "takes in train a philosophical machinery of self-consciousness, subjectivity, and imagination, of post-Kantianism in general, that for me runs out of control; and . . . closes out a possible question as to whether . . . self-consciousness is the cause or the effect of skepticism" (*In Quest of the Ordinary* 45).

35. See *OTB* 52–53.

36. Still, Matthew Arnold's definition of the moral in his essay on Wordsworth is applicable here: "A large sense is of course to be given to the term *moral.* Whatever bears upon the

question, 'how to live,' comes under it" (*Poetry and Criticism* 338). I am looking at Wordsworth's "ethical" side in a less prescriptive sense, of course—more for insight into how we *do* live—particularly in relation to the fact of death and the necessity of skepticism than for advice on *how* to live.

CHAPTER 1

1. Although this may be overstating the case, Gadamer himself has admitted that encounters with French post-Heideggerian thought such as that of Derrida has increased his awareness of his own Romantic roots: "Since my confrontation with the French continuation of Heideggerian thought, I have become aware that my efforts to 'translate' Heidegger testify to my own limits and especially indicate how deeply rooted I am in the romantic tradition of the humanities and its humanistic heritage" ("Text and Interpretation," in Diane P. Michelfelder and Richard E. Palmer, eds., *Dialogue and Deconstruction,* 24).

2. My attention was drawn to this passage (and to the significance of this essay) by Mark C. Taylor's *Altarity.* See esp. 6–11. Taylor's emphasis on Hegel's essay as advocating "inwardization" (*Erinnerung*) underplays both its difference from the later Hegel and its exploration of the *tension* between spiritual inwardness and religious objectivity in the Incarnation.

3. I thank Raimonda Modiano for alerting me to the relevance of Nancy's argument to my own.

4. See Frances Young, *Sacrifice and the Death of Christ,* 49–50.

5. See Girard's reading of the Oedipus myth in *Violence and the Sacred,* 68–88, and *The Scapegoat,* 25–46.

6. Girard, *Violence and the Sacred:* "From the outset of this study, after all, I have regarded violence as something entirely communicable. The tendency of violence to hurl itself on a surrogate if deprived of its original object can surely be described as a contaminating process" (30). In the case of twins, which are "harbingers of indiscriminate violence," many cultures have "one common concern: the fear of pollution." The connection between contagious disease and violence comes in the fact that " 'Bad' violence is by definition a force that works on various levels—physical, familial, social—and spreads from one to the other" (57–58).

7. See Angus Fletcher, " 'Positive Negation.' "

CHAPTER 2

1. In response to the 1815 edition of *Poems* Blake wrote "Natural Objects always did & now do Weaken deaden and obliterate Imagination in Me Wordsworth must know that what he Writes Valuable is Not to be found in Nature" (*The Complete Poetry and Prose of William Blake* 665).

2. See especially "Inscriptions and Romantic Nature Poetry," in Geoffrey Hartman's *Unremarkable Wordsworth,* 31–46.

3. See Ferdinand de Saussure's *Course in General Linguistics,* 65–70, and Claude Lévi-Strauss's *Savage Mind,* 18–30. Though Lévi-Strauss embraces the materiality of the signifying side of the sign ("Signs resemble images in being concrete entities but they resemble concepts in their powers of reference" [18]), Saussure backs off from the idea of words' materiality ("The sound-image is sensory, and if I happen to call it 'material,' it is only in that sense, and by way of opposing it to the other term of the association, the concept, which is generally more abstract" [66]).

4. See Barbara Johnson's succinct review of this history in her essay "Writing," in Frank Lentricchia and Thomas McLaughlin's *Critical Terms for Literary Study.*

5. See L. E. Marshall's discussion of Byron's use of words as things that effect curses in "'Words are Things,'" 816.

6. See "The Ethics of Particularity," in Irving Massey's *Find You the Virtue*, 31–52.

7. See Andrzej Warminski's analysis of the similarly problematic status of the body in this essential Wordsworthian analogy as it is implied in the episode concerning the drowned man of Esthwaite: "The analogy body is to soul as garment is to body links, and verifies the link between, God's Book on the one side and man's books on the other.... Nevertheless, a trouble is introduced into this tropological system of analogies by the surfacing of the drowned man's corpse. For what happens is that the *corpse* is introduced into the slot in the analogy occupied by the body. And the analogy now reads: the corpse is to the soul as the garments are to the corpse" ("Facing Language" 28).

8. Paul de Man's early work clearly articulated the ambiguity of this sense of "thingness" as well as its connection with death. In "The Rhetoric of Temporality" (1969), he says of the second quatrain of "A Slumber," "She has now become a *thing* in the full sense of the word, not unlike Baudelaire's falling man who became a thing in the grip of gravity, and, indeed, she exists beyond the touch of earthly years. But the light-hearted compliment has turned into a grim awareness of the de-mystifying power of death, which makes all the past appear as a flight into the inauthenticity of a forgetting" (*Blindness and Insight* 224). In the earlier (1960) article "Intentional Structure of the Romantic Image," he notes the general tendency of Romantic poetic language to engage in a futile struggle to attain the status of a natural object: "Poetic language seems to originate in the desire to draw closer and closer to the ontological status of the object, and its growth and development are determined by this inclination. We saw that this movement is essentially paradoxical and condemned in advance to failure" (*The Rhetoric of Romanticism* 7).

9. See *OTB* 195n, in which Levinas states his preference for "a responsibility stronger than death" to Heidegger's being-for-death as an "anxiety over the limitation of being."

10. See my "Catachresis and the Romantic Will," 27.

11. Alan Bewell, *Wordsworth and the Enlightenment*: "The Boy of Winander illustrates a central feature of Wordsworth's anthropology of death: that the dead receive a dual burial, in earth and in narratives. Language and burial can thus be seen not only as two of the most important social and socializing human institutions, but also as complementary symbolic mediums that came into being at approximately the same time for the same purpose—to deal with death by reasserting symbolically our original belief in immortality" (212).

12. Andrzej Warminski rightly reads the passage about the boy's encounter with the drowned man as a process of aestheticization, in terms similar to my own: "He is not frightened by the spectacle of the drowned man because he had read of such sights in *books*. It is a spirit coming from books that now re-inspirits the corpse and renders it an aesthetic object with ideal meaning, a veritable work of art.... Such a turn is what Paul de Man in his last work called 'aesthetic ideology,' and the drowned man is a veritable model of it, aesthetic ideology incarnate, as it were" ("Facing Language" 27–30). Still, Warminski, like de Man, uses the incarnational model as a straw man, a "blind" thematic position—"At least on the thematic level the text is unequivocal in its being *for* an incarnational (sacrificial, resurrectional, aesthetic, dialectical) model of language and the text" (27)—to be deconstructed by an "insightful" theory of textuality. Not only does this ideologically rigid reading prevent Warminski from articulating how this incarnational model (whose phenomenological richness he understands very well) confronts problems of textuality, but it also makes his view of Wordsworth's text too uniform. *The Prelude* is about the struggle *toward* incarnational expression; the simple division of Wordsworth's text into "incarnational" and "textual" levels elides the important distinctions among passages in which, as an essential part of the development narrated in *The Prelude*, incarnational generation of meaning is a greater or lesser force.

13. Two Gadamerian ideas are in the background of this point: one is that textuality itself,

and by implication Wordsworth's incarnational poetic text, involves a kind of reification, but one that is an intermediate stage in the process of interpretation; this reified text does not constitute or even ground interpretation: "From the hermeneutical standpoint—which is the standpoint of every reader—the text is a mere intermediate product [*Zwischenprodukt*], a phase in the event of understanding that, as such, certainly includes a definite abstraction, namely, the isolation and reification involved in this very phase" ("Text and Interpretation," in Michelfelder and Palmer, eds., *Dialogue and Deconstruction,* 31). The second is Gadamer's critique of the fundamentality of the subject/object split, leading to his promotion of a hermeneutic conversation that treats the dialogue itself as prior to the subject: what emerges in authentic conversation is "the logos, which is neither mine nor yours and hence so far transcends the interlocutors' subjective opinions that even the person leading the conversation knows that he does not know" (*TM* 368). My point here is not simply that Wordsworth anticipated Gadamer, but rather that these ideas in both Gadamer and Wordsworth reflect some of the implications of pursuing an "incarnational" mode of thought that is released from the idea of a subject manipulating a system of signs.

14. It must be kept in mind that this is a distinction in function only; most words are both signs and things. For example, the words of *The Prelude* still speak to us as "living things" even as their semiotic function enacts a "death" of the signifying poem into the signified life outside of the poem. As Gadamer points out, a poetic text is unique because it combines the referential function of a text, which disappears before its meaning (what I am calling, in terminology that Gadamer would not use, its existence as a set of signs), with the autonomy of a self-originating text (what I am calling words-as-things): "In a literary work, a peculiar tension is generated between the directedness to meaning inherent in discourse and the self-presentation inherent in its appearance" ("Text and Interpretation," in Michelfelder and Palmer, eds., *Dialogue and Deconstruction,* 43).

15. As the translator's note points out, "represent" translates *vertreten* (to deputize or act as a substitute for) rather than *vorstellen* (to afford a representation or idea), but the point still holds, since, in the sense I am using, it is the act of substitution, whether human or poetic, that is at issue, and which is contained in both senses.

16. See Brian Caraher's *Wordsworth's Slumber and the Problematics of Reading,* 119–20 for additional textual evidence, including the capitalized final "She" and "Me" in a late (1848) manuscript of the poem, that Wordsworth was at pains to stress "the sudden difference the irrevocable loss of the woman means for the speaker" (120).

17. See *TI* 232–36.

18. The consolidation of the Lucy poems as an integrated sequence was of course largely the work of late Victorian editors, though some of the connections were initially suggested by Wordsworth's correspondence and the ordering of the poems in editions during his lifetime. For an account of the poems' editorial history, see Caraher, *Wordsworth's Slumber,* esp. 101–3.

19. See Geoffrey Hartman, "A Touching Compulsion," in *The Unremarkable Wordsworth* 27.

20. Hans-Georg Gadamer, *Neuere Philosophie II:* "Die Freiheit des Denkens ist der wahre Grund dafür, daß der Tod eine notwendige Unbegreiflichkeit hat" ["The freedom of thought is the true ground for the fact that death has a necessary ungraspability"] (171).

21. I do not mean to imply, of course, that Wordsworth subscribed to the Catholicism implied in this interpretation of the Eucharist. His complex position between Catholic objectification and Protestant signification of God's presence will be examined in Chapter 4.

22. Though he is not distinguishing these two types of repetition, and is in fact talking about a process of spiritualization rather than incarnation, Alan Bewell describes the repetition in "Lucy Gray" as a history of death in similar terms: "We are thus given a history of the idea of death that does not proceed referentially or chronologically, but instead resides, like the series of 'translation' narratives in the Bible, in the history of interpretations that this story has given rise to" ("Wordsworth and the Enlightenment" 205). See also Dominick LaCapra's critique of

the oversimplified versions of repetition promoted, at opposite ends of the critical spectrum, by M. H. Abrams and Paul de Man: "The crucial point on which I have insisted is that temporality is best seen as an intricate process of repetition with change—at times traumatically disruptive change that may nonetheless involve the return of the repressed. This process is oversimplified when it is resolved into an option between continuity and discontinuity, 'symbolic' unity and 'allegorical' disjunction" ("The Temporality of Rhetoric" 147).

CHAPTER 3

1. The terms "narrative" (*histoire*) and "discourse" (*discours*) are borrowed from Emile Benveniste via Louis Marin. See Louis Marin, "The Autobiographical Interruption," esp. 599–603, and "Toward a Theory of Reading in the Visual Arts," esp. 295–96. I have used these terms to explore the autobiographical rhetoric of books 1 and 6 of *The Prelude* in "The Emergence of the Autobiographical Figure" and "Catachresis and the Romantic Will."

2. Michel Foucault reads *Don Quixote* in this way, suggesting that as a consequence Don Quixote's "reality" is purely intralinguistic: "Don Quixote's truth is not in the relation of the words to the world but in that slender and constant relation woven between themselves by verbal signs" (*The Order of Things* 48).

3. The word "figure" is inevitably problematic, since it suggests the stasis of representational images (as in the human "figure") as well as the process of figuration, which, as de Man points out, is characterized by the active divergence of referent from grammar. From the latter point of view, "figural grammar" is an oxymoron; however, since Wordsworth indeed creates a very paradoxical "figural grammar," the terminology seems appropriate, suggesting the hypostasis of grammatical structures, but also gesturing toward their inevitable subversion by the figural dimension of language. I will use "trope," with its connotations of a "turn," to refer to the figural dimension of language characterized by performative divergence from grammatical structure.

4. For more on the philosophical history of this concept see *TM* 9–19. See also Philippe Lacoue-Labarthe and Jean-Luc Nancy, *The Literary Absolute*, on the Athenaeum fragments of the Schlegel brothers: "Hence the constant and crucial motif of *Bildung* throughout the fragments, in its two values of formation as putting-into-form and formation as culture. Man and work of art alike are what they are only insofar as they are *gebildet*, having taken on the form and figure of what they ought to be" (47).

5. On "Vadracour and Julia" as a tale of unnatural suppression, see Hartman, *Wordsworth's Poetry*, 243. For an outline of the tale's biographical and political significance, see Carl Woodring, *Politics in English Romantic Poetry*, 108.

6. For a discussion of the history of these terms (with the opposite purpose of enriching the meaning of "figure") see Erich Auerbach, "Figura," in *Scenes from the Drama of European Literature*, 11–76.

7. See Edward Said, *Beginnings*, esp. 32–35, 174.

8. In contrast to the "metaphysical" sense of metaphor discussed by Jacques Derrida in "White Mythology": "In this case, metaphor is included within metaphysics as that which should penetrate to the horizon or to the depths of the proper, and in the end there regain the origin of its truth. The turning of the sun is then seen as a reflecting circle, returning to itself with no loss of sense, no irreversible expenditure" (71).

9. For a discussion of the line as an image of narrative continuity, see J. Hillis Miller, "Narrative Middles." With reference to *Tristram Shandy*, Miller points to the "contrast between the featureless straight line and the line curved to become a sign, so carrying meaning and becoming a plot, but at the same time becoming transgressive, deviant" (381).

10. See Derrida, "White Mythology," esp. 52–53.

11. Gerald Bruns presents this Gadamerian view of legal hermeneutics in terms of its historicity as well as its textuality:
> Interpretation in this event will be an adjudication of past and present, or between a written text, the history of the understanding of it (that is, the history of its application), and the question currently to be decided. The law will be that by which we understand our present situation, even as our situation will throw its light upon the law or help us to understand the law more fully, or in a way that will enable the law to remain forceful instead of lapsing into a merely documentary existence. ("Law as Hermeneutics" 317)

12. Marjorie Levinson sees Wordsworth's project in the latter terms: "The larger boon sought by the poet and offered to his contemporary reader was the displacement of ideological contradiction to a context where resolution could be imagined and implemented with some success" (*Wordsworth's Great Period Poems* 5–6). This perception of Wordsworth is shared by Jerome McGann, who says of the "Ode: Intimations of Immortality," "The poem annihilates its history, biographical and socio-historical alike, and replaces these particulars with a record of pure consciousness.... That Wordsworth's was a false consciousness needs scarcely to be said" (*The Romantic Ideology* 90–91). Such historically critical approaches are valuable in their efforts to avoid the solipsism of seeing Romanticism only through its own ideology, and in their reaction to the atemporal excesses of semiotics. The danger, however, is that this critical approach to Romantic ideology will not escape the legacy of nineteenth-century historicism, whose attempt to objectify history as an object of "scientific" study established an artificial relation of complete otherness between the historian and his putatively "complete" (because it is observable from the outside) object. This error denies the unavoidable *interaction* between interpreter and object: "For history is not only not at its end, but we its interpreters are situated within it, as a conditioned and finite link in a continuing chain" (*TM* 200).

13. I treat in more detail in Chapter 4 the conflict in Christianity between Jesus' role as the fulfillment or the abrogation of the Jewish law.

14. See Matthew 26:20–29; Mark 14:17–22; Luke 22:14–23.

15. One way in which the violence associated with the Incarnation can be avoided is to emphasize the happy birth of Christ instead of his death and resurrection. According to van Beeck, this is exactly what happened in Romantic theology:
> For [Schleiermacher]—and for the entire period that expressed its religious identity in *Stille Nacht* and *Minuit Chretiens*—Christmas becomes the vantage point from which to reflect on the Christian mystery.... As the new-born Savior, Christ is the model and the source of the peaceful, spiritual joy which is the prerogative of all those who have been reborn as children by the experience of this most holy night, this feast of piety and melody. (*Christ Proclaimed* 558)

Wordsworth's many celebrations of childhood innocence, of course, transfer this theological emphasis to poetic language.

16. The editors of the Norton *Prelude* point out the similarity between the Snowdon scene and *Paradise Lost* 7.285–87.

17. The uneasy uniting of discordant events that Hartman emphasizes throughout his essay is closely linked to the language of incarnation, which attempts to harmonize the transcendental source of meaning and the event of language, though Hartman dismisses the "logocentric or incarnationist thesis," which "haunts the fringes of most studies of literature," as an oversimplification of textual reality (*The Unremarkable Wordsworth* 177).

18. "System," for Lacoue-Labarthe and Nancy in their interpretation of the Schlegels, is a complex term. It is manifested partly as a desire for an absent system inscribed in that—the fragment—which is antisystematic: "The co-presence of the fragmentary and the systematic has a double and decisive significance: it implies that both the one and the other are established in Jena within the same horizon, and that this horizon is the very horizon of the System, whose exigency is inherited and revived by romanticism" (*The Literary Absolute* 42).

19. Draft 3a, in the Norton edition of *The Prelude* 496–99.
20. Thomas De Quincy, "Wordsworth's Autobiographical Poem," *Gentleman's Magazine* 34 (1850): 459–68, quoted in the Norton *Prelude* 553. The role of the fragment in Romanticism has been a topic of much recent study. See Marjorie Levinson, *The Romantic Fragment Poem*; Thomas McFarland, *Romanticism and the Forms of Ruin*; and Tilottama Rajan, *The Supplement of Reading*.
21. See Louis Marin, "The Autobiographical Interruption," 603–4. For a discussion of the "ruse of writing" used to begin *The Prelude*, see my "Emergence of the Autobiographical Figure."
22. For a broad-ranging meditation on the "effortless" in language, see Massey, *Find You the Virtue*, esp. 113–34.
23. For an instructive account of how Rousseau becomes—in ways very different from Wordsworth—a "post-fictional self," see Juliet Flower MacCannell, "The Post-Fictional Self."
24. As Eugene Vance points out, "'I' is deictic: that is to say, rather than being a signifier (such as the word 'book') designating a specific substance whose nature is more or less fixed, 'I' is a special signifier whose referent necessarily varies with the circumstances of its enunciation" ("Augustine's *Confessions* and the Grammar of Selfhood" 2–3).
25. According to Ferguson, in Wordsworth "an education into selfhood involves disclosing the patterns of internal annexation of others which is the fundamental and inescapable mode of the affections" (*Language as Counter-Spirit* 150). Weiskel argues that *The Prelude* is a dialogue, not so much with Coleridge as with invented past selves of the poet (*The Romantic Sublime* 170–71). Friedrich Schlegel saw the "internal dialogue" of the unavoidably divided self as exemplified throughout history in the form of prayer, "a dialogue of the soul with God" (*The Philosophy of Life* 389). According to van Beeck, the incarnate Word's relationship to God the Father affirms Jesus' self, but also his involvement in human dialogue: "This selfhood, however, is not an isolated selfhood, for Jesus' relationship to God precisely enables him to relate to others boundlessly" (*Christ Proclaimed* 424).
26. Raimonda Modiano notes that Coleridge, in his exaggeration of William Bowles's influence on him at the expense of Wordsworth's, uses a theory of gift exchange similar to Lewis Hyde's to establish an ideal of poetic influence, though it is an ideal he himself violates partly by using it against Wordsworth: "Coleridge, while invoking the ethics of gift exchange as a reminder of Wordsworth's sins against him, is the first to violate it.... In Hyde's terms, Coleridge uses the possessive code of property exchange in relation to Wordsworth and the altruistic code of gift exchange in relation to Bowles" ("Coleridge and Wordsworth" 114).
27. In "Poetics of Prophecy," Hartman attempts to explain the relationship between death and chastisement, in which "there is no hint of anything that would compel the mind to link the two terms," in terms of a "'gravitation' effect, whereby unrelated incidents fell toward each other" (in *The Unremarkable Wordsworth* 170). Similarly, Gayatri Spivak sees here "a metonymic though not logical or metaphoric connection... suggested through contiguity" ("Sex and History in *The Prelude* [1805]: Books IX–XIII" 199). David Ellis argues that it can only be explained within a logic of difference: "The difference between what [the boy] had anticipated and what actually happened is so great that the former becomes a source of guilt" (*Wordsworth, Freud and the Spots of Time* 20). Richard E. Brantley interprets the scene theologically, but in moral, rather than rhetorical terms: "At the heart of this spot of time is a lesson in Christian humility, and when the passage is so understood we are less likely to be repelled by the proposition that the persona has done something for which the death of his father is a chastisement" (*Wordsworth's "Natural Methodism"* 44).
28. This sense of gift giving as a separation of the gift from the giver relies on Levinas's notion that "giving has meaning only as a tearing from oneself despite oneself" (*OTB* 78), and is opposed, at least in emphasis, to Marcel Mauss's converse notion that gift giving is dangerous because it is the communication of one's spiritual essence: "One gives away what is in reality a

part of one's nature and substance, while to receive something is to receive a part of one's spiritual essence. To keep this thing is dangerous, not only because it is illicit to do so, but also because it comes morally, physically and spiritually from a person" (*The Gift* 10). Where Mauss emphasizes the essential communication of spiritual content in the transaction, Levinas emphasizes the existential experience of alterity—which disrupts the very idea of an essential "content"—in the transaction.

29. See Louis Marin's "Autobiographical Interruption." The translation of narrative into the discourse of dialogue has a prominent liturgical function, related directly to the continuing role of the Incarnate Word in the religious community. Rose A. Zak points out that "the Psalms may be seen as a lyrically interpretive prophecy of the life of Christ, but their function in contemporary liturgical structures affirms their role as providing a space for dialogue rather than for narrative" ("Dialogue and Discourse in Stravinsky's 'Symphony of Psalms' " 360).

30. The word "experience," with its double sense of the immediate act of experiencing and the residual, permanent content of what is experienced, provides a linguistic example of this combination of permanent closure and fluid immediacy. Gadamer points out that in German the combination of these meanings in the word *Erlebnis* did not become common until the nineteenth century: "Unlike the verb erleben, the noun *Erlebnis* became common only in the 1870's.... Both meanings obviously lie behind the coinage *Erlebnis*; both the immediacy, which precedes all interpretation, reworking, and communication, and merely offers a starting point for interpretation—material to be shaped—and its discovered yield, its lasting result." Also, because of the primary link between experience and the self, an experience cannot be objectified as a teleological "concept": "The notion of experience also implies a contrast between life and mere concept. Experience has a definite immediacy which eludes every opinion about its meaning" (*TM* 60–61, 67).

CHAPTER 4

1. In terms compatible with another strand of my argument—that incarnational theory offers an interpretive alternative to contemporary semiotic theories—Charles Altieri argues that a consideration of Wordsworth's "ideal of lyric eloquence" enables an engagement with the world that cannot be accomplished by the prevailing modes of late twentieth-century critical theory:

> Such emphases then offer two fundamental contributions to contemporary theory: they define the values possible if we treat poetry as direct, passionate personal utterance, therefore sharply at odds with both the dramatic model basic to New Criticism and the models of textuality governing both deconstruction and new historicist semiotics; and they allow us to make claims for the social significance of poetry without having to rely on a cult of irony or the languages of demystification. The display of passions becomes both an index of powers with which the reader can identify and a projected test of their value in engaging the world beyond the text. (*Canons and Consequences* 132–33)

2. To the limited sense in which the relationship between "incarnation" and "representation" parallels the relationship between "feeling" and "thought" that occasioned so much discussion in the nineteenth century, the explicit tension between these realms in *The Excursion* helps to explain the poem's oft-noted "Victorianism." Stephen Prickett notes Arnold's separation of the realms that the Romantics had united: "What is much more significant is [Arnold's] willingness to abandon the idea of psychic unity at the centre of the Wordsworth/Coleridge idea of poetry as a union of thought *and* feeling in favor of Mill's view of poetry as a matter of pure feeling opposed to 'science' and cognitive content" (*Words and "The Word"* 63–64).

3. David Wellbery points out that this notion of signs as tools reflects the Enlightenment, rather than the modern conception of the sign: "For Saussure and for contemporary semiotics,

language is a social institution, a semiotic (or semiological) system that is sustained by and sustains the collective. But language is this social, systematic, institutional sense is not known— is not an object of study—in the eighteenth century. In the eighteenth-century view, language is one set of instruments... which rational beings use to mark, externalize, manipulate, and communicate their mental representations" (*Lessing's "Laocoon"* 18).

4. Charles Taylor traces this Enlightenment separation of epistemology from ethics from Descartes's theory of procedural reason through Locke's disengaged "punctual self," which takes a supposedly value-free stand toward an objectified world (*Sources of the Self* 156, 160ff). For different purposes, Richard Rorty traces the development of a representational theory of meaning to the post-Cartesian development of a separate category called "mind" (*Philosophy and the Mirror of Nature* 17–69). In his resurrection of the challenge of Pyrrhonian skepticism, David Hiley discusses the reduction, after Descartes, of skepticism's concerns from moral and social questions to purely theoretical and epistemological ones (*Philosophy in Question* 65).

5. Taylor argues against the possibility of "neutral" selves "defined in abstraction from any constitutive concerns": "[Selves] are not neutral, punctual objects; they exist only in a certain space of questions, through certain constitutive concerns. The questions or concerns touch on the nature of the good that I orient myself by and on the way I am placed in relation to it" (*Sources of the Self* 50). Though Gadamer claims not to be concerned with ethics, because "even immoral beings try to understand one another" ("Reply to Jacques Derrida," in Michelfelder and Palmer, eds., *Dialogue and Deconstruction*, 55), he makes a similar statement in theological terms about the necessary contextualization of self-understanding: "*Selbstverständnis* has a pietistic undertone suggesting precisely that one cannot succeed in understanding oneself and that this foundering of one's self-understanding and self-certainty should lead one to the path of faith. *Mutatis mutandis* this applies to the hermeneutical usage of this same term" ("Letter to Dallmayr," in Michelfelder and Palmer, eds., *Dialogue and Deconstruction*, 97).

6. This point is made by Donald H. Reiman in his *Intervals of Inspiration* 155–56.

7. See also Thomas Heller, "Structuralism and Critique," *Stanford Law Review* 36 (1984): 191, quoted by Stanley Fish in *Doing What Comes Naturally* 25: "The claim to a meta-status for theory may be seen as a claim to institutional power for the practitioners of theory."

8. Martha Nussbaum's work also provides an example of the point I tried to make at the end of the previous chapter, which is even more relevant here: the several oppositions outlined between "representational" and "incarnational" thought are not simple oppositions because, as we saw in the previous chapter, the "incarnational" must emerge from, and thus must contain within it a dialectical tension with, the "opposing" representational side of the spectrum. Nussbaum points out that the "Aristotelian" ethics of contingency luck is not the opposite of the "Platonic" ethics of rational self-sufficiency, so much as it is a critical adjustment of that to which it is opposed. After listing characteristics of the two sides under *A* (the Platonic view) and *B* (the Aristotelian view), she notes that "*B* is not the polar opposite of *A*: it is the balanced combination of the elements stressed and cultivated in *A* with the elements that *A* avoids and shuns" (*The Fragility of Goodness* 20).

9. In Mary Jacobus, "Apostrophe and Lyric Voice in *The Prelude*," esp. 174.

10. How ocular metaphors have turned philosophy toward representation and epistemology is discussed at length by Richard Rorty in *Philosophy and the Mirror of Nature*.

11. Kenneth Johnston goes so far as to say that, by 1815, in the wake of *The Excursion*'s poor public reception, autobiography replaces philosophical system: "By his references to *The Recluse*, we can see that the categorization of 1815 supplants an architectural model by an autobiographical one: the cathedral becomes the man, as Wordsworth's tactics shift from applying his poetry to life, to applying his life to his poetry and making the 'system' of his works coterminus with his life" (*Wordsworth and "The Recluse"* 337).

12. This complex association between baptism and death is echoed in the otherwise mediocre sonnet "Baptism" in the *Ecclesiastical Sonnets*. The concluding sestet claims that baptism inside the church is appropriate partly because
> There, should vain thoughts outspread their wings and fly
> To meet the coming hours of festal mirth,
> The tombs—which hear and answer that brief cry,
> The Infant's notice of his second birth—
> Recall the wandering Soul to sympathy
> With what man hopes from Heaven, yet fears from Earth.
>   (3.20.9–14)

As he is being baptized, the infant's cry bounces off the sepulchers within the church, establishing an echoing dialogue between the spiritual rebirth of baptism and the fact of human mortality.

13. Kant, *Prolegomena*:
> But as a boundary itself is something positive, which belongs as well to that which lies within, as to the space that lies without the given complex, it is still an actual positive cognition, which reason only acquires by enlarging itself to this boundary, yet without attempting to pass it; because it there finds itself in the presence of an empty space, in which it can conceive forms of things, but not things themselves. But the setting of a boundary to the field of the understanding by something, which is otherwise unknown to it, is still a cognition which belongs to reason even at this standpoint, and by which it is neither confined within the sensible, nor straying without it, but only refers, as befits the knowledge of a boundary, to the relation between that which lies without it, and that which is contained within it. (133–34)

14. See Andrew Cooper's analysis of this Romantic process in poets other than Wordsworth in *Doubt and Identity in Romantic Poetry*: "Through the reader, the poem's words become flesh as in reality the meanings of the soul become flesh through the expressions of the body" (186).

15. I am aware that I am reversing the valorization of Roland Barthes's use of these terms. For him, the writerly text embodies a positively valued polysemy—"The writerly text is a perpetual present, upon which no *consequent* language (which would inevitably make it past) can be superimposed; the writerly text is *ourselves writing*, before the infinite play of the world (the world as function) is traversed, intercepted, stopped, plasticized by some singular system (Ideology, Genus, Criticism) which reduces the plurality of entrances, the opening of networks, the infinity of languages"—whereas the readerly is the "negative, reactive value" to the writerly; readerly texts are "products (and not productions), they make up the enormous mass of our literature" (*S/Z* 4–5). Readerly texts are "committed to the closure system of the West, produced according to the goals of this system, devoted to the law of the Signified" (7–8). This ascription of ideological domination to the readerly is a classic example of how a theory based on signs can ignore the dominance that is also inherent in the writerly. As Gadamer says, writing is control: "The art of writing... consists in the fact that the writer so controls the world of signs making up the text that the return of the text into spoken language succeeds" ("Letter to Dallmayr," in Michelfelder and Palmer, eds., *Dialogue and Deconstruction*, 96). For Levinas, as I noted in the previous chapter, the interlocutor or reader interrupts the totality of the "said" text, returning it to the untotalizable incarnate temporality of "saying." *The Excursion* similarly suggests that readerliness encourages polysemy, and that writerliness exerts a dominating totalization. The autobiographical voice of *The Prelude* does seem to fit Barthes's description of "*ourselves writing*, before the infinite play of the world," but that is precisely because the autobiographer's involvement in his own subject prevents a dominating "writer" from emerging (except, as I have noted, briefly at the end) as he would in the presentation of a theory.

16. I use M. M. Bakhtin's handy opposition between monological authority and dialogical

critique without intending to invoke exactly his sense of the dialogical; Bakhtin's emphasis on contemporaneousness, laughter, and the genre of the novel makes his theory of dialogue less appropriate to Wordsworth than Gadamer's sense of dialogue as a presubjective context of historically mediated conversation. See M. M. Bakhtin's *The Dialogic Imagination,* esp. 4–40.

17. See my "Emergence of the Autobiographical Figure" for a discussion of this rhetoric at the beginning of *The Prelude.*

18. This active sense of reading as incarnation of meaning is in accord with the side of Gadamer that emphasizes receptivity and hearing in the hermeneutical process (a part of Gadamer's thought that was developed into a full-blown theory of reception by his student Hans Robert Jauss). Gadamer criticizes Derrida for not taking the "reading" side of writing into account: "If Derrida is going to insist that signs are ambiguous and for this reason wants *écriture* to somehow speak like an inner voice, he should not forget that writing is intended to be read.... One cannot read what is written without understanding it—that is, without expressing it and thereby making an intonation and modulation that anticipates the sense of the whole" ("Hermeneutics and Logocentrism," in Michelfelder and Palmer, eds., *Dialogue and Deconstruction,* 118).

19. Charles Taylor, *Sources of the Self:* "It becomes an embarrassment to religion that it should be bound to belief in particular events which divide one group from another and are in any case open to cavil. The great truths of religion are all universal. Reason extracts these from the general course of things. A gap separates these realities of universal import from the particular facts of history. These latter cannot support the former" (273).

20. This goes against the tenor of much recent Wordsworth criticism, from Marjorie Levinson to Alan Liu, which sees Wordsworth as programmatically excluding the historical in favor of the private.

21. For extended discussions of this struggle in *The Prelude,* see my articles "The Emergence of the Autobiographical Figure" and "Catachresis and the Romantic Will."

22. Early version, printed in *"The Tuft of Primroses" with Other Late Poems for "The Recluse,"* 86–88.

23. This latter notion reflects Coleridge's perception of the "tautegorical" relation of analogy, in which a concept *literally* exists on two levels at once, as opposed to the "allegorical" relation of metaphor. In commenting on John 3:6 ("That which is born of the flesh, is flesh; that which is born of the Spirit, is Spirit"), Coleridge says, "Neither do I regard the words, *born again,* or spiritual life, as figures or metaphors. I have only to add, that these analogies are the material, or (to speak chemically) the base, of symbols and symbolic expressions; the nature of which is always tautegorical, that is expressing the same subject but with a difference, in contra-distinction from metaphors and similitudes, which are always allegorical, that is, expressing a different subject but with a resemblance" (*Aids to Reflection* 204).

24. F. X. Shea, S. J., sees Romanticism as reflecting just such a Catholic view of incarnation: "The relationship between God and man which the Christian faith in Incarnation implies is a relationship that defines [*sic;* I assume this is a misprint for "defies"] final definition.... It states that the transcendent and the mundane are one" ("Religion and the Romantic Movement" 290).

25. "I cannot act with those who see no danger to the constitution in introducing Papists into Parliament," Wordsworth writes in an 1813 letter to the Reverend Francis Wrangham (*Letters of William and Dorothy Wordsworth* 3.2.108).

26. See Stephen Gill, *William Wordsworth: A Life,* 397–98, and G. B. Tennyson, *Victorian Devotional Poetry: The Tractarian Mode,* 14–23, 94–96.

27. David Hiley sees a similar problem in Montaigne's skeptical emphasis on "custom," and he points out usefully that the interpretation of Montaigne's (or Michel Foucault's similar) strategy in terms of its relative conservatism misses the point that the skeptical argument cannot be placed in the service of either a conservative or a radical epistemology; the argument is against the kind of epistemological totalization implicit in both:

Montaigne's interpreters have seen in this skeptical strategy opposite dangers. His reform-minded critics believed it produces a wooden adherence to the status quo. The orthodox and faithful accused him of a dangerous relativism that undermined the truth of traditional values. In this respect, Michel Foucault's critics resemble Montaigne's. He is alternately accused of anarchy and conservatism. Both charges issue, I think, from failure to appreciate the degree to which his work on institutions and modern power departs from more familiar forms of political writing. Political theorizing, either explicitly or implicitly, seeks to organize social and political life as a whole. Montaigne and Foucault, alike, oppose the possibility of total organization whether on the basis of fundamental political principles, human reason, or utopian ideals. ("The Politics of Skepticism" 27)

28. Stephen Prickett points out that "Wordsworth's ... argument is not that Paley, Ray or Derham are guilty of any kind of philosophic error, but simply that they are a lot of 'pedants' " (*Romanticism and Religion* 84).

29. Wordsworth, "Preface to *Lyrical Ballads*": "We have no knowledge, that is, no general principles drawn from the contemplation of particular facts, but what has been built up by pleasure, and exists in us by pleasure alone. The Man of science, the Chemist and Mathematician, whatever difficulties and disgusts they may have had to struggle with, know and feel this" (in *PrW* 1:140).

30. See Charles Taylor's discussion (*Sources of the Self* 338–47, 382–89) of how the radical Enlightenment ran into problems because its extreme materialism gave it no way to articulate its own moral sources—hence the late eighteenth century's desire to reinstate a way to articulate moral positions both through the Kantian autonomous rational agent that grew out of that Enlightenment epistemology, and through the contrary Romantic means of an expressive involvement in and with nature.

31. Immanuel Kant, *Lectures on Philosophical Theology:* "Moreover, it is morality alone which gives me a *determinate* concept of God. It teaches me to know him as a being having every perfection" (111). Coleridge points out that belief and understanding are organically related as two different stages of growth: "In spiritual concernments to believe and to understand are not diverse things, but the same thing in different periods of growth. Belief is the seed, received into the will, of which the understanding or knowledge is the flower, and the thing believed is the fruit" (*Aids to Reflection* 195).

32. Gadamer notes that "Heidegger has critically and insightfully spoken of the 'superficiality of the Greeks' with respect to their ocularity, their *eidos*-oriented thinking, their leveling of the *logos* into logic of referential thought" ("Letter to Dallmayr," in Michelfelder and Palmer, eds., *Dialogue and Deconstruction*, 95). Similarly, Rorty traces to the Greeks the ocular metaphor that directed philosophy toward theories of representation: "The notion of knowledge as the assemblage of accurate representations is optional.... [I]t may be replaced by a pragmatist conception of knowledge which eliminates the Greek contrast between contemplation and action, between representing the world and coping with it. A historical epoch dominated by Greek ocular metaphors may, I suggest, yield to one in which the philosophical vocabulary incorporating these metaphors seems as quaint as the animistic vocabulary of pre-classical times" (*Philosophy and the Mirror of Nature* 11).

33. Taylor describes Descartes as initiating
a very different concept of reason from Plato's. Just as correct knowledge doesn't come anymore from our opening ourselves to the order of (ontic) Ideas but from our constructing an order of (intra-mental) ideas according to the canons of *évidence*; so when the hegemony of reason becomes rational control, it is no longer understood as our being attuned to the order of things we find in the cosmos, but rather as our life being shaped by the orders which we construct according to the demands of reason's dominance.... We could say that rationality is no longer defined substantively, in terms of the

order of being, but rather procedurally, in terms of the standards by which we construct orders in science and life. (*Sources of the Self* 155–56)

34. As Taylor points out, such an inward route is Augustinian: "We can thus see the crucial importance of the language of inwardness for Augustine. It represents a radically new doctrine of moral resources, one where the route to the higher passes within" (*Sources of the Self* 139).

35. Bewell examines Wordsworth's ambivalent attitude toward the political controversy over the hortatory power of Methodist preaching, whose language shared the living power of poetry: "Methodist preaching raises the... explicitly political issue of the role that impassioned language (poetry and preaching) and charismatic leaders play in either controlling the poor or inciting them to disorder and violence" (*Wordsworth and the Enlightenment* 115).

36. James D. Boulger argues that the Wanderer and the Solitary represent the regenerate and unregenerate Puritan-Calvinist pilgrims. See *The Calvinist Temper in English Poetry* 416–20.

37. For more on the role of the "imaginative will" in book 6 of *The Prelude*, see my "Catachresis and the Romantic Will."

38. Cavell stresses the fundamentality of violence in the skeptical impulse by saying that "the loss of presentness (to and of the world) is something that the violence of skepticism deepens exactly in its desperation to correct it, a violence assured in philosophy's desperation to answer or refute skepticism, to deny skepticism's discovery of the absence or withdrawal of the world" (*In Quest of the Ordinary* 173–74).

39. René Girard, *Violence and the Sacred*: "Blood serves to illustrate the point that the same substance can stain or cleanse, contaminate or purify, drive men to fury and murder or appease their anger and restore them to life" (37).

40. See Coleridge, *Aids to Reflection*:

> Forgiveness of sin, the abolition of guilt, through the redemptive power of Christ's love, and of his perfect obedience during his voluntary assumption of humanity, [is] expressed, on account of the resemblance of the consequences in both cases, by the payment of a debt for another, which debt the payer had not himself incurred. Now the impropriation of this metaphor—(that is, the taking it literally) by transferring the sameness from the consequents to the antecedents, or inferring the identity of the causes from a resemblance in the effects—this is the point on which I am at issue: and the view or scheme of redemption grounded on this confusion I believe to be altogether un-Scriptural. (286–87)

41. Raimonda Modiano has pointed out in a private correspondence, with some justification, that my reading of the gift in terms of Hyde's rather idealistic logic gives it an overly positive cast. I do maintain that Wordsworth operates within such a logic at the end of *The Prelude*, and that this logic is part of his incarnational thought, but I certainly do not mean to deny the other side of gift giving in general—that it can partake of structures of coercion and obligation. The "negative" side of incarnational anti-economism can certainly be interpreted in the terms of gift theory as well as in the terms that I use, and it can certainly be argued successfully (as Modiano herself has done in "Coleridge and Wordsworth: The Ethics of Gift Exchange and Literary Ownership") that the relationship between Wordsworth and Coleridge is characterized precisely by a *violation* of the idealistic theory of the gift that Hyde proposes.

42. See Jacques Derrida, *Of Grammatology*, 144–57.

43. For Girard, sacrifice is a form of violence—"all sacrificial rites... reproduce certain forms of violence" (*Violence and the Sacred* 114)—but because sacrifice is *controlled* violence, restricted to rituals focused on single victims, "the sacrificial process prevents the spread of violence by keeping vengeance in check" (18). Western systems of justice are no different in principle: "Our penal system operates according to principles of justice that are in no real conflict with the concept of revenge. The same principle is at work in all systems of violent retribution" (16). There is, however, a sharp difference in efficacy between the diversion of violence in sacrificial systems and the constraint imposed by an abstract system of law: "The

break comes at the moment when the intervention of an independent legal authority becomes *constraining*.... In fact, retribution still holds sway, but forged into a principle of abstract justice that all men are obliged to uphold and respect" (21).

44. See *Metamorphoses*, book 9. See also Sophocles, *The Women of Trachis*, and the similar story of the poisoned coat given by Medea to Jason's new bride in Euripides' *Medea*. See Girard's reading of the Sophoclean version of the story in *Violence and the Sacred*, 41–42.

45. Henri Hubert and Marcel Mauss, *Sacrifice:* "Fundamentally there is perhaps no sacrifice that has not some contractual element. The two parties present exchange their services and each gets his due" (100).

46. In his discussion of *Peter Bell*, Bewell contends that Wordsworth's recognition of the violent origins of Christianity reconciles the Enlightenment's use of that fact as a critique of revealed religion with the moral truth of Christianity: "Rather than arguing, as Bayle and his Enlightenment followers did, either that there is no connection between religious ideas and moral conduct or that reason and revelation are fundamentally irreconcilable, *Peter Bell* demonstrates that it was through the violence of a superstitious imagination that religious ideas were first revealed to early humans and they made the transit from barbarism to a world of Christian love" (*Wordsworth and the Enlightenment* 127). The present discussion suggests both an "incarnational" and a "representational" way in which he accomplishes this task.

Works Cited

Aarsleff, Hans. *From Locke to Saussure.* Minneapolis: University of Minnesota Press, 1982.
———. *The Study of Language in England, 1780–1860.* Minneapolis: University of Minnesota Press, 1983.
Abrams, M. H. "English Romanticism: The Spirit of the Age." In *Romanticism and Consciousness: Essays in Criticism,* edited by Harold Bloom, 91–119. New York: Norton, 1970.
———. *Natural Supernaturalism: Tradition and Revolution in Romantic Literature.* New York: Norton, 1971.
Altieri, Charles. *Canons and Consequences: Reflections on the Ethical Force of Imaginative Ideals.* Evanston: Northwestern University Press, 1990.
Arnauld, Antoine. *The Art of Thinking: Port-Royal Logic.* Translated by James Dickoff and Patricia James. The Library of Liberal Arts. New York: Bobbs-Merrill, 1964.
Arnold, Matthew. *Poetry and Criticism of Matthew Arnold.* Edited by A. Dwight Culler. Boston: Houghton Mifflin, 1961.
Auerbach, Erich. *Scenes from the Drama of European Literature.* Translated by Ralph Mannheim. Theory of History and Literature, vol. 9. Minneapolis: University of Minnesota Press, 1984.
Augustine, Saint. *On the Holy Trinity.* Edited by Philip Schaff. A Select Library of the Nicene and Post-Nicene Fathers of the Christian Church 3. New York: Charles Scribner's Sons, 1917.
Austin, J. L. *How to Do Things with Words.* Second Edition. Edited by J. O. Urmson and Marina Sbisà. Cambridge: Harvard University Press, 1975.
Bakhtin, Mikhail M. *The Dialogic Imagination.* Edited by Michael Holquist. Translated by Caryl Emerson and Michael Holquist. Austin: University of Texas Press, 1981.
Barthes, Roland. *S/Z.* Translated by Richard Miller. New York: Hill & Wang, 1974.

Beeck, Frans Jozef van. *Christ Proclaimed: Christology as Rhetoric.* New York: Paulist Press, 1979.
Bernasconi, Robert, and Simon Critchley, eds. *Re-reading Levinas.* Bloomington: Indiana University Press, 1991.
Bewell, Alan. *Wordsworth and the Enlightenment: Nature, Man, and Society in the Experimental Poetry.* New Haven: Yale University Press, 1989.
Blake, William. *Blake's Poetry and Designs.* Edited by Mary Lynn Johnson and John E. Grant. Norton Critical Edition. New York: Norton, 1979.
———. *The Complete Poetry and Prose of William Blake.* Revised Edition. Edited by David Erdman. New York: Anchor, 1988.
Boulger, James D. *The Calvinist Temper in English Poetry.* De Proprietatibus Litterarum, Series Maior 21. The Hague: Mouton, 1980.
Brantley, Richard. *Wordsworth's "Natural Methodism."* New Haven: Yale University Press, 1975.
Brown, Colin. *Jesus in European Protestant Thought, 1778–1860.* Studies in Historical Theology 1. Durham, N.C.: Labyrinth Press, 1985.
Bruns, Gerald L. "Law as Hermeneutics: A Response to Ronald Dworkin." In *The Politics of Interpretation,* edited by W.J.T. Mitchell, 315–20. Chicago: University of Chicago Press, 1983.
———. "Stanley Cavell's Shakespeare." *Critical Inquiry* 16 (Spring 1990): 612–32.
———. "What Is Tradition?" *New Literary History* 22 (Winter 1991): 1–21.
———. "Wordsworth at the Limits of Romantic Hermeneutics." *The Centennial Review* 33 (Fall 1989): 393–419.
Bultmann, Rudolf. *The Gospel of John: A Commentary.* Translated by G. R. Beasley-Murray et al. Philadelphia: Westminster Press, 1971.
———. *Theology of the New Testament: Complete in One Volume.* Translated by Kendrick Grobel. New York: Charles Scribner's Sons, 1951 (vol. 1), 1955 (vol. 2).
Caputo, John D. *Radical Hermeneutics: Repetition, Deconstruction, and the Hermeneutic Project.* Bloomington: Indiana University Press, 1987.
Caraher, Brian G. *Wordsworth's "Slumber" and the Problematics of Reading.* University Park: Pennsylvania State University Press, 1991.
Cascardi, Anthony J. "From the Sublime to the Natural: Romantic Responses to Kant." In *Literature and the Question of Philosophy,* edited by Anthony J. Cascardi, 101–31. Baltimore: Johns Hopkins University Press, 1987.
Cavell, Stanley. *In Quest of the Ordinary: Lines of Skepticism and Romanticism.* Chicago: University of Chicago Press, 1988.
Clough, Arthur Hugh. *The Poems of Arthur Hugh Clough.* Edited by A. L. Norrington. London: Oxford University Press, 1986.
Cohen, Richard A., ed. *Face to Face with Levinas.* SUNY Series in Philosophy. Albany: SUNY Press, 1986.
Coleridge, Samuel Taylor. *Aids to Reflection.* 1840. Edited by Henry Nelson Coleridge. Kennikat Press Scholarly Reprints. Port Washington, N.Y.: Kennikat Press, 1971.
———. *Collected Letters.* 6 vols. Edited by Earl Leslie Griggs. Vol. 1, *1785–1800.* Oxford: Oxford University Press, 1956–71.

---. *Collected Works.* 10 vols. to date. Edited by Kathleen Coburn. Bollingen Series 75. Princeton: Princeton University Press, 1969–.
Condillac, Etienne Bonnot de. *An Essay on the Origin of Human Knowledge.* Translated by Nugent. 1756. Language, Man, and Society: Foundations of the Behavioral Sciences. New York: AMS Reprints, 1974.
Cooper, Anthony. *Doubt and Identity in Romantic Poetry.* New Haven: Yale University Press, 1988.
Curran, Charles. *Faithful Dissent.* Kansas City, Mo.: Sheed & Ward, 1986.
De Man, Paul. *Blindness and Insight.* Second Edition. Theory and History of Literature 7. Minneapolis: University of Minnesota Press, 1983.
---. "Intentional Structure of the Romantic Image." In *Romanticism and Consciousness: Essays in Criticism,* edited by Harold Bloom, 65–77. New York: Norton, 1970.
---. "Pascal's Allegory of Persuasion." In *Allegory and Representation: Selected Papers from the English Institute, 1979–80,* edited by Stephen J. Greenblatt, 1–25. Baltimore: Johns Hopkins University Press, 1981.
---. "Political Allegory in Rousseau." *Critical Inquiry* 2 (Summer 1976): 649–75.
---. *The Rhetoric of Romanticism.* New York: Columbia University Press, 1984.
De Quincey, Thomas. *Collected Writings.* 14 vols. Vol. 11, *Literary Theory and Criticism.* Edited by David Masson. London: A. C. Black, 1896–97.
Derrida, Jacques. *Of Grammatology.* Translated by Gayatri Chakravorty Spivak. Baltimore: Johns Hopkins University Press, 1976.
---. "White Mythology: Metaphor in the Text of Philosophy." Translated by F.C.T. Moore. *New Literary History* 6 (Autumn 1974): 5–74.
Dillenberger, John, and Claude Welch. *Protestant Christianity Interpreted through Its Development.* New York: Charles Scribner's Sons, 1954.
Dykstal, Timothy. "Conversation and Political Controversy." In *Compendius Conversations: The Method of Dialogue in Early Enlightenment,* edited by Kevin J. Cope, 306–20. New York: Peter Lang, 1992.
Ellis, David. *Wordsworth, Freud and the Spots of Time: Interpretation in "The Prelude."* Cambridge: Cambridge University Press, 1985.
Euripedes. *The Medea.* Translated by Rex Warner. In *The Complete Greek Tragedies: Euripedes 1,* edited by David Grene and Richard Lattimore, 55–108. Chicago: University of Chicago Press, 1955.
Ferguson, Frances. *Wordsworth: Language as Counter-Spirit.* New Haven: Yale University Press, 1977.
Ferry, David. *The Limits of Mortality: An Essay on Wordsworth's Major Poems.* Middletown: Wesleyan University Press, 1959.
Feuerbach, Ludwig. *The Essence of Christianity.* Translated by George Eliot. Great Books in Philosophy. Buffalo, N.Y.: Prometheus Books, 1989.
Fish, Stanley. *Doing What Comes Naturally: Change, Rhetoric, and the Practice of Theory in Literary and Legal Studies.* Durham: Duke University Press, 1989.
Fletcher, Angus. "'Positive Negation': Threshold, Sequence, and Personification in Coleridge." In *New Perspectives on Coleridge and Wordsworth: Selected Papers from the English Institute,* edited by Geoffrey Hartman, 133–64. New York: Columbia University Press, 1972.

Foucault, Michel. *The Order of Things: An Archaeology of the Human Sciences.* Translated by Alan Sheridan-Smith. New York: Vintage Books, 1973.
Gadamer, Hans-Georg. *Gesammelte Werke.* 7 vols. to date. Vol. 4, *Neuere Philosophie II: Probleme/Gestalten.* Tubingen: J.C.B. Mohr (Paul Siebeck), 1985–.
———. *Philosophical Hermeneutics.* Edited and translated by David E. Linge. Berkeley and Los Angeles: University of California Press, 1976.
———. *The Relevance of the Beautiful and Other Essays.* Edited by Robert Bernasconi. Translated by Nicholas Walker. Cambridge: Cambridge University Press, 1986.
———. "Text and Interpretation." In *Hermeneutics and Modern Philosophy*, edited by Brice Wachterhauser, 377–96. Albany: SUNY Press, 1986.
———. *Truth and Method.* Second Revised Edition. Translation revised by Joel Weinsheimer and Donald G. Marshall. New York: Crossroad, 1990.
Gill, Stephen. *William Wordsworth: A Life.* Oxford: Clarendon Press, 1989.
Girard, René. *The Scapegoat.* Translated by Yvonne Freccero. Baltimore: Johns Hopkins University Press, 1986.
———. *Things Hidden Since the Foundation of the World.* Translated by Stephen Bann and Michael Metteer. London: Athlone Press, 1987.
———. *Violence and the Sacred.* Translated by Patrick Gregory. Baltimore: Johns Hopkins University Press, 1977.
Haney, David P. "Catachresis and the Romantic Will: The Imagination's Usurpation in Wordsworth's *Prelude*, Book VI." *Style* 23 (Spring 1989): 16–31.
———. "The Emergence of the Autobiographical Figure in *The Prelude*, Book I." *Studies in Romanticism* 20 (Spring 1981): 33–63.
———. "Viewing 'The Viewless Wings of Poesy': Keats, Gadamer, and Historicity." *Clio* 18 (Winter 1989): 103–22.
Hartman, Geoffrey. *Saving the Text: Literature/Derrida/Philosophy.* Baltimore: Johns Hopkins University Press, 1981.
———. *The Unremarkable Wordsworth.* Theory and History of Literature 34. Minneapolis: University of Minnesota Press, 1987.
———. *Wordsworth's Poetry 1787–1814.* 1964. Reprint. New Haven: Yale University Press, 1975.
Hegel, G.W.F. *Early Theological Writings.* 1948. Translated by T. M. Knox. Reprint. Philadelphia: University of Pennsylvania Press, 1975.
———. *Hegel's Phenomenology of Spirit.* Translated by A. V. Miller. New York: Oxford University Press, 1978.
Heidegger, Martin. *Being and Time.* Translated by John Macquarrie and Edward Robinson. New York: Harper & Row, 1962.
Hiley, David R. *Philosophy in Question: Essays on a Pyrrhonian Theme.* Chicago: University of Chicago Press, 1988.
———. "The Politics of Skepticism: Reading Montaigne." Typescript of essay in *History of Philosophy Quarterly.* Forthcoming.
Hoffman, Piotr. *Violence in Modern Philosophy.* Chicago: Chicago University Press, 1989.
Hooker, Richard. *Of the Laws of Ecclesiastical Polity* (abridged). Edited by A. S. McGrade and Brian Vickers. London: Sidgewick & Jackson, 1975.

Hubert, Henri, and Marcel Mauss. *Sacrifice: Its Nature and Functions.* Translated by W. D. Halls. 1964. Reprint. Chicago: University of Chicago Press, 1981.
Hyde, Lewis. *The Gift: Imagination and the Erotic Life of Property.* New York: Random House, 1983.
Jacobus, Mary. "Apostrophe and Lyric Voice in *The Prelude.*" In *Lyric Poetry: Beyond New Criticism,* edited by Chaviva Hosek and Patricia Parker, 167–81. Ithaca: Cornell University Press, 1985.
Johnson, Barbara. "Writing." In *Critical Terms for Literary Study,* edited by Frank Lentricchia and Thomas McLaughlin, 39–49. Chicago: University of Chicago Press, 1990.
Johnston, Kenneth. *Wordsworth and "The Recluse."* New Haven: Yale University Press, 1984.
Kant, Immanuel. *Foundations of the Metaphysics of Morals and What is Enlightenment?* Translated by Lewis White Beck. New York: MacMillan, 1990.
———. *Lectures on Philosophical Theology.* Translated by Allen W. Wood and Gertrude M. Clark. Ithaca: Cornell University Press, 1978.
———. *Prolegomena to Any Future Metaphysics That Can Qualify as a Science.* Translated by Paul Carus. LaSalle, Ill.: Open Court, 1902.
LaCapra, Dominick. "The Temporality of Rhetoric." In *Chronotypes: The Construction of Time,* edited by John Bender and David Wellbery, 118–47. Stanford: Stanford University Press, 1991.
Lacoue-Labarthe, Philippe, and Jean-Luc Nancy. *The Literary Absolute: The Theory of Literature in German Romanticism.* Translated by Philip Barnard and Cheryl Lester. Intersections: Philosophy and Critical Theory. Albany: SUNY Press, 1988.
Land, Stephen K. "The Silent Poet: An Aspect of Wordsworth's Semantic Theory." *University of Toronto Quarterly* 52 (Winter 1973): 157–69.
Latimer, Dan. "Real Culture and Unreal Nature: Wordsworth's Kingdom of Dissimilitude." *New Orleans Review* 14 (Spring 1987): 45–54.
Lazareth, William. "Love and Law in Christian Life." In *Piety, Politics, and Ethics: Reformation Studies in Honor of George Wolfgang Forell,* edited by Carter Lindberg, 103–17. Sixteenth-Century Essays and Studies 3. Kirksville, Mo.: Sixteenth-Century Journal Publishers, Northeast Missouri State University, 1984.
Levinas, Emmanuel. *Otherwise Than Being or Beyond Essence.* Translated by Alphonso Lingis. Martinus Nijhoff Philosophy Texts, vol. 3. The Hague: Martinus Nijhoff, 1981.
———. *Totality and Infinity: An Essay on Exteriority.* Translated by Alphonso Lingis. Duquesne Studies Philosophical Series 24. Pittsburgh: Duquesne University Press, 1969.
Levinson, Marjorie. *The Romantic Fragment Poem: A Critique of a Form.* Chapel Hill: University of North Carolina Press, 1986.
———. *Wordsworth's Great Period Poems: Four Essays.* Cambridge: Cambridge University Press, 1986.
Lévi-Strauss, Claude. *The Savage Mind.* Chicago: University of Chicago Press, 1966.

Liu, Alan. *Wordsworth: The Sense of History.* Stanford: Stanford University Press, 1989.
Lockridge, Laurence S. *The Ethics of Romanticism.* Cambridge: Cambridge University Press, 1989.
Lyotard, Jean-François. "Levinas' Logic." In *The Lyotard Reader,* edited by Andrew Benjamin, 275–313. Oxford: Basil Blackwell, 1989.
MacCannell, Juliet Flower. "The Post-Fictional Self: Authorial Consciousness in Three Texts by Rousseau." *MLN* 89 (May 1974): 580–99.
McFarland, Thomas. *Romanticism and the Forms of Ruin: Wordsworth, Coleridge, and the Modalities of Fragmentation.* Princeton: Princeton University Press, 1981.
McGann, Jerome. *The Romantic Ideology: A Critical Investigation.* Chicago: University of Chicago Press, 1983.
McGowan, John P. *Representation and Revelation: Victorian Realism from Carlyle to Yeats.* Columbia: University of Missouri Press, 1986.
Marin, Louis. "The Autobiographical Interruption: About Stendhal's *Life of Henry Brulard.*" *MLN* 93 (May 1978): 597–617.
———. *Food for Thought.* Translated by Mette Hjort. Baltimore: Johns Hopkins University Press, 1989.
———. "Toward a Theory of Reading in the Visual Arts: Poussin's *The Arcadian Shepherds.*" In *The Reader in the Text: Essays on Audience and Interpretation,* edited by Susan R. Suleiman and Inge Crosman, 293–324. Princeton: Princeton University Press, 1980.
Marshall, L. E. "'*Words* Are *Things*': Byron and the Prophetic Efficacy of Language." *Studies in English Literature* 25 (Autumn 1985): 801–22.
Massey, Irving. *Find You the Virtue: Ethics, Image, and Desire in Literature.* Fairfax, Va.: George Mason University Press, 1987.
Mauss, Marcel. *The Gift: Forms and Functions of Exchange in Archaic Societies.* Translated by Ian Cunnison. New York: Norton, 1967.
Michelfelder, Diane P., and Richard E. Palmer, eds. *Dialogue and Deconstruction: The Gadamer-Derrida Encounter.* Albany: SUNY Press, 1989.
Miller, J. Hillis. *The Disappearance of God.* Cambridge: Harvard University Press, 1963.
———. "Narrative Middles: A Preliminary Outline." *Genre* 11 (Fall 1978): 375–87.
Mills-Courts, Karen. *Poetry as Epitaph: Representation and Poetic Language.* Baton Rouge: Louisiana State University Press, 1990.
Mitchell, W.J.T., ed. *The Politics of Interpretation.* Chicago: University of Chicago Press, 1983.
Modiano, Raimonda. "Coleridge and Wordsworth: The Ethics of Gift Exchange and Literary Ownership." *The Wordsworth Circle* 20 (Spring 1989): 113–20.
Nancy, Jean-Luc. "The Unsacrificeable." *Yale French Studies* 79 (1991): 20–38.
The New Oxford Annotated Bible with the Apocrypha: Revised Standard Version. Oxford: Oxford University Press, 1973.
Nietzsche, Friedrich. *The Gay Science.* Translated by Walter Kauffman. New York: Vintage Books, 1974.
———. *The Will to Power.* Translated by Walter Kauffman and R. J. Hollingdale. Edited by Walter Kauffman. New York: Vintage Books, 1968.

Nussbaum, Martha C. *The Fragility of Goodness: Luck and Ethics in Greek Tragedy and Philosophy.* London: Cambridge University Press, 1986.
Ong, Walter J., S.J. *The Presence of the Word: Some Prolegomena for Cultural and Religious History.* 1962. Reprint. Minneapolis: University of Minnesota Press, 1981.
Ovid. *Metamorphoses.* Translated by Rolfe Humphries. Bloomington: Indiana University Press, 1955.
Prickett, Stephen. *Romanticism and Religion: The Tradition of Coleridge and Wordsworth in the Victorian Church.* Cambridge: Cambridge University Press, 1976.
———. *Words and "The Word": Language, Poetics, and Biblical Interpretation.* Cambridge: Cambridge University Press, 1986.
Rajan, Tilottama. *The Supplement of Reading: Figures of Understanding in Romantic Theory and Practice.* Ithaca: Cornell University Press, 1990.
Reiman, Donald H. *Intervals of Inspiration: The Skeptical Tradition and the Psychology of Romanticism.* Greenwood, Fla.: Penkevill, 1988.
Rorty, Richard. *Philosophy and the Mirror of Nature.* Princeton: Princeton University Press, 1979.
Rousseau, Jean-Jacques. *The First and Second Discourses.* Edited by Roger D. Masters. Translated by Roger D. Masters and Judith R. Masters. New York: St. Martin's Press, 1964.
Said, Edward. *Beginnings: Intention and Method.* New York: Basic Books, 1975.
Saussure, Ferdinand de. *Course in General Linguistics.* Edited by Charles Bally and Albert Sechehaye, in collaboration with Albert Riedlinger. Translated by Wade Baskin. New York: McGraw-Hill, 1959.
Schelling, Friedrich Wilhelm Joseph von. *System of Transcendental Idealism.* 1800. Translated by Peter Heath. Charlottesville: University of Virginia Press, 1978.
Schiller, Friedrich von. *Naive and Sentimental Poetry* and *On the Sublime.* Translated by Julias A. Elias. New York: Frederick Ungar, 1966.
Schlegel, Friedrich. *The Philosophy of Life and the Philosophy of Language.* Translated by A. J. Morrison. London, 1847.
Schneidau, Herbert. *Sacred Discontent: The Bible and Western Tradition.* Baton Rouge: Louisiana State University Press, 1976.
Scott, Charles E. *The Question of Ethics: Nietzsche, Foucault, Heidegger.* Bloomington: Indiana University Press, 1990.
Serres, Michel. *Hermes: Literature, Science, Philosophy.* Edited by Josué V. Harari and David F. Bell. Baltimore: Johns Hopkins University Press, 1982.
Shea, F. X., S.J., "Religion and the Romantic Movement." *Studies in Romanticism* 9 (Fall 1970): 285–96.
Sheats, Paul D. "Wordsworth's Retrogrades and the Shaping of *The Prelude.*" *Journal of English and Germanic Philology* 71 (Oct. 1972): 473–90.
Solomon, Harry M. "Reading Philosophical Poetry." In *The Philosopher as Writer: The Eighteenth Century,* edited by Robert Ginsburg, 122–39. London: Associated University Presses, 1987.
Sophocles. *The Women of Trachis.* New York: Oxford University Press, 1978.
Spivak, Gayatri Chakravorty. "Sex and History in *The Prelude* (1805): Books IX–

XIII." In *Post-Structuralist Readings of English Poetry*, edited by Richard Machin and Christopher Norris, 193–226. Cambridge: Cambridge University Press, 1987.
Stewart, Dugald. "Account of Adam Smith." In Adam Smith, *Essays on Philosophical Subjects*, edited by I. S. Ross, 269–351. Oxford: Clarendon Press, 1980.
Taylor, Charles. *Human Agency and Language: Philosophical Papers 1.* Cambridge: Cambridge University Press, 1985.
———. *Sources of the Self: The Making of the Modern Identity.* Cambridge: Harvard University Press, 1989.
Taylor, Mark C. *Altarity.* Chicago: University of Chicago Press, 1987.
Tennyson, G. B. *Victorian Devotional Poetry: The Tractarian Mode.* Cambridge: Harvard University Press, 1980.
Vance, Eugene. "Augustine's *Confessions* and the Grammar of Selfhood." *Genre* 6 (March 1973): 1–28.
Warminski, Andrzej. "Facing Language: Wordsworth's First Poetic Spirits." *Diacritics* 17 (Winter 1987): 18–31.
Warren, Robert Penn. *World Enough and Time: A Romantic Novel.* New York: Random House, 1950.
Weinsheimer, Joel. *Philosophical Hermeneutics and Literary Theory.* New Haven: Yale University Press, 1991.
Weiskel, Thomas. *The Romantic Sublime: Studies in the Structure and Psychology of Transcendence.* Baltimore: Johns Hopkins University Press, 1976.
Wellbery, David. *Lessing's "Laocoon": Semiotics and Aesthetics in the Age of Reason.* Cambridge: Cambridge University Press, 1984.
Woodring, Carl. *Politics in English Romantic Poetry.* Cambridge: Harvard University Press, 1970.
Wordsworth, William. *"Poems, in Two Volumes," and Other Poems, 1800–1807.* Edited by Jared Curtis. The Cornell Wordsworth. Ithaca: Cornell University Press, 1983.
———. *The Poetical Works of William Wordsworth.* 5 vols. Edited by Ernest de Selincourt. Second Edition. Oxford: Clarendon Press, 1963–66.
———. *The Prelude: 1799, 1805, 1850.* Edited by Jonathan Wordsworth et al. New York: Norton, 1979.
———. *The Prose Works of William Wordsworth.* 3 vols. Edited by W.J.B. Owen and J. W. Smyser. Oxford: Oxford University Press, 1974.
———. *"The Tuft of Primroses" with Other Late Poems for "The Recluse."* Edited by Joseph F. Kishel. The Cornell Wordsworth. Ithaca: Cornell University Press, 1986.
———. *The White Doe of Rylestone.* Edited by Kristine Dugas. The Cornell Wordsworth. Ithaca: Cornell University Press, 1988.
Wordsworth, William, and Dorothy Wordsworth. *The Letters of William and Dorothy Wordsworth.* 7 vols. Edited by Ernest de Selincourt. Second Edition. Revised by Mary Moorman and Alan G. Hill. Vol. 3, *The Middle Years; Part 2: 1812–1820.* Oxford: Oxford University Press, 1967–88.
Young, Frances. *Sacrifice and the Death of Christ.* 1975. Reprint. London: SCM, 1983.
Zak, Rose A. "Dialogue and Discourse in Stravinsky's 'Symphony of Psalms.'" *Criticism* 22 (Fall 1980): 357–75.

Index

Aarsleff, Hans, 31–32
Abrams, M. H., 2, 7
acknowledgment. *See* Cavell, Stanley, on acknowledgment vs. knowledge
allegory, 51, 54
Altieri, Charles, 41–42, 136–37, 183–84, 245 n. 1
Anglicanism, 172–81
animism
 and death, 78
 and expressivism, 8
 and incarnation, 5–12, 75–77
 and skepticism, 8–11, 56, 64
Arnauld, Antoine, *The Art of Thinking: Port-Royal Logic*, 15, 47–48
Arnold, Matthew, 41, 238–39 n. 36, 245 n. 2
Auerbach, Erich, 242 n. 6
Augustine, Saint, 21–28, 132, 137, 195, 197, 250 n. 34
Austin, J. L., 19, 70
autobiography
 in *The Excursion*, 150–51, 155–56, 162
 as exemplary dialogue, 33
 vs. objective theory, 162
 in *The Prelude*, 103–13, 116–19, 123–39
 as route to death, 86

Bakhtin, Mikhail M., 247–48 n. 16
Barthes, Roland, 41, 247 n. 15
Bataille, Georges, 58, 230
Baudrillard, Jean, 34
Beeck, Frans Jozef van, 116–17, 243 n. 15, 244 n. 25
Benjamin, Walter, 125
Benveniste, Emile, 242 n. 1
Bewell, Alan, 81, 96, 141–43, 229, 241 n. 22, 250 n. 35, 251 n. 46
Bildung
 and incarnational subject, 43
 in *The Prelude*, 106–7, 126–27, 136–38, 141, 210–11, 221–22
 public vs. private, 165
 in Wordsworth and Altieri, 184
binary thought. *See also* incarnation; representation; theoretical discourse
 in Hegel, 51–52
 vs. incarnational thought, 17–18, 35, 66–67
 in *The Prelude* vs. in *The Excursion*, 146
 in Romanticism/Enlightenment opposition, 14–18
 and signs, 143–44
 Solitary's critique of, 193–94
Blake, William, 32, 70, 239 n. 1
Blumenberg, Hans, 144
Book of Common Prayer, 173–74
Boulger, James, 250 n. 36
Brantley, Richard, 236 n. 11, 244 n. 27
Brown, Colin, 50

262   Index

Bruns, Gerald, 11–12, 36, 235 n. 3, 243 n. 11
Bultmann, Rudolf, 23, 24

Calvin, John, 165, 201–3
Calvinism, 175, 201, 224
Caputo, John D., 235 n. 3
Caraher, Brian, 98–100
Cascardi, Anthony, 235–36 n. 5
Catholicism
  in *The Excursion*, 174–79, 224
  and incarnation, 174
Cavell, Stanley
  on acknowledgment vs. knowledge, 66–68, 92, 94, 183
  on autobiography, 103
  on death, 63–64, 79, 91–92, 94
  on ethics and epistemology, 36
  on Romantic criticism, 238 n. 44
  on skepticism as animism, 6–12, 56, 76, 212
Cervantes, Miguel de, *Don Quixote*, 104
Chandler, James, 71
Christianity
  and the Enlightenment, 14–15
  and Judaism, 60–61
  and rational economy, 215
  and sacrifice, 57–62, 215, 228–34
  and violence, 59–62, 225–26, 232–34, 251 n. 46
churches, 13, 109, 178–81, 205–6
Clough, Arthur H.
  "Natura Naturans," 67–68
  "Qui Laborat, Orat," 67–68, 204
Coleridge, Samuel Taylor, 32, 115
  as addressee of *The Prelude*, 33, 104, 134–39
  on desynonymy, 6
  on symbol and allegory, 16, 51, 87, 248 n. 23
  on words as things, 24–25, 35–36, 77
  and Wordsworth, 13
  WORKS
  Aids to Reflection, 215, 248 n. 23, 249 n. 31, 250 n. 40
  Biographia Literaria, 5, 63–64, 207–8
  "Frost at Midnight," 5
  letters, 24–25, 77
  The Rime of the Ancient Mariner, 10, 76, 212
  Table Talk, 144
  "To William Wordsworth," 136

Condillac, Etienne Bonnot de, 32–33
contagion, 60–61, 220–22, 239 n. 6, 250 n. 39
Cooper, Andrew, 247 n. 14
creation, divine and human, 74–77
Curran, Charles, 174
curses, 22–23

Davies, Hugh Sykes, 98–99
death. *See also* Cavell, Stanley, on death; incarnation, and mortality; Levinas, Emmanuel, on death
  as fantasy, 99–100
  and forgetfulness, 82–83
  as ground of knowledge, 62–64, 79, 80
  and language, 39–40, 84–85
  into nature, 82
  of other, 94
  postponement of, 102
  and repetition, 96–97, 241–42 n. 22
  in "spots of time," 63, 119–21
  unthinkability of, 91, 96
De Man, Paul, 16, 17, 41, 44
  and Gadamer, 114
  on grammar vs. performance, 105–6
  on symbol and allegory, 30–31
  on words as things, 240 n. 8
denotation vs. prescription, 186
De Quincey, Thomas, 18, 128
Derrida, Jacques, 41, 89, 111, 165, 216, 242 n. 8
Descartes, René, 197–98, 199, 246 n. 4, 249–50 n. 33
dialogue
  and incarnation, 116–17, 160
  as interruption, 138–39
  philosophical, 149
  in *The Prelude*, 32, 132, 134–36
Dillenberger, John, 173–74
Dilthey, Wilhelm, 11
discourse vs. narrative, 104–5, 111–12, 130, 242 n. 1
Dryden, John, 149
duty, 200, 205
Dykstal, Timothy, 149

eating, 52–54, 76
economic systems, 215–17, 220
Einfühlung, understanding as, 11–12
elegy, 73–74, 79, 86
Ellis, David, 244 n. 27

Index

empiricism, 25, 189–90
Enlightenment, 13–15. *See also* incarnation, and Enlightenment thought; Romanticism, and the Enlightenment
epistemology
　and ethics, 7–8, 35–44, 90, 92–97, 136–39, 144, 145, 181–209, 246 n. 4
　and Kant, 7, 12, 162
　in Lucy poems, 90–92
　and moral theology, 185–86
epitaphs, 78–79, 230
　oral vs. written, 158
　as words/things, 80
ethics. *See also* epistemology, and ethics
　empirical vs. rational, 189–90
　expressivist, 136–37
　as interruption, 94–95
　and law, 182, 185, 195, 199–209
　and questioning, 182–83
　and representation, 186–99, 201
　as "saying," 37–38
　and subjectivity, 41–44
Eucharist
　in Catholicism, 224
　and incarnation, 14–15
　as memorial of death, 120–21
　and reading, 52–53
　Real Presence in, 173–74
　as repetition, 97–98
　as representational and ethical, 137
　and signs/things, 15, 47–48, 64
　as subjective fiat, 49
Euripedes, *Medea*, 251 n. 44
example, ethical communication via, 136–38
excursive power, 163–67
expressivism, 8, 136–37

factories, 220–21, 223–25
fate, 211–14
Ferguson, Adam, 142
Ferguson, Frances, 3, 16, 62–63, 90, 92, 119, 162, 244 n. 25
Ferry, David, 17
Feuerbach, Ludwig, 204
figure vs. trope, 108–9, 242 n. 3
figures, supersession of, 103–4, 111–12, 146–47, 210–11
Fletcher, Angus, 62, 115–16
Foucault, Michel, 41, 242 n. 2, 248–49 n. 27
fragment, 128–29
Frank, Manfred, 30

French Revolution
　and Solitary, 221–22
　Wordsworth's crisis regarding, 106–12

Gadamer, Hans-Georg
　on *Bildung*, 106
　on death, 96–97
　and Derrida, 169, 216, 239 n. 1
　on dialogue, 134, 152, 240–41 n. 13, 247–48 n. 16
　on *Erlebnis*, 245 n. 30
　on hearing, 152–53, 248 n. 18
　on historicity, 3–4, 65, 72
　on incarnation, 18–19, 132
　on language and interpretation, 22, 29, 76–77, 78, 127–28, 216, 248 n. 18
　on legal hermeneutics, 113–14
　and Levinas, 115, 238 n. 31
　on questioning, 182
　on repetition, 98
　on Romantic thought, 12, 15–16, 49, 239 n. 1
　on signs, 30–31, 48, 53, 66, 144, 147–48, 215, 247 n. 15
　on textuality, 169–70, 171–72, 240–41 n. 13
gift, theory of, 132–33, 135, 165, 214–16, 244–45 n. 28
Gill, Stephen, 236 n. 12, 248 n. 26
Girard, René
　on Christianity, 59–62, 210, 226
　on death, 63
　on desymbolization, 61
　on differentiation, 59, 213–14, 216–17, 220
　on law, 226
　and Levinas, 213–14
　on rivalry, 59, 212–13
　on sacrifice, 59–62, 221, 226, 250 n. 43
Godwin, William, 24, 184, 189
Goodman, Nelson, 41
grammar, figural, 104–12, 118–19, 131–32
　vs. tropological performance, 113, 122–27, 128, 134

Haney, David P., 30, 80, 242 n. 1, 244 n. 21, 248 nn. 17, 21, 250 n. 37
Hartley, David, 184
Hartman, Geoffrey, 11, 41, 70, 123, 126, 236 n. 9
　on death, 62

on incarnation, 243 n. 17
on troth and truth, 9, 55
on words and wounds, 71
hearing
  hermeneutic priority of, 25–26
  vs. sight, 95, 151–54
Hegel, G.W.F., 42, 133
  and incarnation, 49–55
  on penal law, 210–14
  Phenomenology of Spirit, 49–50, 57, 66
  on sacrifice, 57–62
  "The Spirit of Christianity and Its Fate," 50–55, 60–61, 210–14
  and Wordsworth, 137–38, 172, 177
Heidegger, Martin, 48, 71, 78, 91, 93, 94, 182, 240 n. 9
Heinzelman, Kurt, 71
Heller, Thomas, 246 n. 7
Herder, Johann Gottfried, 74
hermeneutics
  legal, 113–14, 243 n. 11
  Romantic, 15–16, 117
Hiley, David R., 9, 184, 236 n. 8, 246 n. 4, 248–49 n. 27
history. *See also* Gadamer, Hans-Georg, on historicity
  and Anglicanism, 173, 176, 178–81
  and animism, 6
  in contemporary criticism, 71
  and incarnation, 12, 17, 115–19, 144, 178
  in *The Prelude,* 107–8, 116–17
  usurping theory, 167–68
  Wordsworth's denial of, 41, 248 n. 20
Hoffman, Piotr, 10
Hooker, Richard, 203
Hubert, Henri, 57, 223
Hume, David, 47, 89, 142
Husserl, Edmund, 152
Hutchinson, Mary, 132
Hyde, Lewis, 132–33, 215, 244 n. 26

ideology, 4, 35, 65
incarnation
  and Anglicanism, 172–81
  as *Aufhebung,* 49–50
  and the body, 72–73
  and Catholicism, 174
  and contemporary criticism, 2–3, 16–18, 71
  vs. counter-spirit, 18–19, 27, 72–73, 177–78, 209, 222
  and criminal judgment, 119–20
  as critical concept, 4
  as demythologizing, 61–62, 114–15, 144–45
  and early Christianity, 20–23
  vs. embodiment, 18
  and empiricism, 25
  and Enlightenment thought, 13–15, 49
  as event, 19, 160–61
  Gadamer on, 18, 19
  as gift, 132–35, 215
  in Hegel, 49–55
  and impurity, 215–17
  as interruption, 87, 161
  and Jesus as Word, 20, 23–24
  in Levinas, 38–40
  and materiality of language, 54
  and mortality, 19, 26–27, 39–40, 62–63, 66–67, 76–102 passim, 119–21, 133–34
  as philosophical concept, 13
  in poetry and religion, 27–29, 181
  and postmodern sign, 31, 34–35
  as preontological, 38
  and repetition, 98
  and representation, 16–17, 19–20, 27, 29–35, 38–39, 69, 97–98, 143–47, 152–55, 181, 186–209 passim, 230–34, 245 n. 2, 246 n. 8
  reversed, 170–71
  and subjectivity, 12, 115, 117–18, 145
  summary of, 144–45
  as theological concept, 2, 13–29, 97–98, 116–17, 119–20, 168
  vs. theory, 4–5, 143–45
  and transcendence, 123–25, 129–31, 135–36, 158–60, 161–62, 163, 217–18
  as tropological performance, 113–14, 118–19, 122–27, 139
  and violence, 59, 61, 63, 121, 225–34 passim
infinity, 28–29, 36–39, 75

Jacobus, Mary, 152
James, William, 194
Jauss, Hans Robert, 236 n. 16, 248 n. 18
John, Saint, 20, 197
Johnson, Barbara, 239 n. 4
Johnson, Samuel, 164
Johnston, Kenneth, 246 n. 11
Judaism, Hegel on, 50

Index

Kant, Immanuel, 41, 43
  epistemology of, 5–10 passim, 12, 154, 162, 235 n. 5, 236 n. 7, 247 n. 13
  moral theory of, 139, 183–85, 195, 223, 225, 249 n. 31
Keach, William, 71
Keats, John, 166
  "Ode on a Grecian Urn," 6
  "Ode to a Nightingale," 70, 130
Keble, John, 181

Lacan, Jacques, 34, 55
LaCapra, Dominick, 236 n. 14, 241–42 n. 22
Lacoue-Labarthe, Philippe, 43, 125–26, 128–29
Land, Stephen K., 17
language. *See also* word(s)
  Adamic, 31–32
  Augustine on, 21–24
  as counter-spirit, 84
  and death into "said," 38–40
  as event, 19, 22–24, 49, 137
  materiality of, 51–56
  as natural, 74–76
  ownership of, 65–67
  poetic and religious, 27–29, 181, 237 n. 19
  and sacrificial violence, 56–62
  as "shrines so frail" and "visionary power," 26, 35, 73–74, 83, 86
  spoken, 23
  and theology, 20–22, 23, 54, 165
  and thought, 18, 22
Last Supper, 51–52
Latimer, Dan, 77, 81
law
  and ethics, 181, 185, 195, 199–209
  penal, 210–14, 250–51 n. 43
  in Protestantism, 201–4
  religious, 226
  as representational and hortatory, 185–86, 200–209, 211
  and sacrifice, 223, 225–26
  and violence, 209–14
Lazareth, William, 201–3
Levinas, Emmanuel, 36–40, 238 n. 32
  on death, 39, 78, 94, 102
  and Gadamer, 115, 238 n. 31
  on gift, 244–45 n. 28
  and Hegel, 213
  on incarnation, 38–40, 43, 100–101, 115, 117
  on infinity, 36–37, 87, 183
  on interruption, 87, 138–39
  on relation to other, 37–38, 43, 64, 78, 94, 120, 208
  on "saying" and "said," 37–39, 56, 78, 87, 138, 188
  on sight vs. hearing, 153
  on skepticism, 238 n. 30
  on subjectivity, 42–44, 100–102, 115, 117, 138, 145, 167
  Totality and Infinity vs. *Otherwise Than Being,* 36–40, 238 n. 32
Levinson, Marjorie, 71, 243 n. 12, 244 n. 20, 248 n. 20
Lévi-Strauss, Claude, 71, 239 n. 3
liberty, figure of, in *The Prelude,* 107–9
liminality, 77, 126
Liu, Alan, 41, 71, 248 n. 20
Locke, John, 47
  and punctual self, 33, 40, 144, 246 n. 4
  and signs, 8, 24, 29, 31–32, 74, 89, 199
Lockridge, Laurence, 237–38 n. 28
love, Christian, 50–53
Luther, Martin, 201–3
Lyotard, Jean-François, 36, 149, 186

MacCannell, Juliet Flower, 244 n. 23
McFarland, Thomas, 244 n. 20
McGann, Jerome, 3, 243 n. 12
McGowan, John, 70
McGrade, A. S., 203
MacIntyre, Alasdair, 36
Marin, Louis, 14–15, 33–34, 47–49, 52, 129, 242 n. 1
marriage, 19, 67, 77, 79–80
Marshall, L. E., 240 n. 5
Mary (mother of Jesus), 174–75, 176
Massey, Irving, 71–72, 121, 131, 237 n. 17
Mauss, Marcel, 57, 223, 244–45 n. 28
meaning
  and concealment, 48
  and utterance, 22–23
Miller, J. Hillis, 16–17, 242 n. 9
Mills-Courts, Karen, 17, 236 n. 15
Milton, John, 156–57, 168, 170, 215
  Lycidas, 79
  Paradise Lost, 123–24, 243 n. 16
Modiano, Raimonda, 71, 244 n. 26, 250 n. 41
Montaigne, Michel de, 248–49 n. 27
moral sources, 92, 192, 249 n. 30
muse, invocation of, 157

Nancy, Jean-Luc, 43, 57–58, 125–26, 128–29, 230–32
narrative
    vs. discourse, 104–5, 111–12, 130, 242 n. 1
    as interpretation, 65, 112
nature
    and animism, 5
    education in, 80–81, 106
    and the human, 75, 126, 181, 219–20
    as inner source, 7–8
    as interrupting voice, 95–96
Nessus, coat of, 84, 177–78, 222, 233–34
new historicism, 71
Nietzsche, Friedrich, 89, 147, 160
Nussbaum, Martha, 148–49, 156, 183, 246 n. 8

objectivity, materiality and, 51–56
Oedipus, 59, 221, 226
Ong, Walter J., S.J., 23, 236 n. 10
ontology, 7–8
Ovid, *Metamorphoses*, 222
Oxford Movement, 181

Paley, William, 189, 249 n. 28
Pascal, Blaise, 134
Paul, Saint, 20, 23, 186, 215, 228, 230
performance, tropological, 105–11, 113, 122–27, 128, 134
Plato, 147–48, 197–99
poetry
    philosophical, 141–43
    and religion, 27–29, 181
Pope, Alexander, 89, 124, 142
poststructuralism, 41, 71
Poulet, Georges, 11
prescription vs. denotation, 186
Prickett, Stephen, 6, 236 n. 11, 237 nn. 18, 19, 245 n. 2, 249 n. 28
Protestantism, 175–79

question, hermeneutic role of, 41, 182–83

Rajan, Tilottama, 236–37 n. 16, 244 n. 20
rationalism, 5, 189–90
reader, role of, 162, 165, 170, 232, 247 n. 15
reading, 118
    and eating, 52–54
    and incarnation, 248 n. 18

reason, instrumental vs. substantive, 40, 148, 197–99, 223, 245–46 n. 3, 249–50 n. 33
reception theory, 236 n. 16, 248 n. 18
reflection, 51
Reiman, Donald, 246 n. 6
religion
    and law, 226
    and objectivity, 51–53,
    and poetry, 27–29, 181
    and violence, 60
repetition, 97–98, 241–42 n. 22
representation. *See also* incarnation, and representation; sign(s)
    Catholic vs. Protestant, 174–79
    and inner word, 21–22
    and sacrifice, 57–58
    rivalry, 59–62, 212–13
Robinson, Henry Crabb, 70
romance, 107–8
Romanticism
    and animism, 5–12
    and contemporary criticism, 2–3, 15–17, 29–31, 41–42, 70–72
    and contemporary philosophy, 7–8, 43–44, 49, 239 n. 1
    and the Enlightenment, 5–6, 13–16, 30–31, 34
    and the fragment, 244 n. 20
    and history, 3–4, 71, 243 n. 12
    and intentionality, 12
    and the postmodern sign, 34, 89
    and skepticism, 8–13
Rorty, Richard, 36, 149, 194, 246 nn. 4, 10, 249 n. 32

sacrifice, 57–62, 133, 215, 222–34, 250 n. 43
Said, Edward, 109
Saussure, Ferdinand de, 21, 29–31, 34, 71, 236 n. 13, 245–46 n. 3
scapegoat, 59–62
Schelling, Friedrich Wilhelm Joseph von, 207–8
Schlegel, August Wilhelm and Friedrich, 43, 142, 242 n. 4, 243 n. 18, 244 n. 25
Schleiermacher, Friedrich, 12, 243 n. 15
Schneidau, Herbert, 114–15
Scott, Charles, 182–83
self
    as deictic, 244 n. 24
    determined by signs, 89

effacement of, 150, 156, 158–60, 161–62, 166, 168
  extra-textual, 123–26, 129–31, 135–36
  and inaccessible sources, 116–17
  punctual, 33, 40, 49, 85, 144, 155–56, 246 nn. 4, 5
semiological vs. semiotic, 236 n. 13
Serres, Michel, 216–17
Shaftesbury, third earl of (Anthony Ashley Cooper), 149
Shea, F. X., S.J., 248 n. 24
Sheats, Paul D., 104
Shelley, Percy Bysshe, 32
  Adonais, 79
  Mont Blanc, 6
sight
  vs. hearing, 95, 151–54
  as representational, 249 n. 32
sign(s). *See also* Gadamer, Hans-Georg, on signs; incarnation, and representation; representation
  in American criticism, 237 n. 21
  effacement of, 159, 172
  in Enlightenment, 147–48
  Enlightenment and postmodern, 30–31, 34, 66, 89, 147–48, 245–46 n. 3
  exposure of self as, 38, 138
  and things, 47–48, 84–85, 88, 157, 166, 175–79, 206
skepticism. *See also* Cavell, Stanley, on skepticism as animism
  as acknowledgment, 36
  and animism, 8–11, 56, 64
  and death, 63–64, 76
  Levinas on, 238 n. 30
  and politics, 248–49 n. 27
  Pyrrhonian, 9, 236 n. 8, 246 n. 4
  and violence, 10, 250 n. 38
Socrates, 57–58, 163, 230
solipsism, 99, 191–93, 199
Solomon, Harry M., 142
Sophocles, *The Women of Trachis*, 251 n. 44
Spivak, Gayatri, 244 n. 27
Stewart, Dugald, 32
subjectivity. *See also* self
  as anachronistic, 167
  as autonomous, 40–41, 86, 98–100
  in Enlightenment and postmodern representation, 33–34
  as ethical individuality, 41–44
  and Eucharist, 49
  and expressivism, 8
  in Hegel, 52–53
  incarnational, 42–43, 98–102, 115, 117–18, 145
  as openness to other, 37–38, 43, 134
  in poststructuralism, 41–44
  as reflection, 125–26
  and sacrifice, 57–58
  and solipsism, 99, 191–93
  in theoretical discourse, 147–49, 159, 163, 247 n. 15
sublime, the, 121, 162–63
subordinationism, 20, 27
sun, image of, 110–11, 113, 125, 196–99, 204, 207, 242 n. 8
symbol, 16, 48, 51
system
  vs. event, 32–33
  as vision of the absolute, 125–26, 243 n. 18

Taylor, Charles
  on animism, 6–8
  on Augustine, 195, 197
  on Christianity, 14
  on ethics, 36, 92, 182, 192, 249 n. 30
  on narrative, 65, 112
  on punctual self, 33
  on Saussure, 34
  on theoretical discourse, 148, 167
Taylor, Mark C., 239 n. 2
teleology, autobiographical, 109, 112, 127
temporality, apocalyptic, 126–27
Tennyson, Alfred, Lord, *In Memoriam*, 79
Tennyson, G. B., 248 n. 26
texts, admonitory, 205–6
textuality
  Derrida on, 169–70
  Gadamer on, 169–72, 240–41 n. 13, 241 n. 14
  in *The Prelude* and *The Excursion*, 168–72
theology
  and human language, 54
  Romantic, 243 n. 15
theoretical discourse, 4–5. *See also* Gadamer, Hans-Georg; incarnation, and representation; Taylor, Charles, on theoretical discourse
  detachment of the subject in, 147–51, 167
  vs. incarnational discourse, 143–44

Tooke, Horne, 32
trope vs. figure, 108–9, 113, 242 n. 3
tropological performance. *See* performance, tropological
troth, truth and, 9, 55, 56, 64, 67

unity, non-differentiation and, 61–62, 213–14

Vance, Eugene, 244 n. 24
Vickers, Brian, 203
violence
  and Christianity, 59–62, 212, 225–26, 232–34, 251 n. 46
  effacing differences, 220
  in *The Excursion*, 214, 217–34 passim
  and Hegel, 56–57, 60–62, 210–14
  and incarnation, 61, 121, 225–34 passim
  and language, 56–57
  and law, 209–14
  and sacrifice, 250 n. 43
  and skepticism, 10, 250 n. 38

Warminski, Andrzej, 3, 75, 240 nn. 7, 12
Warren, Robert Penn, 50
Weinsheimer, Joel, 237 n. 20
Weiskel, Thomas, 118, 162–63
Welch, Claude, 173–74
Wellbery, David, 34, 245–46 n. 3
will, divine and human, 206–8
Wittgenstein, Ludwig, 41, 64
Woodring, Carl, 242 n. 5
Word (of God), 20–24, 114–15, 127, 132
word(s). *See also* language
  Augustinian inner, 21–24
  divine and human, 21–24, 78, 127–28
  as events, 70, 78
  as funerary monuments, 78–79
  as things, 24–25, 31, 55, 69–80, 84–89, 97, 118, 137, 172
  as things or signs, 47–49, 53–56, 61, 64–68, 88, 156, 215, 233–34, 241 n. 14
Wordsworth, Dorothy, 80, 94, 132, 151
Wordsworth, William
  and Augustine, 23–28
  and autonomous subject, 41
  and contemporary criticism, 2–3, 16–17, 29–31, 44, 243 n. 12, 248 n. 20
  and Enlightenment thought, 15, 31–33, 49, 189, 204
  on ethics, 184–85, 189
  and French Revolution, 106–12
  on hearing vs. sight, 25–26, 151–54
  and Hegel, 49, 66, 76, 83, 137–38
  and Levinas, 40
  on poetry and religion, 27–29, 181
  on solipsism, 191–93
  theology of, 181
  WORKS
    "Anecdote for Fathers," 146
    "Composed When a Probability Existed of Our Being Obliged to Quit Rydal Mount as a Residence," 170–71
    Descriptive Sketches, 125
    Ecclesiastical Sonnets: part 2, no. 25 ("Mother! whose virgin bosom was uncrost"), 174–75; part 2, no. 30 ("For what contend the wise?—for nothing less"), 175–76; part 2, no. 40 ("Holy and heavenly Spirits as they are"), 176; part 3, no. 18 ("A genial hearth, a hospitable board"), 159; part 3, no. 20 ("Dear be the Church that, watching o'er the needs"), 247 n. 12
    "Elegiac Stanzas" on Peele Castle, 79
    "Essay on Morals," 184–85, 189
    "Essay, Supplementary to the Preface" of 1815, 27–29, 181, 192
    "Essay Upon Epitaphs" (1), 12, 63, 79–80, 96, 230
    "Essay Upon Epitaphs" (3), 1, 5, 19, 72–73, 84, 177–78, 209–10, 222
    The Excursion: Preface, 162; Prospectus, 156–57; book 1, 166, 168; book 2, 150, 166, 181, 221; book 3, 193–94, 219–20; book 4, 146–47, 151–54, 164, 174, 185–86, 190–93, 195–200; book 5, 62, 88, 150, 158–60, 173, 178, 187, 193, 205–6; book 6, 158, 178–79; book 7, 167, 200, 217, 218; book 8, 157, 160–62, 223–25; book 9, 164, 222–23, 225–34; the Pastor in, 58, 157–62, 217–18, 226–34; the Poet in, 162, 165, 170; *The Prelude* and, 40, 143, 146–47; the Solitary in, 154, 174, 193–94, 219–22; the Wanderer in, 147–56, 163–72, 218–19, 222–25
    "Hart-Leap Well," 76, 88, 181
    "I Travelled Among Unknown Men," 92–93
    letters, 177, 248 n. 25
    "Lines Left Upon a Seat in a Yew-Tree," 70
    "Lucy Gray," 241 n. 22

"Methought I Saw the Footsteps of a Throne," 90, 91
note on "The Thorn," 24, 73, 97
"Ode: Intimations of Immortality," 62, 91, 96, 131, 243 n. 12
"Ode to Duty," 200, 205, 206
Peter Bell, 251 n. 46
"Preface to *Lyrical Ballads*," 249 n. 29
The Prelude (1805): book 1, 86, 102, 120, 164, 208–9; books 1–8, 104; book 5, 26, 35, 73–75, 80–89, 100; book 6, 28, 40, 94, 208; books 7–9, 104–5; book 9, 86, 102, 105–8, 124, 127; book 10, 108–13; book 11, 25, 116, 118–20, 128, 133–34, 209; book 12, 229; book 13, 33, 122–39
The Prelude (1850), 5–6, 10, 75, 86, 87, 118, 229
The Prelude, MS W, 77, 126

The Recluse, 126, 130, 141–43
Salisbury Plain, 229
"She Dwelt Among the Untrodden Ways," 92, 93–94, 137
"A Slumber Did My Spirit Seal," 77, 82, 83, 96–100, 240 n. 8
"Strange Fits of Passion Have I Known," 94–95, 98, 100–101
"The Tables Turned," 3
"Three Years She Grew In Sun and Shower," 82, 95–96
"Tintern Abbey," 7–8, 70, 96, 152–53, 168–69, 231
"We Are Seven," 146
The White Doe of Rylestone, 176–78

Young, Frances, 228

Zak, Rose A., 245 n. 29

www.ingramcontent.com/pod-product-compliance
Lightning Source LLC
Chambersburg PA
CBHW031547300426
44111CB00006BA/203